New Horizons

Ashland Oil & Refining Co.

The Story of **Ashland Inc.**

Ashland Oil, Inc.

New Horizons

The Story of **Ashland Inc.**

Jeffrey L. Rodengen

Edited by Melody Alder

Also by Jeff Rodengen

The Legend of Chris-Craft

*IRON FIST: The Lives
of Carl Kiekhaefer*

*Evinrude-Johnson and
The Legend of OMC*

*Serving The Silent Service:
The Legend of Electric Boat*

The Legend of Dr Pepper/Seven-Up

The Legend of Honeywell

The Legend of Briggs & Stratton

The Legend of Ingersoll-Rand

*The Legend of Stanley:
150 Years of The Stanley Works*

The MicroAge Way

The Legend of Halliburton

The Legend of York International

The Legend of Nucor Corporation

*The Legend of Goodyear:
The First 100 Years*

The Legend of AMP

The Legend of Cessna

The Legend of VF Corporation

The Spirit of AMD

The Legend of Rowan

The Legend of American Standard

The Legend of Federal-Mogul

The Legend of Pfizer

The Legend of Amdahl

The Legend of Echlin

*Connected:
The History of Inter-Tel*

*Applied Materials:
Pioneering the Information Age*

The Boston Scientific Story

Publisher's Cataloging in Publication

Rodengen, Jeffrey L.
New Horizons: The Story of Ashland Inc./Jeffrey L. Rodengen.
1st ed.
p. cm.
Includes bibliographical references and index.
ISBN 0-945903-42-1

1. Ashland Inc. 2. Petroleum industry and trade. 3. Chemical industry. 4. Petroleum chemicals industry. I. Title

HD9569.A74R64 1998   338.2
                            QBI98-39

Write Stuff Enterprises, Inc.

1515 Southeast 4th Avenue • Fort Lauderdale, FL 33316
1-800-900-Book (1-800-900-2665) • (954) 462-6657

Library of Congress Catalog Card Number 97-062155

ISBN 0-945903-42-1

Completely produced in the United States of America
10 9 8 7 6 5 4 3 2 1

TABLE OF CONTENTS

INTRODUCTION

"Almost every month additional properties or companies are acquired by the Ashland group. Although most of these additions are comparatively small, their acquisition is of vital importance. Every acquisition makes its distinctive contribution; otherwise, there would be no justification for the addition, since increased size, alone, has no merit.

— Paul Blazer, 1956

"Strategy is the process of having carefully thought out a course of action. That's one thing I believe Ashland does well ... to think about the strategy behind the business, driving the actions we take, well in advance."

— Paul Chellgren, 1997

THE STORY OF ANY CORporation, to a certain extent, runs parallel to the course of history. Global events — wars, recessions and social phenomena — have always influenced the trends of businesses, even causing some companies to fail or be acquired by other corporations. World War II, followed by the postwar boom, for example, sent Ashland's profits soaring. The 1929 stock market crash and the 1973 OPEC oil crisis, on the other hand, plunged the economy into a tailspin, forcing Ashland to struggle for survival. And Americans' increasing concern for the environment influenced Ashland to be much more conscientious regarding pollution and waste management.

The oil industry is particularly vulnerable to global events, because the price of oil, upon which the world relies for transportation and energy, tends to rise and fall in tandem with world events. It is extremely difficult for oil companies to constantly respond to those cycles, but respond they must, or else be left behind.

Early in its history, Ashland learned how to be proactive. It learned how to anticipate and prepare for global events — before they took the world by surprise. In essence, Ashland learned how to diversify. Over time, the company broadened its spectrum of products and services to include those that were not so heavily influenced by the ever-changing price of oil. In other words, Ashland would control its own destiny.

By the time Paul Chellgren took over as CEO in 1996 and chairman in 1997, the company described its strategy as "responsible growth" — an appropriate doctrine for what the company's philosophy had been even from its earliest days of operation, when it was a single refinery in eastern Kentucky.

Ashland Inc.'s legacy can be traced back to its founder, Paul Blazer, who, in 1924, became manager of a refinery known as Ashland Refining Company, a subsidiary of Swiss Oil. By the end of his first year at the helm, Blazer turned what was once a floundering operation into a profit center for Swiss Oil, increasing its output over 36 percent. Over the next few years, Blazer made a number of strategic acquisitions to help the company's distribution, so that by the time the stock market crashed in 1929, Ashland Refining Company was well-positioned to survive. In 1935, Blazer became president and CEO of Swiss Oil, and the following year, he merged Swiss Oil and Ashland Refining to create the Ashland Oil & Refining Company. Without articulating it, the tenet of responsible growth had already been adopted.

Ashland was still almost exclusively involved in refining at this time, but the company gradually reduced its vulnerability to the price of crude oil by expanding into chemicals, road construction, convenience stores, automotive products and coal. By the end of 1997, Ashland had combined its refining and marketing operations with the USX-Marathon Group in a joint venture to create Marathon Ashland Petroleum LLC, the nation's sixth largest petroleum refiner.

When the joint venture began operation in January 1998, all of Ashland's diversified businesses operated exceedingly well. Ashland Chemical had become the largest distributor of chemicals and plastics in North America, in addition to being a global producer and marketer of hundreds of specialty chemicals. Valvoline, likewise, was among the top three brands of motor oil in the United States and was gaining international popularity. The APAC construction group was America's largest highway contractor. Arch Coal emerged as the No. 2 coal producer in the United States. Ashland's SuperAmerica convenience store chain merged with Marathon's Speedway to create Speedway SuperAmerica LLC, one of the nation's top 10 convenience store chains.

As the millennium approaches, Ashland Inc. is in an enviable position. The company ended fiscal 1997 with net income of $279 million — giving Ashland even more reason to celebrate its 75th anniversary in 1999. But the success did not come by chance. It came through a team of committed employees, through excellent service, proactive planning and, of course, through responsible growth.

FOREWORD

by
Frank C. Carlucci
Former U.S. Secretary of Defense and current Ashland Inc. board member

AS A MEMBER OF ASHLAND'S board of directors since 1989, I've witnessed a number of important changes in the company, but none quite as far-reaching as those that have occurred in 1998. In that year alone, the company merged its refining and marketing operations into a joint venture with Marathon, married its two coal companies to form Arch Coal, Inc., and announced it was relocating its corporate headquarters to Covington, in northern Kentucky.

That's a lot of adjustments for one year, and some have argued that Ashland is no longer the company it once was. To a certain extent, that is true. The role of the smaller, independent refiner has become increasingly difficult in this highly competitive industry. OPEC seems to be fraying at the edges as it struggles to cut back on daily oil production and reduce the worldwide glut of oil in the market. By merging with Marathon, Ashland has taken a necessary step to ensure it has the critical mass to maintain the prosperity and viability of the company.

The mass consolidation that is transpiring in the refining industry dates roughly back to when I was first elected to Ashland's board of directors. President Bush passed the Clean Air Act

Amendments in 1990, which tightened standards for lower emissions and cleaner fuel. As a result, Ashland's debt increased substantially after the company nearly doubled its investment in refining to comply with the new laws. By the late 1990s, the refining industry as a whole is still reeling from the effects of these investments, and is responding by selling assets and consolidating to improve returns.

However, one thing that hasn't changed about Ashland is its continued dedication to the state where it was founded and where it prospered. In 1998 Ashland's board of directors voted unanimously for the company to move its corporate headquarters to Covington. Before Ashland officially announced its intentions to the public, there was wide speculation in the local media that the company would move to Ohio. Such a move would have meant an enormous loss to Kentucky, but Ashland is well aware of the positive impact it has had on the state. I think it is a tribute to Ashland that the company elected to remain in its home state.

Ashland and Kentucky have a solid relationship that reaches back to the days before the Great Depression, when Paul Blazer first managed the single refinery in Catlettsburg. Even then, the Bluegrass State kept Ashland safely iso-lated from Standard Oil's monopoly of the oil indus-try, and ever since, Kentucky has been very hos-pitable to Ashland. After the hostile takeover attempt by the Belzbergs in 1986, for example, the Kentucky legislature lost no time in passing a law to protect Ashland and other companies from further such hostile attempts.

Of course, the relationship between Ashland and Kentucky is a reciprocal one. Not only does Ashland provide the state with hundreds of jobs, thus strengthening Kentucky's economic and cultural development, but it has been extremely generous over the years, donating time and funds to the University of Kentucky, the United Way, and many other nonprofit organizations. Ashland, in addition, has been a proponent of several environmental causes, such as River Sweep to clean up the Ohio River. And Ashland's dedication to education has gone above and beyond what is expected of a *Fortune* 500 com-pany. Even as far back as the 1930s, Ashland encouraged Kentucky lawmakers to improve public schools. Now Ashland is behind numer-ous educational causes, including the Ashland Inc. Teacher Achievement Awards and The

Ashland Foundation, which makes frequent con-tributions to colleges and universities.

Ashland is a private company that makes a major public contribution. And as a former pub-lic servant, it has been a pleasure for me to be associated with the people of Ashland. For they are not just committed to the company — they're committed to society as well.

FRANK C. CARLUCCI HAS SERVED ON Ashland's board of directors since 1989 and is chairman and a partner in The Carlyle Group, a merchant bank based in Washington, D.C. He served as Secretary of Defense from 1987–1989. In 1987, he served as National Security Advisor to President Reagan. Prior to that he was chairman and CEO of Sears World Trade. Mr. Carlucci has a long history of government service, including positions as Deputy Secretary of Defense, Deputy Director of Central Intelligence, Ambassador to Portugal, Undersecretary of Health Education and Welfare, Deputy Director of OMB and Director of the Office of Economic Opportunity.

ACKNOWLEDGEMENTS

A GREAT NUMBER OF PEOPLE assisted in the research, preparation and publication of *New Horizons: The Story of Ashland Inc.* The principal archival research was accomplished by my gifted and resourceful research assistant, Sharon Peters.

This work would not have been possible without the generous assistance of many Ashland executives, employees and retirees. I am particularly grateful for the insights provided by Paul Chellgren, chairman and chief executive officer; Fred Brothers, executive vice president; John Hall, retired chief executive officer and chairman of the board; Thomas Feazell, senior vice president, general counsel and secretary; Harry Zachem, retired senior vice president, public affairs; and Charlie Luellen, retired president and chief operating officer.

I am indebted to Dan Lacy, vice president, Corporate Communications, for his suggestions and collegial guidance in all phases of the manuscript. I am also grateful to Ruth Rust, assistant to Mr. Lacy; Margaret Thomson, director of shareholder and employee communications; Lesli Christian, former editor, *The Ashland Source;* and Amy Burrus, former advertising supervisor, for their assistance in research and stringent attention to detail.

Bill S. Conley, art supervisor, Carolyn Kersey, photography supervisor, and Tim Fuller, art director of *The Ashland Source,* also provided valuable help.

Several former top executives greatly enriched the book by discussing their experiences at the helm of the company. The author extends particular gratitude to these men for their candid recollections and anecdotes: James Boyd, senior vice president and group operating officer; David D'Antoni, senior vice president and president, Ashland Chemical Company; Marvin Quin, senior vice president and chief financial officer; James O'Brien, senior vice president and president, The Valvoline Company; Charlie Potts, senior vice president and president, APAC, Inc.; Carl Pecko, vice president, Planning; William Hartl, retired vice president, Investor Relations; and William R. Sawran, vice president and chief information officer, and president, Ashland Services.

Also providing valuable insights were: Kenneth Aulen, administrative vice president and controller; Philip Block, administrative vice president, Human Resources; Robert Bell, retired administrative vice president; John Biehl, senior vice president of administration, Valvoline; Nancy Blazer, daughter-in-law of Founder Paul Blazer; Jim Burkhardt, former director of planning and analysis, Valvoline; Lamar Chambers, auditor, Ashland Inc., and former vice president and controller, Marathon Ashland Petroleum; William Chellgren, retired company controller; Johnnie Daniels, retired secretary to Rex Blazer; John Dansby, retired administrative vice president and treasurer; race car driver Gil DeFerren; Bill Dempsey, vice president and managing director, Valvoline International; Larry Detjen, senior vice president of North American Products, Valvoline; W.H. Dysard, legal consultant for Ashland; James Fout, retired group vice president, Petroleum Marketing; J.L. "Corky" Frank, president, MAP; Duane Gilliam, executive vice president, MAP; Jack Gordon, retired former president, Valvoline International; Kevin Henning, senior vice president, Supply and Transportation, MAP; Bob Huge, former manager of editorial services; Cleve Huston, vice president, Valvoline, and president, First Recovery; Marty Kish, vice president of Communications, Valvoline; John Kebblish, retired vice president and former president, Ashland Coal; Steven Leer, president and chief executive officer, Arch Coal, Inc.; Fran Lockwood, vice president of Technology and Product Development, Valvoline; Randy Lohoff, senior vice president of Human Resources, and Health, Environment and Safety, MAP; Sam Marrs, retired director of air transportation; race car driver Mark Martin; Robert McCowan, retired vice chairman of the board, External Affairs; Rodney Nichols, vice president of Human Resources and Labor Relations, MAP; Scotty Patrick, group vice president of Petrochemicals and Technical, Ashland Chemical; Gary Peiffer, senior vice president, Finance and Commercial Services, MAP; John Pettus, retired president, SuperAmerica; Randy Powell, vice president of Human Resources, Valvoline; Jack Rousch, NASCAR team owner; Bill Seaton, retired vice chairman of the board and chief financial officer; Veronica Thistle, retired secretary to President J. Howard Marshall; Michael Toohey, director, Federal Government Relations; John Van Meter, president, Ashland International; race car driver Derrick Walker; Doris Webb, daughter of Founder Paul Blazer; Richard White, senior vice president of Marketing, MAP; Charles Whitehead, director of selection and placement; Jerry Wipf, vice president, Valvoline and president, Valvoline Instant Oil Change; and Riad Yammine, executive vice president of Strategic Planning and Business Development, MAP.

As always, the author extends a special expression of thanks to the dedicated staff of Write Stuff Enterprises, Inc. Proofreader Bonnie Freeman and transcriptionist Mary Aaron worked quickly and efficiently. Particular thanks goes to Alex Lieber, executive editor; Melody Alder, Jon VanZile and Catherine Lackner, associate editors; art directors Sandy Cruz, Jill Apolinario and Kyle Newton; Fred Moll, production manager; Colleen Azcona and Jill Thomas, assistants to the author; Marianne Roberts, office manager; Bonnie Bratton, director of Marketing; Ivan Bial, marketing and sales manager; Rafael Santiago, logistics specialist; and Karine Rodengen, project coordinator.

1924 — Paul Blazer becomes general manager of a refinery in Catlettsburg known as Ashland Refining Company, a subsidiary of Swiss Oil.

1936 — Blazer is elected president and CEO of Swiss Oil and Ashland Refining and consolidates the two companies into Ashland Oil & Refining Company.

1947 — Blazer expands Ashland Oil by purchasing the government-owned aviation fuel plant now known as Catlettsburg's No. 2 Refinery.

1948 — Rexford Blazer, nephew of Paul Blazer, becomes president of the Allied Oil Division, and Ashland merges with that company.

SECTION ONE

THE PAUL BLAZER YEARS

IF NOT FOR THE BRILLIANCE AND FERvor of Paul Blazer, what is now known as Ashland Inc. could never have existed. What started as a single refinery in Catlettsburg, Kentucky, became — by the time Blazer died — a large and quite successful company. Blazer was steadfast in his hard work and dedication and instilled in the company a drive and a passion that fueled Ashland's success. Blazer's influence — and his legend — still live strong, for it was his spirit and exacting principles that molded what was once Ashland Oil & Refining Company into Ashland Inc., a diversified corporation whose products touch all of our lives.

1950 — Ashland merges with Freedom-Valvoline to become the 19th largest oil company in the country.

1951 — Paul Blazer's health continues to weaken, and Rex Blazer is elected president; his uncle Paul remains chairman of the board.

1956 — Paul Blazer approves the installation of a Udex unit to produce petrochemicals; Ashland Oil is listed at 134 by *Fortune* 500.

1966 — Paul Blazer Sr. dies from natural causes.

An Ashland refinery crew (circa late 1920s). In 1928, refinery workers broke the world record for cleanout of the then state-of-the art Dubbs unit.

CHAPTER ONE

THE FOUNDING FATHER

"It is impossible to separate the story of Paul G. Blazer from that of Ashland Oil. For the success of one is the success of the other."

— *The Courier-Journal*, 1956[1]

OCTOBER 22, 1936, BEGAN as just another day for the industrial town of Ashland in northeastern Kentucky. But on this autumn day, Paul Blazer struck a deal that would forever change the town, the oil industry and the fortunes of thousands. Blazer, a tower of a man, with a razor-sharp intellect and tremendous ambition, signed the documents to create Ashland Oil & Refining Company, which would grow to become a significant force in the history of the American oil industry.

By many standards, it was a modest merger, a consolidation of Swiss Oil Corporation of Lexington, Kentucky, and its subsidiary, Ashland Refining Company, which Blazer had managed since its inception in 1924. At the time, Ashland Oil & Refining Company claimed assets of just $6.43 million, so few paid the transaction much attention.[2]

By the conclusion of the 20th century, however, Ashland Oil & Refining would merge with, acquire or form joint ventures with more than 100 other companies. Its product line would expand from oil to chemicals to paving to coal, and Ashland would become a *Fortune* 500 company, with international holdings and sales in the billions.

Along the way, Ashland struggled for survival. During the mid-1930s, in the midst of the Great Depression, it was merely a hopeful little company founded among the Kentucky hills along the mighty Ohio River. Its manager, Paul Blazer, was from the western Illinois flatlands and had happened into the oil business by chance 18 years earlier. The grandson of German immigrants, Blazer was born into a strict family that treasured responsibility and attention to duty above all else,[3] principles he demonstrated throughout his life.

Even in the oil business, where millionaires were often created overnight, no one could have predicted the success Blazer would achieve for himself and his company. In the darkest days of the Depression, fortunes were more often lost than made, and major players in the oil industry were seldom restrained in their quest to eliminate competition from small independents.

Paul Blazer was a forceful presence at Ashland Oil & Refining Company for 30 years, directing its growth, its culture and its destiny, even after he retired. "Paul Blazer holds a position probably unique in the oil industry today," declared a 1956 industry publication. "No company with compa-

By the early 1930s, Paul Garrett Blazer had taken on a prosperous, dignified air, as befitted a top executive earning a high-end income.

rable sales is more closely associated with one individual as is Ashland Oil & Refining Company with Paul Blazer."[4] So pronounced was his influence that "it is impossible to separate the story of Paul G. Blazer from that of Ashland Oil. For the success of one is the success of the other,"[5] *The Courier-Journal* of Louisville pointed out that same year. Decades after his death in 1966, his imprint remains.

Forming the Mold

Paul Garrett Blazer was born September 19, 1890, in New Boston, Illinois, the son of a teacher-turned-newspaper publisher. He grew up quickly and proved his industrious nature at an early age. A football and track star who earned solid grades and graduated from high school at age 16, he excelled in both academics and sports.

At a time when magazines enjoyed enormous popularity, Blazer, like many boys, sold subscriptions for pocket money. But there his similarity to other teenagers ends. Blazer quickly became the most successful salesman in the area. While still in high school — between the ages of 12 and 16 — he hired a full-time adult secretary and paid her salary out of his profits. While not even old enough to vote, he became self-supporting and bought all his own clothes, books and incidentals.[6]

Still, it was unclear what career he would pursue until he was nearly 30. Blazer had something of an eclectic career until he joined the oil business, purely by chance, in 1917. By the time he was 27, he had attended two colleges, but graduated from neither. He had held four jobs and enlisted in the Army during World War I, but served for only a few weeks in the hospital corps. But it was not a lack of focus that created Blazer's erratic résumé; rather, it was his energy and curiosity. He succeeded at nearly everything he tried.

His first college stint, which lasted two years, was close to home. He attended William & Vashti in Aledo, Illinois, a school his family helped found. At age 20, however, he left school and moved across the country to accept an attractive offer from the Curtis Publishing Company of Philadelphia. Curtis, the publisher of the *Saturday Evening Post*, hired him as manager of school subscriptions for the entire United States, at $10,000 per year in salary and commissions.[7] At the time, $1,000 a year was considered an impressive income for an entire family, and suddenly the 21-year-old was earning 10 times that amount.

In Philadelphia, Blazer was exposed to new intellectual, political and social consciousness, and it was this personal awakening that led to his lifelong commitment to a handful of causes. Here Blazer won a place on the Curtis Correspondence Committee, which selected letters written by various departments and reviewed them for clarity, correctness and succinctness.[8] This experience forged in him a talent for effective writing. "The work of the committee and the tremendous influence of the *Saturday Evening Post* and its writers fascinated Blazer," wrote Otto Scott in his 1968 book, *The Exception*. "Years later, he was able to put these perceptions and skills to excellent use as the chief executive officer of an enterprise physically separated from its board of directors and financial backers."[9]

In 1913 Blazer decided to complete his education. After rejecting job offers from both Curtis Correspondence and its rival, Crowell Publishing Company,[10] he returned to Illinois to enroll in the University of Chicago where he joined the Alpha Tau Omega (ATO) fraternity. During this period, Blazer continued hauling in profits from the magazine subscription business he had maintained, even during his years with Curtis, and became business manager of one of the university's two student publications, quickly guiding it to unprecedented profits.[11]

He began courting fellow student Georgia Monroe in the fall of 1915. But in the spring of 1917, with war raging in Europe and just weeks from earning his degree, he dropped out of college and enlisted. Paul Blazer and Georgia Monroe joined the thousands of American couples rushing to the altar before the men marched off to war.[12]

Blazer, however, failed his army physical, because football games and several unfortunate motorcycle episodes had left him with an injured back. He enrolled in the 123rd U.S. Army Hospital Unit, expecting to be shipped overseas, but fate intervened. That summer, while the unit was still training, Blazer's back gave out completely, and he was rushed to the hospital, where he

Paul and Georgia Monroe Blazer in the 1920s. The couple were married in 1917, two years after meeting at the University of Chicago.

spent the next two months in traction.[13] He would never completely recover. For the rest of his life Blazer regularly wore a back brace to lessen his pain, and he was consistently described as having a stiff, forward-leaning gait.

Delving Into the Oil Business

At age 27, Blazer was a jobless, newlywed college dropout, living with his in-laws and hobbling about on crutches. Eventually, he secured a position as advertising service manager for the Chittenden Press in Chicago,[14] writing circulars, soliciting printing work and helping customers develop advertising campaigns. But while the job utilized his writing skills, it left him bored and listless.

Not until Blazer ran into Eric Shatford, an old William & Vashti college friend, did his luck change. After college, Shatford had joined The Great Northern, a marketing company with strong ties to the oil industry. Shatford's father had oil refineries in Illinois, and in addition to marketing their products, The Great Northern had its own refinery. Blazer admitted his boredom, and Shatford offered Blazer a job as advertising manager, which Blazer accepted.[15]

"I soon discovered that Eric's firm didn't really have any need for an advertising manager," Blazer said later. "I could handle his few trade publication ads by working one day or two a month. So ... I suggested that I join the sales department and try to do a little selling in my spare time."[16]

Within a year Blazer was a vice president. Later, a biography described Blazer's aptitude for the oil industry:

"He not only sold with smoothly polished skill, but he applied his mathematically oriented mind toward the balancing of freight rates, refining costs and a fluctuating market to strike the best bargain. These were the sorts of calculations at which he excelled and which he enjoyed. He developed the habit of poring over the trade press to spot clues, trends and directions; he read the technical literature that explained refinery shortcuts and new processes and equipment; and spent a great deal of time visiting and learning from men on various levels in the industry. In modern terms, one would be tempted to call Blazer a market researcher at a time when the term was unknown."[17]

In the middle of 1918, as World War I raged on, Blazer journeyed to eastern Kentucky to examine the crude oil situation, having read about a boom and cheaper crude oil prices there. The place was ripe with opportunity, he realized, and within months, Blazer and Shatford had organized a venture they named The Great Northern Pipeline Company. Their aim was to build a pipeline to carry the abundance of cheaper crude to eager markets in the North.

Construction on the pipeline began in 1919, the same summer the young Blazers had their first son, Paul Jr. Tragically, Georgia's father, who was only 45, was injured in a car accident just days before his grandson's birth. Mr. Monroe died shortly thereafter, and Georgia's mother and younger sister moved in with the young couple. Almost overnight, Blazer became the head of a much-expanded family. While he might have wanted to remain longer with his family at this time of great change, Blazer was obligated to leave Chicago and travel south to Beattyville, Kentucky, to oversee construction of the pipeline.

Soon after a pipeline was completed, Shatford and Blazer were approached by a group of investors who wanted to build an oil refinery. The two young men had by now garnered a solid reputation, and the investors invited them to join the venture. To do that, Shatford and Blazer decided they had to divest themselves of The Great Northern, which they sold to the Warren Oil Company of Pennsylvania.[18] Thus free to pursue their first refinery venture, Blazer and Shatford founded the Southern Refining Company of Lexington, soon renamed the Great Southern Oil & Refining Company. Shatford was president, while Blazer was vice president of sales, earning the same $10,000 salary he had commanded nearly a decade earlier, but this time with a 3 percent ownership.[19]

By mid-1920, the situation in Kentucky was stable enough to move the family south. Blazer packed up his wife, baby son, mother-in-law, young sister-in-law and family canary and moved them to Lexington, where they settled into a stylish neighborhood.

Lexington, the most refined of the commonwealth's cities, seemed to the Blazers deliciously Southern, a gracious and courtly community. They found the pace a wonderful contrast to Chicago and were quickly absorbed by the culture of their adopted city, becoming chaperones for the Alpha Tau

During the 1930s, Swiss Oil crewmen often traveled through mud and snow to reach rural drilling sites. Primitive — and even non-existent — roads required teams of oxen and mules for carrying supplies and equipment.

Omega chapter at the University of Kentucky, located just a few blocks from their house.

With the family settled in, Blazer turned his attention to learning as much as possible about the region, the markets and the competition. He analyzed the oil industry and mastered the finer points of finding, refining and transporting crude. Any source was a spring to be tapped, and "his acquaintances ranged from the uneducated operators in the refineries to the heads of companies," a biographer later wrote.[20]

Within three years, Blazer had become known for his uncanny ability to accurately predict fluctuations in oil prices — a talent that was not mystical, as some supposed, but born of his relentless study of market patterns.

The Great Southern Oil & Refining Company, however, didn't always take advantage of his expertise, and considerable losses sometimes resulted. The most significant occurred in 1923, when Blazer recommended against sending a shipment on credit to Aetna Oil, which had been floundering for some time. Blazer was concerned about Aetna's ability to pay, and he predicted that the price of crude was about to drop. Aetna, if it paid at all, would insist upon paying the lower price, Blazer said. And he was right. Prices fell, Aetna went bankrupt, and the Great Southern sustained a loss of more than $300,000.[21] It was an event that marked the beginning of the end of Blazer and Shatford's partnership. In the fall of 1923, seven months after his second child and only daughter, Doris, was born, Blazer resigned from the Great Southern.

Success During Failure

Blazer was in an enviable position, for he had several offers from which to choose. In the end, he joined Swiss Oil Corporation, headed by charismatic Oklahoma wildcatter J. Fred Miles. As an inducement, Miles, who had founded the company in 1918, promised Blazer the company would buy or build a refinery of Blazer's choice for the young man to run. He further pledged that this refining operation would be a new company, an arm of Swiss Oil, of which Blazer would be president. Blazer would also hold 10 percent ownership.[22]

Unfortunately, the terms of the deal changed once Blazer accepted the job. Instead of being president, Blazer learned he was to be general manager. Instead of being given 10 percent ownership, Miles offered to loan Blazer the money to buy 10 percent of the stock of the company.[23] By the time the deal was hammered out, it was Christmas 1923. Blazer was supporting two children, a wife, mother-in-law and sister-in-law, and he hadn't worked for two months. He had already turned down his other offers, and Miles knew it. There seemed to be nothing to do but accept the revised terms.

Despite the other changing terms, Blazer was still allowed to select his own refinery. When his top choice — a refinery in Latonia, Kentucky — was ruled out because the owner reneged on his promise to sell,[24] Blazer settled on a refining operation located on the banks of the Big Sandy River at the train stop known as Leach, near Catlettsburg, Kentucky, not far from Ashland.

A 1918 share certificate for Swiss Oil, six years before the company bought the Catlettsburg refinery and organized a subsidiary, Ashland Refining Company.

On January 26, 1924, Swiss Oil's board of directors voted to purchase the Catlettsburg Refinery for $212,000 and to organize a subsidiary corporation named Ashland Refining Company, with Paul Blazer as general manager.

Unknown to Blazer, Swiss Oil was in significantly bad financial shape at that time. On the same day the board had voted to buy the Catlettsburg Refinery, it had agreed to pay $91,000 to Union Gas and Oil for an option to purchase

that company for $5 million.[25] The purchase would bring 486 producing oil wells and 70 producing gas wells on 13,000 acres in nearby Lawrence and Johnson counties — all under the Swiss Oil umbrella.[26] In its enthusiasm for such a desirable acquisition, the board of directors overlooked a crucial fact: Swiss Oil didn't have the money to pay for it. Ashland's parent company, which had been in financial difficulty for years, had embarked on a risky course.

Blazer, 120 miles east of Lexington and unaware of the dire straits Swiss Oil was navigating, moved his family to Ashland. He set up offices in the Second National Bank on busy Winchester Avenue and began to assess the rickety refinery the company had just purchased. It was, before Blazer took over, an unimpressive operation with a spotty history and only 25 employees. Originally constructed by Pennsylvania oil-

Above: The marine operations of Ashland Refining in 1931 were primitive. In the next decade, the company would order its first fleet of ultramodern towboats.

Left: Paul Blazer acquired 50 shares of company stock when he started managing Ashland Refining in 1924.

men to produce lubricating stock during World War I, it had passed through several hands, none of which had been able to craft it into a money-making endeavor.[27] It had also physically deteriorated over the years.

Within the first few months, Blazer spent $25,000 on repairs and $10,000 on new equipment.[28] He also hired Charles Jouett, an experienced refinery superintendent. As an inducement, Miles promised Jouett a 4 percent share of the company, which he then demanded Blazer produce from his 10 percent.[29]

Personnel at Ashland Refining Company in the summer of 1925 consisted of 19 men. Top row, standing: Ben Heath, assistant superintendent; E. Fraily, gauger; Earnest Alley, boiler fireman; Taylor Moore, pipefitter; M. Adams, machinist; Cyrus Wooten, pipefitter; an unidentified Johns-Manville salesman; Ollie Maynard, stillman; an unidentified Johns-Manville salesman; Charles Jouett, general superintendent; Henry Bluebaum, loader; Herbert French, loader; Ben Byron, chemist; Hyman Crog, shipping clerk. Front row: P. Maynard, laborer; Earnest Robinette, stillman; Earl Burns, laborer; Earnest Johnson, oiler fireman; Lee Campbell, laborer; George Hulett, laborer; E. Lynch, laborer.

After Jouett was hired, he and Blazer began to clean house. They fired employees who weren't performing and encouraged the remaining employees by promising they would do all they could to get the refinery on its feet.[30]

No one, as it turned out, would work harder than Blazer, who virtually lived at the refinery until he could turn it around. It wasn't unusual for Blazer to work until 2 or 3 a.m., but his labors paid off handsomely. Within seven months, the refinery was reporting profits of $5,000 a month; within nine months, profits had soared to $10,000 a month.[31] And on the last month of the very year Blazer had taken it over, the refinery made a $20,000 profit.[32] The figures for 1924 told a remarkable story: In 12 months, Blazer had taken the floundering refinery and increased throughput over 36 percent to an annual total of a half-million barrels.[33] This translated to 18 million gallons of refined oil sold, for a total revenue of $1.2 million and $100,000 in products resold to other refiners.[34]

The parent company in Lexington, on the other hand, was mired in debt and desperately searching for financing to complete the Union Oil purchase. Unable to scrape together the needed

$5 million, company officers traveled to the country's financial capitals and explored every avenue, but came back empty-handed.

Finally, James Martin of Pynchon & Company, who sat on Swiss Oil's board of directors, offered Swiss Oil a deal. Pynchon & Company would loan the company $1.75 million in return for a $2 million note — $2 million in Swiss Oil common stock and three additional seats on the board of directors. Author of *The Exception*, Otto Scott would later note:

"Faced with this tremendously loaded choice, the Swiss Oil board of directors gratefully voted for their own rescue and delivered their down payment to the three owners of the Union Oil Company on the very last day of their option. Jonah had swallowed the whale."[35]

J. Fred Miles, who founded Swiss Oil and was its general manager, fell from grace as a result of the frantic search for cash and the subsequent deal with Pynchon. Less than two years later, after an unsuccessful battle to regain the control he had previously enjoyed, he resigned,[36] though in years to come, he would resurface as a competitor.

Blazer, uninvolved in the parent company's internal warfare, was having an extraordinary run in his second year as general manager of Ashland Refining. The plant was manufacturing fuel oils, naphthas, rubber solvent, kerosene, petroleum coke and furnace distillates. Gasoline, the premium version of which was sold under the name Pepper, was also available through several service stations Swiss Oil had acquired.

Diligent about upgrades, Blazer made two important equipment decisions in 1925 and 1926: He added "bubble towers" to two stills for about $100,000, the object being to separate various products during the distilling process; and he added a $125,000 Dubbs thermal cracking unit. Ashland Refining was only the third refinery in the country to possess such a unit,[37] a distinction which quickly elevated its stature within the oil refining business.

Although he spent $285,000 in repairs and improvements in the first two years — more than the refinery had cost originally — Blazer was no spendthrift, as Scott would later point out.

"This breakneck speed was accompanied by rhetoric — and habits — of extreme caution.

Oddly enough, the combination was an accurate reflection of his methods. He was keenly aware that a business is a living organism, vulnerable both to outside attack and to internal illness. It was necessary not only to overcome internal problems, but to exert effort and move forward. But he was chary of glowing promises; he avoided the discussion of glowing opportunities. In his pragmatic view, the dark shadows of possible failure fell across the greenest pastures, even as he galloped toward them. He knew the world, and the frailty of its glitter."[38]

Employee Relations

In June of 1926, Blazer made an important hire when Everett Wells, who majored in economics and law at the University of Illinois, came to work for him. Though at first the two men had little contact, by 1928, Wells would become Blazer's right-hand man in sales, and years later he would become president of the company.

But not all of Blazer's employee relations went as smoothly as with Wells. In 1927, Miles, having founded the Louisville Refining Company after his departure from Swiss Oil, proceeded to raid Ashland Refining of its best employees. Jouett defected, as did all of the top operators and the purchasing agent. Unwilling to shut down operations while he hired new workers, Blazer personally took charge of the refinery, literally moving in and sleeping there.[39]

If Blazer suspected his remaining employees were preparing to leave on a second wave of defections, he didn't show it. He worked shoulder to shoulder with the men, treating them with the same respect he always had. He had a keen understanding of employee relations, as Scott noted in his story of Ashland Oil & Refining Company:

"Miles and Jouett seemed to prove the fragility of labor relationships, but Blazer did not — either then or later — turn against the men in the refinery. On the contrary, he went to extraordinary lengths to establish and maintain his friendships among the operators; years later these friendships were still firm, and extended to their sons. Long after the company had grown beyond the stage where one might have expected such contacts to continue, the chairman of the board and operators in the plant were still on a first name, personal basis."[40]

The Ashland refinery by 1931 had been transformed from an underproducer to a peak performer.

With labor problems at bay, Blazer turned his attention to expanding the company. By the end of 1927, when his third child, Stuart, was born, Blazer's new Dubbs cracking unit was operating at nearly full capacity. His next task was to engineer an efficient way to reach consumers with his refinery products. He realized he needed Swiss Oil's cooperation in this, so he began filing monthly, weekly and sometimes daily business reports with the principals of the parent company in Lexington, which included influential Senator Thomas A. Combs, company president. Scott noted:

"The result was a combination diary, ship's log, persuasion, exhortation, and the equivalent of a business stream of consciousness. The total impact was of intimacy, coherence, and clarity, especially because his readers, like himself, were men whose minds could best be reached through print."[41]

Throughout most of 1929, before the October stock market crash, Swiss Oil embarked on a number of strategic acquisitions at Blazer's suggestion. Swiss Oil purchased four marketing operations: Highland Oil Company of Hillsboro, Ohio, for $25,000; Home Oil Company of Maysville, Kentucky, for $85,000; Southern Ohio Oil Service Company of Pomeroy, Ohio, for $15,000; and Dawson-Pepper Oil Company of Crooksville, Ohio, for $27,000. These new additions would serve as the distribution arm. An additional oil-producing operation — Keaton Oil & Gas Company of Johnson County, Kentucky — was added for $250,000.[42]

Surviving the Times

On October 24, 1929, a wave of panic rolled over a sea of dazed brokers, investors and bankers on Wall Street as the stock market plummeted to an unprecedented and spectacular low. Most industries felt the effects of the stock market's crash immediately and deeply, but the oil business, spurred on by the growing popularity of automobiles, escaped the Depression's worst effects.

In fact, it was an advantageous time for anyone who had cash to buy distressed properties. Undaunted by national events, Swiss Oil in 1930 bought Economy Bulk Sales of Columbus, Ohio, for $40,000.[43] Swiss Oil also bought Tri-State Refinery in Kenova, West Virginia, a floundering refinery that was literally within view of the Catlettsburg operation. At a price of $550,000, it was costly, but it increased the Ashland Refinery's 4,000-barrel-per-day capability by an additional 1,500 barrels a day and added a marketing network that sub-

Among the company's holdings in the 1930s were this towboat, *The Colonel*, and several barges.

stantially increased its reach to distributors and bulk plants. According to a later profile:

"Blazer was now able to sell gasoline through several hundred service stations and more than 50 bulk stations. He could operate a fleet of motor trucks that carried refined products to warehouses, river terminals and railroad sidings, and oil barges that carried refined products to river terminals for sales to major oil companies. ... The brands Blazer now controlled included such recondite but regionally well-known names as Red Pepper Ethyl, Green Pepper Anti-Knock, White Pepper, Tri-State Ethyl, Tri-State Super-Motor and Tri-State Aviation Gasoline."[44]

Although Ashland Refining continued to post profits on the balance sheet, and Blazer had managed to bring the losses at the Tri-State Refinery down from $25,000 to $3,000 a month, the parent company considered selling the refining operations. Swiss Oil investors were feeling the economic pinch from investments in other enterprises, and some simply wanted to cash in their stock and get out of the oil business.

Though Blazer tried to find someone to buy the company, there were no takers.[45] Crude oil prices were down nationwide — average prices for which Ashland crude oil was sold had plummeted from $2.43 a barrel in 1925 to $1.84 a barrel in 1930[46] — and potential buyers had troubles of their own.

With a sale out of the question, Blazer slipped again into an expansion mode and began eyeing the Cumberland Pipeline Company, which owned thousands of miles of gathering and truck lines serving oilfields in Kentucky, West Virginia and Delaware. The pipeline enterprise served, in addition to the Ashland and Tri-State refineries, five refineries owned by Standard Oil of Kentucky, Standard Oil of New Jersey and Atlantic Refining.[47] Within a matter of months, the Cumberland Pipeline, constructed in 1902 for $3.6 million, was Blazer's. Purchased by Swiss Oil for $420,000, it was an even greater bargain than it appeared on the surface, given that there was $100,000 worth of uninventoried crude oil in its lines at the time.[48]

More than two decades later, Blazer called the Cumberland purchase the "most significant

This Wurts Bros garage, like many other service stations in the mid-1930s, sold Ashland's Pepper brand of gasoline.

deal we ever made."[49] Cumberland, which served about 5,000 small oil wells in eastern Kentucky, was losing more than $15,000 a month when Blazer acquired it; within weeks it was making $15,000 per month.[50]

But the significance of the deal had less to do with the immediate impact on the bottom line than with the fact that the system was now complete: Swiss Oil could carry its own crude oil (and that of others) into and out of its own refineries through its own lines, and to its own marketers.

Still, Swiss Oil's financial troubles continued. By the autumn of 1930, the common stock price had fallen to $1 a share, rumors about an impending sale of Ashland Refining were rampant, and a $778,000 payment on bank loans was due in a matter of months. Senator Combs pledged $100,000 in personal funds, as well as the full assets of his lumber company, to keep Swiss Oil going; another shareholder also pledged considerable sums of money.[51] This kept Swiss Oil viable through yet another crisis, but did little to put the company on stable footing.

Blazer, realizing the potential for calamity, took a creative approach to sustaining the parent company: he began buying shares of stock. He bought 69,000 shares, steadying the price at $1 per share.

In the mid-1930s, this converted trolley car was one of several retail outlets for Ashland Refining's Pepper brand of gasoline.

As Scott pointed out, "The child was beginning to support the parent."[52]

Although acquisitions halted over the next four years, and Ashland Refining kept operating at a profit, Swiss Oil, like many companies of the time, was struggling in the aftershock of the market crash and debts it could never seem to overcome. The successes of Blazer and Ashland Refining began gaining attention, and by 1933 "the name of Swiss Oil had receded into the background; the name of Ashland Refining Company had become far better known; the name of Paul Blazer began to carry weight," according to Scott's history.[53]

A Solid Foundation

The years 1931 through 1935 were fraught with events that would have a serious impact on Ashland. During this time, Combs abused his senate position by tapping into political friend-ships to ensure that state roads were paved with Ashland Refining asphalt, which prompted a state investigation in 1934. Furthermore, refinery workers were unionized by the American Federation of Labor in 1933, even though Blazer had always maintained good relationships with his employees — even praising them in Ashland's annual report, a practice unheard of at the time.

His sentiments in the report foretold what would be said of him later — that creating a "family-like" atmosphere in his company was important to him. Demonstrating unfailing respect for others was an inherent part of his personality. On the other hand, Blazer was a demanding man who set exceedingly high standards for himself and others. But what most people recall is his common-man approach that never changed, as the Huntington *Herald-Dispatch* described him in a mid-1960s editorial:

"... he was refreshingly homespun. He had none of the airs of the tycoon. His friendly manner was disarming, and those who knew him slightly were sometimes deceived by his apparent simplicity. Yet this was a man who met the most formidable competitors in a business that came to be operated by giants. Not only that, he bested many of them in production miracles and often business deals. And on top of it all, he retained the friendships of those he outwitted and outmanaged."[54]

During the early 1930s, Swiss Oil also was finally able to get out of debt, a feat which Combs proudly announced in a June 15, 1934, letter to stockholders. Dividends were issued to the stockholders (10 cents a share) for the first time since 1930.

Then, on April 7, 1935, Combs died. Blazer was elected president and chief executive officer of Swiss Oil Corporation, as well as Ashland Refining Company. Swiss Oil's headquarters was transferred to Ashland, where Ashland Refining was now reporting earnings about 10 times higher than those of its parent company.

Blazer next set about consolidating the two companies. Proving to the board of directors that his motives were unselfish, he sold back to the company his 10 percent interest in Ashland Refining. Finally, on October 31, 1936, after a year of hashing out the details, Swiss Oil and Ashland Refining Company were consolidated to form Ashland Oil & Refining Company, with a portion of its stock to be sold to the public.[55]

All in all, the mid-1930s were good years for Ashland's employees. Blazer announced that the company would pay wages based on the cost of living — a rarity in the Depression — and salaries increased approximately 5 percent for Ashland employees in 1936. Those with more than six months' seniority also got a bonus in December equal to a week's pay.[56] Due in large measure to Blazer's fortitude, Ashland Oil & Refining Company was now poised to begin its climb to refining industry leadership.

Oxen hauled equipment to remote Kentucky oilfields in a quest for oil, which would one day provide the fuel to transform American society.

CHAPTER TWO

THE KENTUCKY ADVANTAGE

"All our habits, and notions, and associations for half a century are turned topsy-turvy in the headlong rush for riches. … The big bubble will burst sooner or later."

— Daniel Yergin, *The Prize*[1]

PAUL BLAZER'S DECISION TO buy a refinery near Ashland, Kentucky, proved to be perhaps the single most important factor in his company's eventual success. A river town about 120 miles from Lexington, it was, and is, quite removed from the culture and tempo of the rest of the Bluegrass State. The area is so hilly that any smoke, haze or fog that originates there is trapped for some time. It was these stone-faced hills that presented a severe challenge to transportation in the early days, thus contributing to the area's isolation.

Most of the various adventurers and opportunists who settled there were drawn by the valley's abundant natural resources and its proximity to the busy Ohio River — another advantage of the refinery, since Blazer was able to avoid costly railroad rates by transporting oil with towboats.[2] Ashland, within the Appalachian chain, was nestled in one of the nation's finest virgin hardwood forests and situated atop a geological confluence that yielded rich deposits of coal, oil and natural gas.

The town itself had been industrial from its earliest days. Pig iron producers, attracted to the region's timber, coal, limestone and iron ore deposits, had operated in the vicinity since the early 1800s. Ashland soon became the transportation link for furnace operations that lined the river to the north and south. Railroad lines sprang up to meet the demands of new industry, and steamboats plied the river, transporting iron up and down the Ohio to Pittsburgh and Cincinnati. The lumber industry flourished until the early 1900s, with mill after mill sprouting throughout the valley.

When Blazer founded Ashland Refining, the area was experiencing a time of great prosperity and growth. The American Rolling Mill Company (Armco), headquartered in Middleton, Ohio, bought two local operations — the Ashland Iron and Mining Company in 1921 and Norton Iron Works in 1928. The city's population doubled during the 1920s, from 14,729 to 29,074.[3]

It was actually at Catlettsburg, near the city of Ashland, where the Ashland refinery was located. Catlettsburg thrived from the mid-1800s until the 1930s as a busy trading post and steamboat landing. By 1900, Catlettsburg had become the center of one of the "largest hardwood timber markets in the world," according to *The Kentucky Encyclopedia*.[4]

At the start of the oil boom, oil derricks were typically flimsy structures, as depicted in this photo from the early 1920s. *(Photograph courtesy of Stephens County Historical Museum.)*

Catlettsburg, like Ashland, is located on the Ohio River, but it also borders on the Big Sandy, a double-forked river that winds its way through much of eastern Kentucky. The Big Sandy was the primary means of moving products into and out of the remote mountain communities of the resource-rich Appalachians, while the Ohio provided a north-south route. Furs, pelts, herbs, corn, sorghum and chickens were transported on push boats to Catlettsburg during the early 1800s. Eventually, rafts stacked with huge logs headed to sawmills, steamboats filled with passengers and livestock, and barges piled high with coal joined the push boats, according to Big Sandy biographer Carol Crowe-Carraco.[5]

Around the turn of the century, the little town of Catlettsburg boasted a race track, an opera house and 21 saloons.[6] The town never reached its full potential, however, due in large part to four major fires and four giant floods that destroyed most of the downtown over the years.

Oil in Kentucky

The first oil discovered in Kentucky had spewed forth a full century before Paul Blazer got into the business. The find occurred in 1819 in the valley of South Fork of the Cumberland River, in the south-central part of Kentucky, several counties away from Ashland. Martin Beatty of Abingdon, Virginia, encountered oil at several hundred feet while drilling for salt water. Ten years later, a salt-seeking well drilled in Cumberland county became what is regarded as the first commercial well in Kentucky. As was typical in that era, the oil encountered "was bottled and sold as medicine to be used both internally and externally for a variety of ills in both humans and animals,"[7] according to *The Kentucky Encyclopedia*. These early finds were not, strictly speaking, regarded by most experts as "oil propositions, since the man who drilled was looking for salt."[8]

However, once the value of oil was established, Kentucky drillers wasted little time. Widespread prospecting for oil and gas began in the late 1860s, and wells were drilled in Allen, Barren, Boyd, Clinton, Floyd, Johnson, Knott, Letcher, Magoffin and Pike counties in the 1880s and 1890s.[9]

The first year of recorded oil production in Kentucky was in 1883, when drilling brought in 4,755 barrels.[10] Following the turn of the century, production grew, and there were additional important discoveries: Ragland pool in Bath County, Warfield Fork in Martin County, Compton pool in Wolfe County, Sunnybrook pool in Wayne County, the Big Sandy gas field in Floyd County, Big Sinking pool in Lee County and Bowling Green pool in Warren County.

These oilfields provided sufficient crude oil to keep Ashland Oil & Refining busy for many years to come. However, eastern Kentucky, where it all started, was not, it later turned out, the most oil-rich region. Notable oilfield discoveries at the opposite end of Kentucky wound up being far more significant. Thanks largely to finds in the western part of the commonwealth, Kentucky was producing 27.2 million barrels a year by the 1950s.

The Bubble Rises

Ashland, Catlettsburg and the surrounding hills and hollows were clearly not places for the faint of heart. But neither was the oil industry. The oil business from its inception was a highly speculative, exceptionally risky enterprise, a volatile blend of controversy and chaos.

By the middle of the 20th century, oil had become "central to the security, prosperity and the very nature of civilization,"[11] commented Daniel Yergin, author of *The Prize: The Epic Quest for Oil, Money and Power*. When Blazer entered the fray in the 1920s, the oil business was poised to fulfill that prophesy. The path to the top was characterized by challenge, trauma and threat, made all the more intense by the speed with which the oil business was forced to mature.

Only since the mid-1800s had oil been seen as something of great value and potential, something to be actively sought, processed and marketed. From earliest recorded history until well into the 19th century, oil had been regarded primarily as a medicine, believed to have a curative effect on such maladies as festering wounds, diarrhea and gout. Would-be entrepreneurs sopped it from the pools where it oozed out of the earth in dark globs, collected it in vats and sold it in bottles.

Only in the Middle East were more utilitarian uses found for the crude oil that seeped out of the ground. In ancient times, oil was used as a building mortar, caulk and road surfacer in Babylon and Jericho.[12] But in the United States, no applications beyond the long-standing medicinal benefits were explored until 1854.

George Bissell, a New Englander, realized that the viscous black liquid he had seen skimmed off pools in Pennsylvania was flammable. He concluded it might be the perfect illuminant to replace the various sputtering, unreliable products then currently in use. To that end, he managed to attract a group of investors and contracted with a chemist to analyze a bottle of crude. After establishing in the lab that it was easily distillable into a fluid (kerosene) that burned with a dependable, unwavering glow, he was encouraged to move ahead. Various skimming techniques didn't yield the quantities of crude oil the investors projected they would need, so they embarked on a search for better refining methods.

That's when they dispatched E.L. Drake, an ex-railroad man and jack-of-all-trades, to Titusville in northwestern Pennsylvania, where there seemed to be an unusual abundance of the dark crude pushing its way out of the earth. Drake labored there unsuccessfully for two years until, in the spring of 1859, he joined up with blacksmith Billy Smith. They decided to erect a drilling device not unlike those used to drill for salt water, in hopes of somehow striking and extracting the rivers of crude oil they imagined might be flowing underground.

Drake and Smith erected a derrick, began drilling and on August 27, 1859, the little opera-

---

Oil was once thought to have healing powers, as this 1897 advertisement for Petrolina ointment shows. *(Photograph courtesy of Corbis.)*

Above: The first producing oil well was nursed into existence in Titusville, Pennsylvania, the result of the prodigious efforts of E.L. Drake, a former railroader, and blacksmith Billy Smith (foreground). *(Photo courtesy of Schoenfeld Collection from Three Lions.)*

Below: Soon after the Drake-Smith hit in 1859, prospectors began drilling oil wells throughout northwestern Pennsylvania.

tion struck oil. Ill-prepared for the subsequent flow, Smith and his two sons scrambled to find receptacles in which to trap the stream of crude oil issuing steadily from the hole they had bored. Once they filled every available bucket, tub, wash-basin and barrel, they began a frantic search for bigger vessels and eventually bought every empty whiskey barrel in the county.

The oil rush had begun. Within weeks, derricks dotted the area, which came to be called the Oil Regions, and pastoral farmlands became a frenzied circus of buying, selling, drilling, pumping and transporting. By 1860, Pennsylvania had 25 producing wells and 21 oil refineries.[13]

Frequent periods of turbulence and chaos punctuated the next several decades. Prices plummeted regularly as production frequently outpaced demand. Teamsters charged exorbitant rates to transport the crude to refineries (which prompted oilmen to construct a network of underground pipelines). Deals were often forged in fraud, future speculation flattened many a fortune, and ne'er-do-wells from nearly every walk of life were drawn by get-rich stories. Still, public clamor for kerosene grew, and it was obvious that oil was a path to considerable wealth.

The Standard Monopoly

The oil boom did not escape the attention of John D. Rockefeller, a pious, persistent young man. By the age of 20, Rockefeller was running a successful produce-shipping firm in Cleveland, and by the age of 26, he had added a high-performing refinery to his holdings.

Rockefeller leapt quickly into the oil business, immersed himself in it, and as early as the mid-1860s was, according to Yergin, bent on "total dominance and mastery over the world oil trade."[14] The young entrepreneur's motto: "Pay nobody a profit."[15]

Rockefeller got his fingers into several aspects of the oil business, and on January 10, 1870, five men, led by Rockefeller and Henry Flagler (who later developed much of South Florida), established the vehicle that would allow them to control the industry: the Standard Oil Company, incorporated in Ohio. By the spring of 1872, Rockefeller was, according to Yergin, "master of the largest refinery group in the world. He was ready to take on the entire oil industry."[16] By 1879, Standard controlled almost every foot of pipeline into and out of the Oil Regions, the only place where oil was being drilled in any appreciable quantity. By 1880, Standard Oil refined 90 to 95 percent of all the oil produced in the United States.[17] Rockefeller also had a hand in the transportation and marketing sector of the business. Yergin detailed the Standard Oil techniques and tentacles:

> *"Rockefeller's firm acquired its own tracts of land on which grew the white oak timber to make its own [oil] barrels; it also bought its own tank cars and its own warehouses in New York and its own boats on the Hudson River."[18]*

Moreover, Rockefeller's organization — larger and more powerful than any of its competitors — used its clout to set up deals with the railroads through which it received rebates on freight rates (while its competitors paid full freight), thereby reaping enormous pricing and profit advantages. Not content with that windfall, Rockefeller worked out yet another arrangement with the railroads whereby Standard received a percentage of every dollar its competitors spent on shipping.

Before his monopoly was dissolved in 1911, Rockefeller was "King of the World," as this editorial cartoon depicts. *(Photograph courtesy of Corbis.)*

For many years, Rockefeller pointedly stayed out of one part of the oil business — drilling and production — which he regarded as entirely too speculative. Finally, in the 1880s, Standard entered that realm as well and by 1891, it was providing more than 20 percent of America's output of crude.[19]

Standard had become a most formidable presence. The oil giant swallowed up many independent operators, who found it almost impossible to stay in business and compete against the almost unlimited resources and incredible reach of the company. In 1882, Standard Oil gathered all of its varied holdings under the umbrella of the Standard Oil Trust, a complicated legal maze designed to centralize control.[20]

Rockefeller's ruthless domination of the oil industry touched off a powder keg of protest. Nearly a dozen states, including Ohio and Texas, launched legal actions of one sort or another, primarily anti-monopoly suits, which failed to stop Rockefeller. When the Ohio Supreme Court ordered the trust dissolved in 1892, the company simply reorganized in New Jersey and transferred all its assets there.[21] Public outcry ensued, erupting in rallies and demonstrations against Standard Oil. Politicians, sensing a cause they could exploit, grew very interested in the company's activities and strategies.

Ida M. Tarbell finally accomplished what politicians, judges, oilmen and refiners could not. A renowned journalist (whose father and brother were both oilmen), Tarbell wrote a series of 24 investigative articles on Standard Oil for *McClure's* magazine. The first ran in November 1902, and month after month, the articles told the story "of machination and manipulation, of rebates and brutal competition, of the single-minded Standard and its constant war on the injured independents," Yergin said.[22]

The articles were much read and much discussed, and public sentiment against Standard Oil grew ever more vociferous. Immediately after Theodore Roosevelt was elected president in 1904, his administration began an investigation of Standard Oil and the petroleum industry. Two years later, the government brought suit against Standard Oil, charging it under the Sherman Antitrust Act of 1890 with conspiracy to restrain trade.

By 1909, after the dispute had been hashed over for years in court, a federal judge ruled in the government's favor and ordered Standard Oil dissolved. Though the company appealed to the Supreme Court, the dissolution order was upheld, and in 1911 the breakup could no longer be forestalled.

At that point, according to Yergin, Standard Oil enjoyed incredible control over the industry: "It transported more than four-fifths of all oil produced in Pennsylvania, Ohio and Indiana. It refined more than three-fourths of all United States crude oil; it owned more than half of all tank cars; it marketed more than four-fifths of all domestic kerosene exported; it sold to the railroads more than nine-tenths of all their lubricating oils. It even deployed its own navy — 78 steamers and 19 sailing vessels."[23]

Standard Oil was divided into seven separate entities. The largest, Standard Oil of New Jersey, eventually became Exxon; others eventually became Mobil, Chevron, Sohio, BP, Amoco, Conoco and Sun.

With the separation complete, competition was finally reinstated in the oil business. Although the separate entities spun from Standard were major forces to be reckoned with, the gates of free enterprise were more open than they had been for decades.

From Kerosene to Gasoline

America, in the midst of the Industrial Revolution, was changing rapidly. Thomas Edison had perfected the incandescent lightbulb in 1879, and the first motor car was produced in 1895. Both inventions would change the course of history, and of the oil industry.

By the turn of the century, much of America, and a significant part of the rest of the world, was illuminated by kerosene. Various businesses and industries had begun to extend their hours well into the night, and the future of the oil business seemed limitless, thanks to the world's reliance on kerosene.

Then, in 1879, George Westinghouse developed a system for transmitting electricity. By 1902, 18 million incandescent lightbulbs were in use, and electric light was seen as highly superior to the flame produced by the kerosene lamp. Edison might have single-handedly, if unwittingly, brought the oil industry to its knees were it not for the well-timed appearance of another invention: the automobile.

Though custom-made cars were available at the end of the 19th century, it wasn't until Henry Ford perfected the assembly line method of mass production that these new vehicles were priced within the reach of consumers. The Model T, introduced in 1908, cost $850, an impressive

Henry Ford's assembly line, as shown here in 1913, made automobiles more affordable, thereby increasing the demand for oil. *(Photograph courtesy of Corbis.)*

sum, but one that many could afford. Ford continued to streamline production and lower costs. "When I'm through, everyone will be able to afford one, and about everyone will have one," he said.

Luckily for the oil business, his prediction was correct. Each of the 902,000 automobiles in service by 1912 required thousands of times more refined crude than each kerosene lamp, thereby guaranteeing the oil industry a market for some decades to come.

Refineries hurriedly redirected their techniques to produce more gasoline, which had previously been an insignificant byproduct of the refining process. Suddenly it seemed likely that for the first time in years, demand would surpass the ability to supply. For although exploration had finally extended beyond Pennsylvania to California, Texas, Oklahoma, Ohio and Louisiana (there were also small finds in Arkansas, Kentucky and West Virginia), it was obvious the existing reserves would shortly prove inadequate for the growing demand.

It was an era of dizzy prosperity. In the early 1920s, consumerism replaced Americans' traditional frugality as the ethic of the day, industry boomed and a cooperative government lowered taxes and raised tariffs. Eight million automobiles bumped over the roads in 1920; by 1929 that number would nearly triple to 23 million.

The Bubble Bursts

The economy soared during "the Roaring '20s," and the stock market rocketed, artificially inflated by the risky practice of buying on margin. It looked as though the good times would last forever, but in September 1929, stock prices began to slide.

On the first day of real panic, October 24, blue-chip certificates of companies like General Electric, Johns-Manville and Montgomery Ward tumbled, in some cases losing 25 percent of their value. On October 29, "Black Tuesday," frantic investors, bankers and investment companies unloaded 16 million shares of stock, triggering the Great Depression, which would consume the livelihoods, dreams and dignity of millions of American workers and families.

At the depth of the Depression, one in five Americans was out of work. Those lucky enough to have savings accounts raided them, and banks failed throughout the country. Demand for goods fell sharply as people concentrated on survival.

In 1930, prospectors hit a well in east Texas that gushed like a geyser. It was an oilfield of unprecedented promise, and the inevitable occurred: Frantic overproduction drove prices into sharp decline.

The timing could not have been worse. In the midst of the Great Depression, demand for most forms of fuel had already diminished for the simple reason that most people could no longer afford them, and now the oil industry was on the brink of complete collapse. In 1931, the governor of Texas shut down production, but with only limited success, as it was impossible to police every well to ensure no contraband oil slipped beyond the Texas borders. The price of a barrel of crude oil, which had been $1 a year earlier, plummeted to 10 cents.

To stimulate economic recovery, U.S. Interior Secretary Harold Ickes set monthly quotas to

reduce oil production, but that action was challenged in the courts. Eventually the government provided only a "suggested" quota for each oil-producing state, something most oil producers honored. Terrified by the precipitous slide of the industry and believing voluntary quotas a promising way of reviving the industry, oil producers felt they had very little choice.

The Location Advantage

Blazer and Ashland Oil & Refining weathered the tumult of the 1920s and 1930s with relative ease, in no small part because Kentucky was only a bit player in the oil rush and was therefore never subjected to the horrendous abuses inflicted on the big boom areas. The refinery operation, while strong, was still small enough to make quick adjustments when the economic climate changed; moreover, the company's debt was extremely low, so it was not imperiled when oil prices fell dramatically.

Thus, it may well have been to Ashland's extreme advantage to have been operating in a place where there was only a moderate supply of oil, and to have been still in its formative years during the pandemonium of the post-Standard Oil and Depression years.

National Refining Company's Labor Day parade served as a sales opportunity for automotive products, as seen here in 1907.

Paul Blazer (right) rarely stayed in his own office. Here he discusses the Dubbs thermal cracking unit with Clay Callihan in 1941.

CHAPTER THREE

UNCHANGING PRINCIPLES

"I believe that modern industry is seldom understood by people outside of industry. Industry is constantly changing; it isn't the same as it was twenty or ten or even five years ago."

— Paul Blazer, 1940[1]

AS ASHLAND OIL & REFINING Company emerged from the challenging era of America's Great Depression, Paul Blazer was prepared to move ahead. In 1936, after consolidating Ashland and its parent company, Blazer stood at the helm of a new business venture ripe with potential. Although conservative, he was not excessively cautious.

As a first step to dramatically increase the size of the company, Blazer purchased $350,000 worth of oil-producing properties in western Kentucky, ensuring a steady flow of crude oil and reducing the company's reliance on wildcatters. Blazer also moved the company's headquarters. Ashland Refining's offices had been located inside the Second National Bank since its founding. In late 1937 Blazer bought a six-story clothing store two blocks away, and on January 15, 1938, employees moved into their new offices in the heart of Ashland.

It was during this time that Blazer, who fervently believed in a flat organization populated by those able to handle a variety of tasks, began to establish some level of specialization and departmentalization. In 1938, he created a Personnel Department, headed by Alex Chamberlain, who established pre-employment testing, making Ashland one of the first businesses in the country to do so. Branching out again, in 1939 Blazer inaugurated the Exploration and Development Department, headed by Sam Wells, a geologist with wide experience throughout Illinois and the Southwest.

Principles to Uphold

Although Blazer was paying more attention to how the company was organized, author Joseph Massie, who Blazer later quoted in his "E Pluribus Unum" address,[2] noted that Blazer "continued to de-emphasize the clear-cut separation of duties."[3]

There were some principles that Blazer had developed in the early days that he refused to abandon. He believed in "strict credit control, which minimized the requirements of working capital" and attention to "small details, especially those relating to costs." Regarding his relationship with independent producers, Blazer wanted to remain close "in order to establish greater security in crude oil supply and close attention to the level of inventories, which provided further security of raw materials supply and decreased the risk from price changes."[4]

In 1938, Ashland employees moved into their new headquarters, a former six-story clothing store.

Blazer was convinced that growth for the mere sake of growth was a fool's approach. From his earliest days at the refinery, he had believed that the company must take certain steps to remain competitive, and that sometimes meant acquiring other properties and growing larger. But he was acutely aware, as he often commented in later speeches, that without thoughtful control, larger size often led to lowered efficiency and profitability.

And, finally, Blazer felt that management had a strong responsibility to the community, its employees and customers. He was determined to maintain the sense of family he had developed with his employees and associates in the early days. In 1956, exactly 20 years after he became head of Ashland Oil & Refining, he made reference to this in his "E Pluribus Unum" speech to the prestigious Newcomen Society, which met in Lexington.

"As Ashland Oil has continued to grow, so have we struggled to maintain the informal,

friendly organization of a small company. We have endeavored to inject into our relations with the public, our employees, customers and stockholders what I like to think of as a small-town, large-family attitude."[5]

Of course, Blazer's speech was far more than just rhetoric. "Mr. Blazer practiced what he preached," said W.H. Dysard in a 1998 interview. Dysard provided Ashland with outside legal counsel as early as 1932. "E Pluribus Unum really spelled out Blazer, what Blazer believed in. … The emphasis is on people, and he meant every word of it."[6]

While he treated business associates as family, Blazer also insisted on hard work. "He paid well," said Veronica Thistle, who worked in the Ashland Sales Department in the mid-1940s, "but he expected a dollar and a half for every dollar that he spent on your salary."[7]

In terms of his family life, Blazer spent long hours at the office or at the refinery, and his time was never wasted. On weekends and school holidays, his children would sometimes accompany him. "There was never any sense of deprivation," said his daughter, Doris Webb. "We always knew Daddy was down at the office, and whenever he wasn't there, he was with us. He didn't golf,

By the mid-1940s, Ashland had assembled an impressive fleet of towboats that was, in the minds of many, among the finest plying the waterways.

didn't fish, didn't have hobbies. The business was his hobby."

He also insisted upon — and demonstrated — flawless integrity. "While he was working, I would keep him company. I would do my homework down at the office or write letters to my friends," Webb recalled in a 1998 interview. "But I always had to bring my own stamps, or wait until we got home. I was not to use the office stamps — those were for the business, not our personal use, he said. We had a company car, too, but we didn't use that for family or social events, just for business."[8]

Blazer's Fleet

With those canons firmly in place, Blazer took bold steps in his first decade as president of Ashland Oil & Refining — years that would be marked by post-Depression upheavals, natural disasters and World War II.

He quickly made a plunge into the transportation of oil and its products by river. When Swiss Oil first purchased the refining operation in 1924, the company owned one boat, *The Colonel*, which pushed one barge with five tanks on its hull. While still heading up the refining operation, Blazer convinced the company to add two more boats to the fleet, *The Scout* in 1926 and the *Ruth Ann* in 1930. And although the additional boats were purported to have enough power to travel as far as Cincinnati, Ohio, and Charleston, West Virginia, they were purchased secondhand and didn't live up to their potential.

So Blazer ordered one constructed to the company's specifications, and in 1936 took delivery of the *Senator Combs*, the first towboat constructed specifically for Ashland Oil & Refining Company's use. It was, according to author James Casto, whose book *Towboat on the Ohio* details transportation on the Ohio River, "one of the finest and most powerful boats on the river."[9]

By 1939, the *Combs* was moving "only 40 percent of the total tonnage transported on the river by the company, with the remainder being handled on a contract basis," Casto wrote.[10] Moreover, Blazer had discovered that American Barge Lines, which moved a good deal of Ashland's products, planned on increasing its rates. Blazer made the decision to build a company fleet. It was, as Joseph Massie, author of *Blazer and Ashland Oil*, notes, a decision that had a profound effect on the company's future. "Other companies were using the river at an increasing rate, but many were leasing rather than buying their equipment."[11]

During the first two years of the 1940s, the company added four more boats to the fleet: the *Jim Martin*, named for Ashland's chairman of the board, in May 1940; the *Ashland* in May 1941; the *Paul Blazer* in December 1941; and the *Tri-State* in May 1942. Each cost about $300,000.

Unlike their predecessors, these were gleaming, ultramodern vessels. The company's in-house publication, the *Ashland Oil Log*, described the *Ashland* with breathless enthusiasm:

"... the galley [has] every modern convenience possible, electric stove, electric coffee urns, ice-boxes, dishwashers — your kitchen at home is probably not as well equipped and couldn't be any cleaner. ... The crew lives in as comfortable surroundings as any that a first class hotel provides. With tiled baths, lounge rooms, radios, soft beds and air circulation, they have all the comforts of home and more."[12]

More importantly, the new boats were faster, more reliable and more powerful than the early boats, able to push far larger barges, an important capability since critical new sources of crude oil were many miles downriver. When World War II began, Ashland was able to expedite its own deliveries rather than queuing up behind others.

The state-of-the-art towboat *Jim Martin* could push larger loads further and faster than its predecessors.

Blazer always had a simple reply when asked about his commitment to inland waterway transportation. As he told a reporter years later, "It cost us more to truck gasoline 10 miles from the refineries to Ashland than to deliver it by barge for 900 miles."[13]

Surviving the Flood

But the Ohio River, so crucial to the success of the company, was also responsible for its near ruination in the late 1930s. On January 26, 1937, the river crested at a record 79.99 feet, causing unprecedented damage and destruction throughout much of the Ohio Valley. More than 12,000 square miles of land in three states was flooded, several hundred people were drowned (published reports put the number anywhere from 250 to 900), thousands were forced from their homes, and hundreds upon hundreds of businesses were put out of operation.

The original Catlettsburg refinery was marooned, the water rising to within 10 feet of the plant. Blazer took control of the company command post, issuing directives and surveying the damaged area regularly by boat. The Blazers set up a second kitchen in the basement of their home and prepared vats of soup and scores of sandwiches, which were transported by motorboat to the 30 men who remained to battle the rising waters and protect the equipment. During this battle, Blazer contracted influenza, but he continued his efforts from his sickbed.

The refinery was shut down for 15 days — a significant loss in earnings — but the fallout was to be felt by the company for months. Distributors and independent filling stations up and down the 250 miles of the firm's holdings were put out of operation for weeks.

Ashland recovered quite quickly, however, and 1938 was a robust year of acquisitions and improvements. Blazer bought a majority interest in Mt. Pleasant Aetna Company, a distributor, and purchased the Burning Fork Oil Company and the Boston & Southwestern Oil Company, two producers with wells in western Kentucky. The company also established a new river terminal in Covington, Kentucky. (Two years later — even before delivery of the last three boats of the fleet — the company purchased 77 acres on the Monongahela River in Floreffe, Pennsylvania, near Pittsburgh, to build yet another modern terminal for shipping by river, rail and truck.)

Strategic Maneuvering

In 1937, Ashland, which had been quietly but effectively making inroads into the asphalt producing business, won a huge contract to sell asphalt to the state of West Virginia, a victory that would lead to many other asphalt expansions in the decades ahead. The refining plant also underwent its first major modernization since 1924 — the installation of a $220,000 combination atmospheric and vacuum unit, expanding the refinery's capacity by 80 percent.

Soon, the company purchased the Illinois-Owensboro Pipeline system, which flowed crude oil from the newly established oilfields in Illinois to Owensboro, Kentucky, a few miles from Louisville. This would provide the much-needed additional crude oil for the company's increased refining capacity.

As it turned out, the pipeline had benefit far beyond that. One of Ashland's competitors, Standard Oil of Ohio, had been a chief user of the Owensboro line, using two-thirds of the crude moved through the pipeline, while Ashland took the other one-third. Additionally, Standard owned a competing pipeline, which carried oil from Illinois. Standard had hoped to acquire the Owensboro system to bolster its edge but moved too slowly, waiting for management approval. Standard suddenly found itself in the potentially unhappy situation of having Ashland in control of a pipeline upon which it had relied rather heavily.

Blazer took his advantage one step further. He offered a compromise that would be to both companies' advantage. Standard of Ohio would be a joint owner of the Owensboro system he had just purchased, but in exchange, Standard was required to allow Ashland to be joint owners of Standard's competing system. Standard agreed. "Thus," as author Otto Scott pointed out, "in one stroke, Ashland had moved from a one-third user in the Owensboro system to one-half, had the resources of a second, parallel system available when they needed it, and had moved from a minority customer in one line to a half-owner in two."[14]

There was another important element of the Owensboro purchase, according to Scott: It was the first real evidence of the "maturity of the management team," the first absolute signal that the team "could reach understandings that required only [Blazer's] assent."[15] For this deal had been executed not by Blazer himself, as had heretofore been the case in every major decision, but by an executive team. Bill Keffer, Ashland's head of pipelines, and Everett Wells, sales manager, were on the scene with the pipeline executives, making the requisite snap decisions, merely keeping Blazer informed by telephone. The Owensboro deal, Scott wrote, "was a benchmark of Ashland Oil & Refining's progress and proved that an executive group existed that could carry the firm past the one-man stage."[16]

Paul Blazer believed that industry was constantly changing and it was important to keep up with those changes. At the same time, he maintained a firm set of principles — a work ethic that went beyond verbal intonation and made its way into his actions and into the actions of those who worked for him. It was this combination that helped Ashland Oil & Refining Company mature during these difficult years. And mature it did — for it was during these post-Depression/pre-World War II years that Ashland began its metamorphosis into Ashland Inc., an energy and chemical company that would someday market throughout the world.

In 1941, workers completed the pipeline from the Cumberland station to the Catlettsburg Refinery. It was the last pipeline Ashland built by hand.

CHAPTER FOUR

INFLUENCING THE NATION

"Neither the wheels of industry nor the arms of war could move without oil."

— Otto Scott, *The Exception*[1]

BY WORLD WAR II, BLAZER AND Ashland had established themselves as a force on the national level. Blazer had always been a networker of the highest order, meeting with and learning from others in the industry, keeping up cordial communication with customers and competitors alike. But in 1938, he began to be an outspoken independent-company proponent.

Congress was considering the Petroleum Divorcement Act, aimed at splitting the industry into its various segments, something that would have a calamitous effect on integrated companies like Ashland. Blazer gave a measured but impassioned presentation before a Senate committee and a year later traveled to Washington twice to make similar points at committee hearings. In future years, he would often be invited to Washington to give his impressions or insights into industry issues.

In 1941, as events in Europe assumed center stage, Ralph Davies, deputy director of the Petroleum Council, summoned a group of oilmen to Washington. Blazer, who was the only executive of a small company to attend, was soon thereafter appointed chairman of District Two (consisting of 15 states) of the Petroleum Administration of War.

A Deal With the Government

The U.S. government was cautiously preparing for greater involvement in the growing war in Europe, and it was clear to the men in Washington that the need for 100-octane gasoline to power aircraft would be far greater than refineries were currently putting out. Refiners were asked to devise plans for greater production. Blazer, after consulting with his company experts, concluded that building another plant would cost more than the company could bear.

It would be much more feasible, Blazer's team suggested, to combine Ashland's operation with a government-built aviation plant. This is what he proposed. Officials in Washington agreed to put up $6.7 million to build a new refining plant in Catlettsburg (although it would actually cost more than twice that figure), and Ashland agreed to invest $250,000 to integrate the new plant into the existing facility.

Then, on December 7, 1941, more than 360 Japanese planes swooped out of the clouds,

---

Ashland adopted the "Flying Octanes" logo to convey the image of an active company on the move.

unleashing dive bombs and torpedoes on an unsuspecting U.S. Pacific Fleet. By the time the attack was over, more than 2,000 military personnel and 400 civilians had been killed. Three of the eight battleships — the backbone of the Navy — were sunk and the other five badly damaged. More than 150 planes were destroyed on the ground.

The construction of the second refinery to help in the war effort was a major coup for a small company like Ashland, and Blazer was delighted. Ashland employees were told by the *Ashland Oil Log* they should "consider the selection of the Ashland Oil & Refining Company for the design and management of this tremendously important plant as a tribute to the personnel of this organization and a recognition of their ability to keep abreast of the latest technical developments in the oil industry and to place them into practical operations."[2]

Equally apparent was that the government needed a ceaseless, unprecedented volume of oil for itself and its allies, and Ashland's relatively remote location near the mountains hundreds of miles inland would be less susceptible, perhaps, to enemy attack or sabotage. Moreover, as Blazer

A service station in Ashland, Kentucky, during the 1940s, where the Pepper brand was sold.

pointed out in his letter to stockholders in the 1942 annual report:

"Because of our geographical location between the area of surplus petroleum products in the Southwest and the area of scarcity in the East, our refinery with its supporting transportation system is able to perform an important service in supplying civilian consumption."[3]

By the 1940s, oil and oil-based products had become so vital to modern civilization that nations could be paralyzed without sufficient supplies. And this dependency, as Scott pointed out, was intensified and magnified with the war:

"In World War II oil was the vital ingredient. Rubber and carbon black were made from it, and bullets could not be made without it. ... The nation without oil was defenseless against its enemies. The ships at sea, the planes in the air, the trucks on the highway, the tanks on the field and the locomotive on the track — all moved on oil. ... Oil heated the home and the barrack and the tent alike; oil produced the asphalt for the highways and the landing strips, was the basis for waterproofing uniforms, for rayon parachutes, for lubricating machinery and greasing wounds and for DDT."[4]

Division and Unity

The construction of the new aviation fuel plant at Catlettsburg was an ordeal that took months longer than anticipated and ultimately cost $16 million. It was a difficult task in difficult times. The government was mobilizing industry of all manner, struggling to establish needs and priorities, and there was not always the manpower, not to mention the resources, to accomplish things quickly. Confusion and conflict were rampant. In 1942, for example, there were 20 major oil companies and 520 independents[5] jockeying for position, attempting to ensure their fair share

The need for tight security at the refineries during the war brought a team of security guards to Ashland Oil & Refining for the first time.

of what were sure to be limited resources during the war effort.

At Ashland, too, things were in flux. There were union problems for the first time since the union had organized there in 1933. The draft board was taking some of the company's most experienced men. Blazer was occupied in Washington almost as much as in Ashland, dealing with the responsibilities of his post with the Petroleum Administration of Wars. The men at the refinery battled back another flood on the Ohio. And orders from Washington forbade Ashland to make its most highly profitable products, in favor of focusing its energy on far less profitable fuel oil.

Guards were positioned at Ashland's gates for the first time; employees were issued company identification badges with photographs; and everyone associated with the company was warned to be tight-lipped, suspicious and vigilant. As the *Ashland Oil Log* warned in a directive to employees in early 1942, caution was the better part of valor:

"Sabotage need not necessarily be by means of bombs — in fact, this is rarely the case. The more common methods of sabotage include malicious damage to vital equipment, damage to water supply or the power systems; contamina- *tion of materials being used or processed; damage or delay to finished products both at the plant and in transit; destruction or alteration or theft of blueprints or other confidential data; damage to technical mechanisms; deliberate creation of fire hazards and injury to personnel."[6]*

A few months later, under the headline "Don't Let Anyone Sabotage Your Mind," employees were warned that "the enemy is trying to divide us and conquer us by a carefully planned campaign of lies," and were advised that they had a responsibility to read the newspapers carefully, listen to news broadcasts and study geography to have full comprehension of the war.[7]

In fact, the *Ashland Oil Log* was, during this era, crammed with challenges for everyone — employees and their families alike — to do their part for the war effort. "Save Cans, Rags and Paper" was a frequent entreaty. "Oil is Ammunition, Use it Wisely!" "Remember Pearl Harbor: Work, Fight, Sacrifice!"

Stories advised everyone to take first-aid training to be able to help in a crisis and to wear sweaters

The Pepper brand of fuels and lubricants, which Ashland picked up during the mid-1940s, was regionally quite popular.

to cut down on home heating costs. There were periodic announcements that rubber drives and scrap metal drives would take place at the company, and employees were asked to locate no-longer-usable bolts and tires to turn over to the government for recycling. Great pressure was put on them to buy bonds; competitions between the divisions were set up in an effort to enlist 100 percent participation in each.

Employees were often reminded to work safely, since industrial accidents amounted to "200 million lost man-hours a year in the early 1940s, time which, had it not been lost, could have been used to build 15,000 large bombers or 30,000 medium bombers or 75,000 fighter planes or 110,000 trainer planes or 195,000 light tanks."[8]

There were also frequent stories extolling the fine contribution the company was making to the war effort:

"Not only is our gasoline used in Army equipment, but our asphalts are providing the cushions needed for the landing of bombers and fighter planes. ... The Marines in Quantico, Virginia, are being trained in tanks using our gasolines. The trucks are using it also. ... We are supplying products to the Navy for shipment to England. These are gathered at an Atlantic port and moved out by tanker."[9]

While the company dealt with new rules and expectations, trauma was a relentless visitor. An explosion at the asphalt plant in April 1943 left one man dead. Two months later, a fire in the plant killed three men, the worst catastrophe the refinery had endured thus far. Early in January 1944, the new aviation fuel plant went online, quickly surpassing the 3,080 barrels a day it was designed to process. A few days later the union voted to strike, a vote that was rejected by the national office, given the nation's need for all plants to keep operating.

The Mother of Necessity

The company was going through a transformation, adjusting to increased demands and the changing landscape, and eventually, in the words of writer Otto Scott, fitting "into a harness of responsibility within a framework of national responsibility."[10]

The extent of this responsibility is shown in the company's 1942 annual report, which Blazer wrote in March 1943:

"The Company has its share of problems resulting from war dislocations. Reflecting the reduced use of gasoline, our production of that product has been greatly reduced, and the yield of fuel oil, our least profitable product, has been correspondingly increased. Because of the difficulty in obtaining repair parts and machinery replacements, we are obliged to depend largely upon second-hand materials which add to our operating problems. Due to the rapid growth of the company, many supervisory positions have been held by young men, who are now in military service. From five to ten years' training is required to prepare them for certain hazardous operating positions in the refinery. Temporarily, some of our older employees are having to work 72 hours per week, which means

In the mid-1940s, company greeting cards displayed this nighttime photo, with the caption "Industry at War."

less efficiency and high manufacturing costs. Most departments of our company are operating 24 hours a day and seven days a week."[11]

The number of Ashland men drafted into military service was not insignificant. By the end of the war, 163 employees had served with the armed forces. Since the all-out effort to operate at full capacity around the clock demanded additional employees, women were for the first time performing work previously reserved for men. Former art teachers, bolstered with re-training in mechanical drawing, were hired into the Engineering Department; chemistry teachers took to the laboratory.

As the company publication pointed out in a 1943 story, "The public has long been accustomed to seeing girls in office and clerical jobs, in stores and banks, but it is a novelty to see them in the laboratory, in drafting rooms and in filling stations."

As desperate as the company was for new workers, it was even more desperate for additional crude oil. In 1941, the oil industry produced 1.4 billion barrels of crude oil,[12] a number that grew each year as war waged, due to frantic exploration efforts by most oil companies, including Ashland Oil & Refining.

Indeed, Ashland pursued new sources of crude oil with zeal, an effort that would serve it

During the war, women began filling positions previously held only by men, as was the case with sisters Henrietta and Barbara Siebert, working in the company's Drafting Department.

well once the war was over. As Blazer explained to shareholders in a letter dated March 1, 1944:

"Because of curtailed operations by many of the independents or smaller oil producers from whom we have always secured the greater part of the crude oil supply for our refinery, we decided last year it would be necessary for our company to engage extensively in exploratory drilling.

"As a result of our drilling, which has proved more successful than anticipated, we have been able to add almost 50 percent to our company-owned crude oil production and thus maintain an adequate supply for our refinery."[13]

Sam Wells, who had been hired in 1941 to direct exploration activities, soon shifted the company's exploration efforts from Illinois to western Kentucky, Indiana and Oklahoma. This necessitated a satellite office in Tulsa, Oklahoma, to keep track of the mid-continent efforts, and later an office in Baton Rouge, Louisiana, to oversee drilling efforts in Louisiana and Mississippi. There were several oil strikes, the most sensational in the Uniontown, Kentucky, area, which spawned perhaps the biggest single drilling spree during the war years.

Ashland acquired little during the war years, but there were several purchases to support the company's frantic efforts to explore and refine: In 1941, Ashland bought a pipeline system and gasoline plant, which used natural gas as a feedstock, from Cleveland's Cumberland Gasoline Corporation. The facilities were located in the Big Sinking district in Lee County, Kentucky. In early 1945, the company purchased a refinery in Pryse, Kentucky, with 412 producing oil wells and 75 miles of gathering pipelines in Lee, Estill and Powell counties. Interestingly, the nucleus of the pipeline system in the latter purchase was one with which Blazer had a previous association. He had overseen the construction of the pipelines 25 years earlier, when he was working for his friend Eric Shatford at The Great Northern Pipeline Company.

Shifting Priorities

Victory in Europe for the Allies finally came on May 7, 1945, when Germany surrendered

With more than 150 of the company's men called off to serve in the war, women worked in new areas, such as the laboratory.

unconditionally. Fighting continued for several more months on the Pacific front. Since 1943, General Douglas MacArthur and Admiral Chester Nimitz had been positioned to invade Japan, but it wasn't until the Allies dropped atomic bombs on Hiroshima and Nagasaki that Japan was brought to her knees. On August 14, 1945, Japan surrendered. World War II was over.

After the war ended, the United States gasoline ration was lifted, and oil companies were able to focus on a new type of consumer. Instead of producing 100-octane fuel for fighter aircraft, refineries needed to produce gasoline for civilian automobiles. Consequently, refineries had to be redesigned. By 1950, gasoline sales were 42 percent higher than they had been in 1945.[14] The postwar demand for gasoline was so great, in fact, that oil companies found it difficult to keep up.

At the same time, the world began to recognize the rich oil resources in the Middle East. In 1943, Everette Lee DeGolyer's appraisal of the oil potential in Saudi Arabia "constituted a eulogy for America's receding place in world oil — the end of its dominion," according to Pulitzer Prize-winning author Yergin. "Its remaining days as an exporter would soon disappear."[15] The prediction came true. By 1948, America's oil exports no longer exceeded its imports.[16]

These changes in supply and demand brought a shift in priorities for American oil companies, and Ashland Oil & Refining Company was no exception. When the fighting ended in 1945, Ashland servicemen began to return from the war, and the company promised, according to official company releases, to produce 800,000 gallons a day of higher octane gasoline for civilian automobile use.[17] Ashland also began emphasizing the burgeoning asphalt segment of its operations and the industrial lubricant business, in which the company had become a leading specialist during the war years.

In fact, the company had been preparing for the war's end for several months before the governments across the Atlantic and across the Pacific had reached agreement to end the fighting. As Blazer wrote on December 30, 1944, in a letter to the stockholders for the annual report:

> *"Second only to the desire to do a good job in the production of war products is the desire to do an equally good job of planning for the postwar period. ... Your company will have its share of problems — many of which cannot be solved in advance. It is believed though that the company will be in a strong financial position and have its investments in facilities sufficiently charged off as to cushion the necessary postwar adjustments."[18]*

On September 6, 1945, Blazer announced that the $16 million government aviation plant would be taken over by Ashland on a six-month lease to negotiate for a long-term lease or outright purchase. As part of that announcement, Blazer disclosed that a public offering had been made the previous week of $5 million in 3 percent, 20-year sinking fund debentures through Chicago, New York, Cincinnati and Louisville investments bankers.

"This offering," he announced, "was immediately oversubscribed, being purchased largely by insurance companies and banks for investment accounts. This financing, together with a public offering in May of $4 million in 4¼ percent convertible preferred stock, which likewise was oversubscribed and is now selling at a premium, puts the company in a strong financial position."[19]

The war years, certainly, had taken a toll. But the company that in 1938 had reported assets of $5.6 million would, by the end of 1945, report assets of $21.8 million. And the company that in 1938 reported a net profit of $566,241 would by the end of 1945 report net profits of $980,000. In less than a decade, the company had more than tripled its value. Ashland Oil & Refining Company seemed quite well-positioned for whatever the postwar years might require.

J. Howard Marshall

Blazer's frequent absences from Ashland, a spate of health problems never adequately diagnosed, despite trips to major medical centers, and the company's rapid growth combined to convince Blazer of the need for another top executive with broad training, a possible successor. In 1944 he hired as Ashland's new president a relatively young petroleum lawyer, J. Howard Marshall, who had served with the Petroleum Administration of War. Blazer, in turn, took the titles of chairman and chief executive officer while Everett Wells became vice president.

Although only 39 when he assumed Ashland's presidency, Marshall had an impressive background. After graduating from Haverford College in Haverford, Pennsylvania, with degrees in physics and chemistry, he earned a law degree from Yale University, graduating magna cum laude. He served two years as assistant dean of the Yale Law School before practicing law with a prestigious San

Francisco law firm. During the war, he was called to Washington, D.C., where he developed powerful friends. His application to Ashland Oil included Supreme Court Justice William O. Douglas and Secretary of the Interior Harold Ickes as references.

A trim Quaker with aristocratic good looks and a listing walk, the result of a childhood bout with typhoid that rendered his left leg three inches shorter than his right, Marshall had the kind of quick intelligence and high energy that Blazer prized.

Within weeks of his arrival in Ashland with his wife — a thespian who appeared in scores of local productions — and their two young sons, Marshall had distinguished himself spectacular-

ly, by showing "unusual initiative," Blazer wrote to shareholders at the end of 1944.[20]

In his written comments to stockholders for the 1945 annual report, Blazer was confident of the future:

"It is believed that our company, heretofore engaged principally in refining, transportation and distribution, is now also firmly established in the producing branch of the petroleum industry. Last year's drilling program has opened numerous semi-proven locations for further drilling as well as pointed the way toward attractive wildcat blocks."[21]

The No. 2 Refinery was purchased by Ashland Oil after the war for about one-eighth of what the U.S. government had paid to construct it.

CHAPTER FIVE

RECOVERY AND EXPANSION

"This is a dream era, this is what everyone was waiting through the blackouts for. The Great American Boom is on."

— *Fortune* magazine, 1946[1]

POSTWAR ADJUSTMENTS WERE many, not only for Ashland Oil, but for the nation. The texture and tempo of American life changed quickly. The first five postwar years, 1946 to 1951, were among the company's most active. Throughout this period, Ashland purchased several more refineries, many miles of pipelines and several significant companies, driving sales upward. In 1946, for example, the company reported net sales of $20.4 million; by 1950, that number had increased to an impressive $145.4 million, and by 1951 net sales rocketed to $205.9 million.

New Allies

Ashland's buying spree, slow at first, escalated to a breathtaking pace by the end of the 1940s. The first purchase was the refinery Ashland had operated throughout the war. After prolonged negotiations between Ashland and the government, Ashland purchased the $16 million aviation fuel plant for the $2.15 million it had offered.

The decision to buy had been an uncharacteristically anguished one. Many company officials viewed the plant as vital to Ashland Oil's future because it had state-of-the-art equipment Ashland's own plant lacked. Also, it was located so close to Ashland's property that, were it to be

purchased by anyone else, Ashland's expansion possibilities would be severely limited.

Those opposed to the acquisition suggested, however, that demand for gasoline in peacetime could languish for several years, hardly justifying a second refinery. Ashland was clearly in a strong negotiating position. The refinery was not particularly appealing to other potential buyers, chiefly because they did not have the crude oil supplies and distribution capabilities in the area that Ashland did. So for a bargain price, Blazer purchased, on December 11, 1947, what would become known internally as the No. 2 Refinery.

During the same months in 1946 that Ashland was negotiating for the No. 2 Refinery, it was holding secret talks with Allied Oil, a relatively young Cleveland-based company. Allied had a refinery in Canton, Ohio, but it was primarily a reseller of fuel oil. Negotiations stalled before the year ended, with each side holding firm its final offer, the figures remaining $500,000 apart. In 1947, the two companies resumed negotiations. Allied's motivation to sell had escalated. The two founders, Floyd R. Newman and W.W. Vandeveer, were facing a vari-

An Ashland gas-station attendant in Kenova, West Virginia, in 1946.

ety of company-related tax problems and financial difficulties, including the need to spend large sums to modernize its refinery.

It would be a marriage of opposites: Allied was bigger in terms of sales — $40 million in 1947 compared with Ashland's $29 million — but its net profits were lower: $1.8 million compared with Ashland's $2.9 million. One of the things that made negotiations more difficult, Scott pointed out, was the two companies' methods of ownership:

"Ashland was a public corporation with stock traded, with connections and a reputation with brokers, with a number of astute financial advisors on its board and near its management. Its *avenues for expansion and capitalization were extensive, its structure complex.*

"Allied Oil, on the other hand, operated along the lines of a simple partnership, although technically it was a corporation. The stock was largely owned by [co-founders] Newman and Vandeveer, and neither wanted to enter the complicated world of shareholders, directors, public reports and exposure involved in a publicly held corporation."[2]

Ashland's No. 1 Refinery, the company's original plant, was expanded greatly over the years until, by 1947, it sprawled far along the river.

Blazer and his team were acutely aware of more subtle differences. As Blazer commented during the protracted discussions, "There is little resemblance, I believe, between the character and psychology of their operation and ours."[3]

It was an observation born of several small incidents. One that rang especially clear was an exchange between Allied's legal counsel, Jim Weeks, and Blazer, when the Blazers were entertaining the Allied executive at the local country club. During small talk about various interests and pastimes, Weeks expressed what Blazer evidently saw as excessive enthusiasm for the concept of vacations. "At Ashland Oil, Jim," Blazer intoned with firm conviction, "our work is our vocation, our avocation and our vacation."[4]

Whatever reservations either or both sides may have harbored, the deal was finalized in 1948, the same year Ashland became one-third owner of Southern Pipeline Company, which brought the company in touch with the Atlantic Ocean for the first time.

The merger with Allied Oil moved Ashland into a new league, according to author Otto Scott.

"[The deal] extended Ashland Oil from a one-refinery company to a company with almost double its former resources. Lake tankers, pipelines, barges, tank cars, salesmen, new customers, new banking connections, more oil and gas leases and partners, and more crude oil and wells entered the firm."[5]

Even more significant, the merger with Allied Oil brought Rexford Sydney Blazer, Paul Blazer's nephew and an Allied Oil executive, into the business. Rex Blazer's joining Ashland

Oil would resonate with import barely three years later, when Paul Blazer suffered his first heart attack.

Rex Blazer, the son of Paul Blazer's brother, Frederick, had wanted to join Ashland two decades earlier. In 1928, when the Ashland name was attached to only the ramshackle refinery in Catlettsburg, Rex had journeyed to Kentucky soon after his graduation from the University of Illinois to ask his uncle for a job.

Paul Blazer turned him down flat, telling his nephew that the company was too small for him to hire a family member. According to the elder Blazer, if his nephew did well, everyone would say it was nepotism. If he didn't, his uncle would have to fire him, and that would cause trouble in the family.[6]

With that, the elder Blazer offered the young man train fare to Cleveland, suggesting that he talk to some friends of his at Allied Oil.

Allied hired Rex Blazer and promptly dispatched him to Ashland for an apprenticeship at Blazer's refinery. At Ashland, Rex learned the ropes the hard way, loading tank cars, assisting in the product laboratory and the like. On his return to Cleveland, he quickly proved himself a skilled, knowledgeable salesman and became Allied's vice president of Sales soon after he turned 30.

With the merger of Allied and Ashland, Rex Blazer, a single father who had lost his first wife to childbirth and his second to divorce, became president of the Allied Oil Division of Ashland.

A Giant is Born

Although the Allied merger eclipsed most other activities at Ashland that year, it was only one among many. Ashland bought a refinery, this time in Niles, Ohio, from Western Reserve Refining Company. Ashland had leased the refinery and later exercised its option to buy it. Although it was small and outdated, it was on the edge of Ashland's distribution area and could be

Rex Blazer was 21 when he first asked Paul Blazer for a job at Ashland Oil & Refining Company, but it wasn't until Ashland merged with Allied Oil that Rex began working for Ashland.

used to refine additional fuel during periods of high demand. Ashland made it hugely profitable in short order.

That same year, Ashland also purchased the Ohio Oil Company's distribution properties in about a dozen Kentucky counties. Ashland had changed a great deal since the war's end:

"Ashland had almost doubled its size; grown beyond the $100 million volume figure. Its market area had been extended from the Ohio River Valley north to Chicago, Cleveland and the Great Lakes. Its pipelines had been stretched east of Pittsburgh to the Atlantic seaboard, south to Louisiana, Texas, the Gulf, west to Kansas and Oklahoma. It had added two refineries and more specialists to its group, extended its products, increased its capacities, added more executives and more young and ambitious men. Its employees grew to 2,000; its stockholders to 9,600. Mr. Blazer and his associates had accomplished this, moreover, without losing control; without even sharing control."[7]

Within months, the company planned further acquisitions. By 1950, Ashland had taken five additional companies under its umbrella, acquiring from National Refining a 10,000-barrel-a-day refinery in Findlay, Ohio, as well as its White Rose gasoline brand and Enarco motor oils. In short order, it bought Frontier Oil in Buffalo, which had an 8,000-barrel-a-day refinery, a fuel market in western New York, and a subsidiary called Frontier Transportation that transported crude to Buffalo through the Erie Canal.

Ashland then merged with Aetna of Louisville, which had not only a refinery, but owned or leased 220 gasoline service stations in Kentucky and Indiana and a large barge fleet. The next acquisition was the Independent Oil Company of Clinton, Kentucky, with two bulk plants distributing to several counties.

In 1948, Ashland Oil & Refining merged with Allied Oil, which was established over two decades earlier to specialize in fuel oil.

Perhaps the most significant deal of the era occurred in 1950 with the Freedom-Valvoline merger. Involved in the manufacture and marketing of lubricating motor oils, Valvoline could trace its roots back nearly a century, and both Freedom and Valvoline were nationally recognized brands. But the owners, Earle Craig and William Bechman, were aging, and the issues of estates and taxes loomed large. Within weeks of initial discussions, a deal was finalized.

With that, Ashland entered more new territory. The Department of Justice, during discussions concerning Ashland's purchase of Frontier Oil, ranked Ashland the 19th largest oil company in the country, and in the spring of 1950, Ashland Oil & Refining Company was listed on the New York Stock Exchange.[8]

The Talent

From its earliest days, Ashland had been a place suitable only for those with an extraordinary work ethic. This remained a constant even as the company matured. Executives were expected to work a minimum of 12 hours a day, and Saturdays were regarded as part of the work week. Paul Blazer, who required little sleep and had no known interests or passions other than work, evidently believed most people should follow his lead. "He ran a tight shop," said W.E. Chellgren, who joined the company in 1953 after the Valvoline acquisition and eventually became the company controller.[9]

It was a challenging culture to many, but Ashland

Above and below: In 1950 Ashland acquired Aetna of Louisville, which had impressive holding, distributing and marketing networks in Kentucky and Indiana.

had developed a reputation as a leader in technology and technique, and it attracted an array of willing young men, eager to make the necessary sacrifices. Against all odds, perhaps, most of them stayed. Even more astonishingly, many of the children of Ashland employees watched their parents toil through long days and nights and weekends, and then went off to college for their degrees and soon thereafter presented themselves at Ashland's doors.

Most of the men who started out with the company in its infancy were still there in the late 1940s — and beyond — helping lead it through the challenges of rapid growth.

Palmer Talbutt, a World War I veteran who joined the refinery staff in 1926 as a Dubbs operator, quickly worked his way through the ranks, eventually becoming a vice president, then director. He remained with Ashland until his retirement.

E.W. Ned Seaton, a Yale graduate and the company's treasurer in 1932, eventually became a director and stayed until his retirement in 1959; his son Bill Seaton, also a graduate of Yale, started with Ashland as an insurance specialist and became an

executive assistant, working for Rex, in 1964. He rose to become a director and vice chairman of the board and CFO.

Everett F. Wells, a University of Illinois graduate who majored in economics and law, accepted an entry-level position at the refinery in 1926, then climbed from sales manager to executive vice president, ascending to the presidency in 1967.

Arthur Points, a graduate of Georgetown College, left a bank job in 1931 to work as an Ashland bookkeeper at a lower salary and rose to controller and then treasurer of the company.

Ed Emrick, a graduate of the University of Illinois, was hired in 1931 for a sales job, shifted quickly to the Accounting Department, and rose to top executive positions, including corporate treasurer, and stayed on until his retirement.

Roland Whealy, with an M.S. in chemical engineering from Iowa State University, joined the company as a chemist in 1935, rising to superintendent of the refineries and a vice presidency.

The list goes on and on. But while there was an abundance of seasoned, senior long-term executives by the middle of the 1940s, there was also an infusion of new, very bright and promising young men.

Even Blazer's son, Paul Jr, entered the fray. After attending Virginia Polytechnic Institute, then serving in the Army in World War II, he graduated from the University of Kentucky and joined Ashland Oil & Refining Company in 1947. The son of the founder "received no favors from management,"[10] according to author Otto Scott. He held various positions, including manager of new product development, and in 1967 was elected a director. Paul Jr. became the first president of The Ashland Foundation in 1968. After suffering a stroke in 1982, he retired the following year.

The Setting

For all the hard work and micro-managing the employees endured, they obviously found aspects of the company attractive.

Dave Miller, Mack Crider and Ralph Romine restore the fluid catalytic cracking tower at the No. 2 Refinery after the company negotiated with the government to buy the plant.

Above: Employees and their children gather for the annual summer picnic in August 1956.

Below: Ashland employees had their own credit union, founded in 1941, further enhancing the sense of family unity.

Some of the appeal was the sheer challenge of surviving — indeed, excelling — in an industry littered with failure. Some of the appeal was the gestures that Blazer unfailingly offered. Demanding and exacting, Blazer was also acutely conscious of the sacrifices his employees were making and went to great lengths to celebrate their victories, their lives and their families.

The Ashland Christmas parties — gay, raucous family affairs — were unparalleled. Circus acrobats, trick dogs and prancing ponies were hired to perform; the meals were lavish; and the children received carefully selected gifts that took days to wrap and tag. Blazer seized every opportunity to compliment or reward a job well done, and he was inconsolable when an employee died, was injured or fell on hard times. He was resolute about helping his employees improve their lives through education; he set up vari-

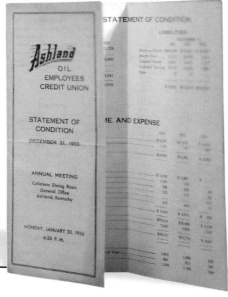

ous means by which Ashland employees could take courses to improve their skills or help increase their opportunities for advancement.

Because the area is geographically isolated, Blazer realized it would be in the best interest of Ashland Oil to nurture an active social life for its employees. Cutthroat softball leagues provided diversion during the long, hazy summer months; bowling (for men and for women) was the winter sport of choice, and the top rollers were awarded giant trophies. There were company picnics and a variety of planned activities for the executives' wives. Female employees started a social club called the Arcoettes in the mid-1940s, and as a group they took tours, arranged luncheons and explored the area together.

The employees looked to each other and the company for much of their stimulation and sustenance, and as the company grew large in the late 1940s, Blazer worried about losing some of the things dear to him. He spoke movingly to employees at the 1949 Christmas party:

"We don't ever want to get like a large corporation. I hope we never get so large that this spirit is gone. I want you to always be sure that someone in this company is interested in your welfare and your problems, whether it is your immediate supervisor or someone higher up."[11]

Community Involvement

Blazer also reminded his employees that each of them had an obligation to the world in which they lived:

"As we grow larger there are certain responsibilities which we must keep in mind. ... We are put into this world to do a good job, not merely to have a good time."[12]

The Blazers had embodied that philosophy for years. Accordingly, the city's Board of Trade honored Ashland Oil & Refining and Blazer at an appreciation dinner in the

Ashland's signs depicting the "Flying Octanes" logo began showing up in the late 1940s. By the 1950s, they were in place throughout the distribution area.

early 1950s for playing an important role "in the economic and cultural development of eastern Kentucky and the Ohio Valley." Blazer and the company, the board said, "have been good citizens and neighbors and have accepted willingly and generously their community responsibilities."[13]

Blazer became an outspoken proponent of a variety of educational causes and rallied for race issues in the 1940s, a time when few prosperous white men concerned themselves with civil rights. He became chairman of the Cincinnati Branch of the Federal Reserve System; served as president pro tem of the Kentucky Traffic Association, a group devoted to strengthening traffic laws in the state (J. Howard Marshall was a committee chairman for the same organization); and was chairman of the state Constitutional Convention to revise the 1891 document, because it contained restrictions making progress in certain areas impossible.

He received in the late 1940s a "Useful Citation" from the University of Chicago, and the University of Kentucky awarded him a medallion for outstanding service to the community. He also contributed quietly and privately to a variety of charities and causes. His wife was active in several local civic organizations and served as a trustee of the University of Kentucky — the first woman to receive such an appointment — from 1939 until 1960.

Marshall, Ashland's president, was involved in a number of professional and regional improvement organizations. For starters, he was among 15 petroleum officials nationwide appointed by the U.S. Secretary of the Interior to the Military Petroleum Advisory Council. He was also a member of the research advisory council of the Kentucky Chamber of Commerce, a vice president of Marketing for the American Petroleum Institute, and chairman of the board of the Ohio Valley Improvement Association, which was aimed at balancing development and conservation concerns in the Ohio Valley.

The pages of the *Ashland Oil Log* were filled with news about employees who contributed to the industry and their communities. Among them, John Rosson, refinery operations manager, was elected president of the regional fire and safety department of the National Petroleum Council; salesman Roy Herrenkohl became president of the Ashland Rotary Club; Jack Wilson, manager of the Cumberland Terminal, became president of the Catlettsburg Rotary Club; and transportation manager M.C. Dupree became vice president of the American Waterways Operators. Employees in all levels of the company did their part.

Difficult Times

Ashland Oil & Refining Company was not without its problems, however. First, although Ashland continued to pour money into its effort to locate oil, the company could never seem to master the art of finding it. Even though it allied itself with a variety of drilling companies, the number of dry holes was alarmingly high, the number of productive holes, by comparison, shockingly low. This realm of the oil business that Blazer had been slow to enter never became the profit generator that he had hoped.

But in the postwar years, exploration efforts continued. In 1946, half of the company's total $8 million investment was tied to producing. Still, the supply of crude could not keep pace with the ever more efficient refineries. As author Scott pointed out, "It was ironic that the Ashland drilling in Oklahoma and Texas, both famed oil areas, was disappointing, while the drilling in Kentucky, Illinois and Indiana, where laymen seldom think great oilfields exist — was much better."[14] This pattern continued for years.

Another disturbing issue had to do with Blazer himself. Now in his 50s, he was experiencing increased difficulties in health. At the time of the Allied signing, he was noticeably pale and thin. Soon, he was diagnosed with diabetes. A few months later, the company doctor informed him he was at risk for heart problems. A hereditary disposition, coupled with stress, long hours and irregular diet, had produced a calamitous situation that seemed destined to result in a heart attack.

By the middle of 1950, a renowned heart specialist in Cleveland informed him a heart attack was mere months away. Although the doctor advised Blazer to ease up at work, nothing would halt the inevitable, the doctor said.

Deciding an Heir

With the doctor's grim news, the question of a successor became compelling. Blazer did not feel comfortable with Marshall. For the first couple of years, the relationship with his hand-picked president had been nothing but cordial, respectful and mutually satisfying. Marshall, a Yale-educated lawyer who had been a law professor before joining Ickes' efforts in Washington during the war, had skills and knowledge Blazer did not, and his work ethic equaled that of his boss. "He was a brilliant man," said Veronica Thistle, who served as Marshall's secretary from 1946 to 1950. "It was like an education to work for him. … He expected the utmost, but you were just glad to do it."[15] Blazer prized the young man and often was heard commenting on the wisdom of his decision to bring Marshall into the company.

But there were incidents that had shaken Blazer's faith in Marshall. In 1947, Blazer had been interested in obtaining a pair of tankers from the government. Marshall, as the expert on Washington affairs, told him that to receive two, they would have to apply for eight. Blazer was stunned to discover a few months later that Ashland had been approved for the purchase of all eight and was now obligated to buy them.

Marshall quickly took action to turn a potentially disastrous situation into a profitable one by forming a partnership with Allied Oil to create the Independent Tank Ships Company. Though the new company sold the tankers off and made a

An Ashland service station in Kentucky during the early 1950s.

Ashland President J. Howard Marshall and Chairman Paul Blazer aboard the *Ashland* in 1948, after the towboat had been rebuilt for greater power.

profit, Blazer still fumed. He could not get over the haunting impression that Marshall's advice had very nearly caused a calamity and put him in grave difficulty with his board of directors. Years later Blazer would identify this event as pivotal in his relationship with Marshall. According to author Scott, "... he had relied upon Marshall and his advice, and had nearly been landed in the soup."[16]

The second incident occurred in the last days of the Allied Oil merger negotiations. In the final draft of the merger documents, Blazer found a clause that he had neither requested nor been informed of. The clause gave Allied's Jim Weeks voting privileges for Vandeveer's and Newman's combined stock — a huge voting bloc. Blazer, knowing that Marshall and Weeks were quite friendly with each other, felt they had conspired to put that clause in, and could foresee the day when together they could exert undue influence in any power

struggle. They could, with that bloc, plus their own voting rights, probably change the direction of the company, and unseat Blazer if they desired.

Blazer never believed the inclusion of that clause was innocent. At the final signing, he presented a document that gave him the voting rights of Vandeveer's and Newman's stock and announced that, unless they signed it immediately, the deal was off. They signed without delay.

These incidents effectively removed Marshall's name from any list of potential successors. Blazer's older son, Paul Jr., was bright and hardworking, yet lacked managerial experience. On July 19, 1950, the afternoon the heart specialist gave his grave prediction, Blazer asked his nephew Rex, the man he had denied a job a quarter-century earlier, to take over the company, and Rex agreed. At this point, Rex was president of both Allied Oil and Frontier Oil. While he split his time between Buffalo and Cleveland, he was ensconced in Cleveland society and discouraged any talk of his moving to Ashland, Kentucky.

Less than five months later, doctors' predictions were sadly realized. Paul and Georgia Blazer were at the beach apartment in La Jolla, California, for the Christmas holidays. After composing the year-end letter to employees, Blazer announced he was feeling ill. A young heart specialist called to their apartment told Mrs. Blazer her husband was in heart failure, and as he arranged for an ambulance, he confided that he did not expect Blazer to live through the night.

Blazer survived, though the recovery was measured in the tiniest increments. The corporate headquarters received almost daily progress reports from Georgia Blazer.

By mid-January, it seemed that the worst was over, and Blazer was soon back in the apartment in California, on the phone, conducting business from his bed. "Daddy always had a phone in his hand, or nearby," daughter Doris Webb would later recall. "He always felt that he could keep in touch that way, keep up with everything that was happening."[17]

His affinity for the phone extended into his personal life as well. "Mother used to go to bed early, and after I had the children, Daddy would call me and we would talk late into the night. He liked to talk about all kinds of things — we had some wonderful talks."[18]

In Ashland, events he had set in motion before his heart attack moved ahead as he had intended. In 1951, the board of directors elected Everett Wells executive vice president. "He will take over most of my work in operations," Blazer had told the board earlier.[19] In addition, the board elected Rexford Blazer as president of Ashland Oil & Refining Company and made J. Howard Marshall vice chairman of the board.

Marshall soon recognized that a shift in power had occurred, and his relationship with Paul Blazer became increasingly strained. By the end of the year, Marshall resigned.

Ashland Oil & Refining Company was now in the capable hands of two Blazers.

The United Carbon acquisition in the early 1960s was part of Ashland's diversification efforts as the company sought to lessen its reliance on the production, manufacture and distribution of fuel oils.

CHAPTER SIX

GAINING MOMENTUM

"The American success story was never better exemplified than in the career of Paul Blazer."

— *The Herald-Dispatch*, 1966[1]

BY THE END OF 1952, WITH REX Blazer as president and a recovered Paul Blazer serving as chairman and CEO, the company reported net sales of $229.4 million, up from $205.9 million in 1951. Also, the company would report that it was refining 110,009 barrels of crude oil a day, up from 93,724 in 1951.

Making Adjustments

There were months — years, in some cases — of adjustments as the various companies that had joined with Ashland in the late 1940s and early 1950s adapted to a new and evolving culture. As Paul Blazer pointed out in his speech to the Newcomen Society, the combining of companies is a complicated affair:

"Every organization has in it much that is good and desirable, but each organization also has its weaknesses and peculiarities. A merger of two companies is far more than a financial transaction. ... There are many problems inherent in the methods of expansion which we have used so extensively. ... The feeling of personal insecurity often associated with mergers must be overcome. It must be replaced with the confidence that there will be greater opportunities and that every employee will be advanced without favoritism. Mergers must not result in stepchildren.

"Mergers frequently require the reconciling of different philosophies of business. Planning and patience are necessary in order to avoid inequities to individuals and to protect personal pride. It is not easy to bring people who have been trained differently into a smoothly functioning team under a consolidated leadership. The acceptance of a certain amount of entrenched inefficiency may be necessary; likewise new talent must be recognized and rewarded. A period of months may be required in which to locate people into positions where their abilities may be utilized and their shortcomings minimized."[2]

Yet even as Ashland prepared to extend a fair measure of leeway to newly acquired employees, the company wasted no time identifying operational problems and correcting them. Considering its experience with the acquisition of poorly performing refineries and turning them around, Ashland knew what had to be done. Very soon following an acquisition, an Ashland team would arrive on site to begin the process of determining how to improve efficiency and profitability. So effi-

---

Rex Blazer served as president of Ashland Oil & Refining from 1951 to 1956 and as chairman of the board from 1957 to 1971.

cient was this process that on more than one occasion the Ashland team showed up at the acquired company's headquarters before the previous owners had finished drafting an announcement to its employees.

Throughout this hectic period, Paul Blazer continued to reassure his associates that he was in good health. Several months after Blazer's nearly fatal heart attack, Personnel Manager Alex Chamberlain discussed with him the possibility of enrollment in the company pension plan. Obviously, Chamberlain assumed that Blazer would one day retire, and provisions should be made for that day. Blazer, however, refused, as Chamberlain wrote.

"Monday evening, September 10 [1951], I discussed with Mr. Blazer the matter of whether or not he should enroll in the Company Pension Plan. He

decided in view of the fact that he would probably continue to work for the company as long as he lives and receive a salary for such services, that he would be ineligible to receive any pension. Any money that he would put into the Pension Plan would, of course, be returned to him with interest. However he feels that he can invest such money to better advantage than 2% interest."[3]

A Relative Status

The dust soon settled once Rex Blazer became president. J. Howard Marshall departed, and Paul Blazer recovered from his illness. There was little confusion about who was in charge, nor any tension relating to the potentially awkward matter of having two top men named Blazer. Paul Blazer continued to be called Mr. Blazer; his nephew was Rex. This simple protocol was understood by all, although no edict was issued.

Years later, Paul Blazer called Rex and was startled when his nephew's secretary answered with "Mr. Blazer's office."

Paul Blazer in the 1950s was spending less time at the office and more time at home. He kept connected to the various workings of the company by telephone.

"Young lady," the company founder announced, "this is Mr. Blazer. Now let me speak to Rex."[4]

A man whose drive and work ethic equaled those of his uncle, Rex Blazer had always been an overachiever. When he graduated from the University of Illinois with a degree in business, it was with 158 credit hours rather than the 120 required.[5] Upon joining Allied Oil, he became a vice president in 10 years and president within 20.

Rex set about the business of running the company with quiet resolve. In addition to being president of Ashland, he remained president of Allied, and was president of Frontier as well. He settled into an unyielding routine: 10 or 11 hours a day at the office (usually taking lunch at his desk), dinner with his family (he remarried several years after he moved to Ashland) and then back to the office until 11 p.m. He usually worked most of the day on Saturday and five or six hours on Sunday, after church. "He rarely missed an evening that he did not come back to the office and work several hours," said Johnnie Daniels, who served as Rex Blazer's secretary for several years.[6]

He may have worked in the shadow of his uncle, but Rex Blazer quickly achieved a reputation as an articulate and informed straight-shooter.

Widely regarded as an excellent speaker, he was soon in great demand. He rapidly distinguished himself as one of the industry's most informed and impressive spokesmen. "Rex was a huge talent," said James Fout, retired group vice president of Petroleum Marketing. "His speeches were superb. His letter-writing skills were without peer, and so he did a tremendous job with our image within the industry."[7]

Over the years, Rex Blazer addressed scores of professional organizations and annual conventions, including the American Road Builders Association meeting in Los Angeles; The Pipe Line Conference of the American Petroleum Institute meeting in Dallas; the National Petroleum Refiners Association meeting in San Antonio; and the Ohio Petroleum Marketers Association meeting in Cleveland.

There were also dozens of appearances before civic and educational groups, including the Psi Upsilon National Convention; the Lexington Kiwanis Club; commencement exercises at Aledo (Illinois) High School; the Ashland Jaycees; and the Ironton Lions Club. Rex was a frequent presence in

The catalytic cracking unit, some of the most advanced technology of the day, rises in the background of the Canton, Ohio, refinery in 1952.

Washington, D.C., speaking before various congressional committees and subcommittees, and was a convincing voice with Kentucky state legislators.

Infused with a strong sense of responsibility to his industry and the community, he became active in a variety of organizations and causes. He served as president of the National Petroleum Council, vice president of the Western Petroleum Refiners Association and was a member of the executive committee of the American Petroleum Institute and a director of both the Asphalt Industry and the Kentucky Oil and Gas Association. His participation in civic and educational organizations included the presidency of the Kentucky Chamber of Commerce; board of directors of the Ohio Chamber of Commerce; member of the Eastern Kentucky Regional Planning Commission; member of the advisory committees of the Ohio Valley Improvement Association and the National Waterways Conference; director of the Kentucky Heart Association; trustee of the Kentucky Independent College

By the late 1950s, Ashland's new service stations featured wide driveways, easy access and complete one-stop automotive service.

Foundation; regent of the University of the South at Sewanee, Tennessee; and a member of the board of directors of the University of Illinois.

He also served as a vestryman and senior warden of Ashland's Calvary Episcopal Church. In short order, he had developed an independent name recognition equal to that of his uncle. It is often said that Paul Blazer built the company and Rex Blazer elevated its status, stature and standing.

Gaining Trust

Rex Blazer's influence was soon felt as much inside the company as outside it. Tall, bright and affable, the characteristics that had propelled him to top salesman at Allied quickly earned him broad respect throughout Ashland.

A tension-free relationship between the two Blazers — so similarly confident, competitive and sensitive — seemed unlikely. Yet they forged a respectful working relationship with only a few turbulent moments.

In 1952, Paul's younger son, Stuart, was killed while serving in the Korean War. Some believed he eventually could have succeeded his father at the helm.

"Stuart could have done anything," said Doris Webb, Paul Blazer's only daughter, in a 1998 interview. "He had everything going for him — he was bright, compassionate, well-educated, good at sports, good with people. He could have excelled in just about any field he chose to enter."[8]

Stuart had tried to enlist in World War II but was turned down because he suffered from a separated shoulder. He had surgery to repair it and was able to enlist for the Korean War. Sadly, he would never return.

"Of course we were devastated," Doris Webb said. "But my parents said they felt some comfort that he died fighting for his country, doing something he felt was important, something he believed in and really had tried hard to do. It wasn't a senseless death, a car accident or something like that."[9]

Ensuring the Future

As Rex Blazer adapted to the Ashland corporate and family dynamics, his uncle gradually shifted his attention to preparing a new generation of company leadership. He took a series of young men under his wing as his executive assistants. They opened and helped respond to his mail and listened in on his many calls, receiving broad exposure to virtually every aspect of the company's operations.

He also established an innovative program to allow promising young men to learn from others within the company. They served as assistants to a variety of those in upper management and were tutored in the full spectrum of corporate life.

J.A. "Fred" Brothers, executive vice president at Ashland Inc. in 1998, said among the reasons he joined Ashland in 1966 was because he was "very impressed with the opportunities for young people."[10] Retired Group Vice President of Petroleum Marketing James Fout agreed, saying, "Ashland provided a great atmosphere for training and development. The company gave me more opportunity than I ever had a right to expect or even thought I could handle. It was loyal to me, and I was loyal to it."[11]

A Downturn

Considering the positive leadership and new business, it was surprising that Ashland recorded a sudden downturn in 1954. Net sales fell more than $9 million to $227.9 million; crude oil refined was down more than 1,000 barrels a day to 108,718; and the number of employees was reduced by 200, down to 4,200. "Oil refining profits have tended to run in cycles," Blazer explained in his 1954 annual report to stockholders. "For the past two years earnings in the refining branch of the oil industry have been smaller than normal. The independent refiners who sell much of their output in the wholesale market are suffering especially."[12]

It was a logical explanation, but some board members felt there might be more at play. Perhaps the elder Blazer, then in his 60s, was los-

A tireless proponent of the oil industry, Rex Blazer was elected president of the National Petroleum Refiners Association in 1959.

ing his Midas touch. Perhaps, they considered, Blazer's health difficulties had diminished his ability to direct the company as he once had. At

Robert E. Yancey Sr. was one of Ashland's transition leaders, linking the era of Paul Blazer with more recent periods. Yancey joined Ashland in 1943 and held pivotal roles, including service as the first president of Ashland Petroleum Company and the first president of Ashland Chemical Company when those divisions were formed. Upon his retirement in 1981, Ashland's annual report for that year noted: "As president of the corporation, Mr. Yancey has won the respect of both oil industry leaders and the federal government as a staunch supporter of the ideal of an independent and competitive refining industry. He put forth Ashland's views during the turbulent decade of the 1970s, when the U.S. oil industry had to cope with unprecedented changes and disruptions."

the first board meeting in 1954, board member Walton Davis read a lengthy statement thanking Blazer for his decades of service to the company. He then suggested it would be in Blazer's best interest to retire. Davis was, he said, speaking for many members of the board.

Blazer listened quietly to the statement. At its conclusion, he calmly thanked the board members for their concern, then promptly dismissed the recommendation. He was feeling quite well, he said, and suggested that the board had somehow developed an exaggerated notion of his condition.

He was, however, acutely aware there was more behind the board members' suggestion that day than concern for his health. He quickly added another duty to his nephew's growing roster — emissary to the directors. Rex began making regular visits to board members, reassuring them of his uncle's continued ability to do the job.

The company's rebound was quick. The problem, it turned out, was just as Blazer had said: one of those cyclical dips. By the following year, the company had reported net sales of $245.8 million, and crude oil production had climbed to 110,383 barrels a day, the result, according to Blazer, of "a more normal relationship between prices for refined products and the cost of crude oil" and also "new refining and transportation facilities."[13] In that year, the company upgraded its refineries, added two new towboats and hired 100 more employees.

Stepping Back

Buoyed by the comeback, Blazer began turning his attention to internal matters. Fearing the Ashland organization had grown "too static," he began shifting leadership into two new responsibilities. Roland Whealy went from general superintendent of the refineries to the post of special assistant to Everett Wells, executive vice president. Bill Humphreys, chief engineer of the refineries, became assistant to Franklin "Chub" Moffitt, head of National Accounts. Gus Litton, formerly an assistant to Humphreys, was made chief engineer. Bob Yancey Sr. became coordinator of refineries.[14]

During this period, Orin Atkins, a University of Virginia Law School graduate who joined Ashland's Legal Department in 1950, was beginning to make a name for himself. Paul Blazer, who was increasingly confined to his home, began to rely more and more on the eyes and ears of Atkins, who became one of Blazer's executive assistants. Atkins strolled the halls, notebook in hand, making notes of his observations and details of various operations.

As author Otto Scott observed, the two men, though quite different, were very helpful to each other, and each felt high admiration for the other.

"The fact was that the two men complemented each other. Atkins' legal training equipped him to concentrate on the issues that arose: to examine them for means and avenues of resolution and this was important. But even more important was that his was a fertile and creative mind in finance. Atkins brought insights to Mr. Blazer that had not been taught to him, but that he discovered for himself. In addition, his manners were good and his instincts gentlemanly; the combination to Mr. Blazer was most attractive. His eyes, experienced in reading men, saw the outlines of a possible corporate heir, and all his faculties began to assess, to weigh and consider this possibility."[15]

In 1955, the year Paul Blazer was selected Kentuckian of the Year by the Kentucky Press Association and Rex became president of the Kentucky Chamber of Commerce, exploration and production efforts were curtailed following lackluster performance. Rumors flew throughout the industry and on Wall Street that Ashland might be absorbed by a larger oil company. Congress also began to show increased interest in support of a user tax on the waterways, legislation that would have an immediate and disastrous effect on Ashland's performance.

Despite the turbulence, by the end of 1955, the company would report sales of $245.9 million and profits of $10 million — a new record for sales and the second highest figure for profits in its history. Blazer took this opportunity to announce that he intended to further limit his involvement with day-to-day activity.

"Having now reached the age of normal retirement I am looking forward to the opportunity, as circumstances permit, of playing a less active role in the affairs of the company. It has been a great privilege for me to have had the opportunity of working for so many years with such capable and loyal associates who have cooperated in building an organization in which all of us take great pride."[16]

In 1956, the gasoline market peaked, an event that was particularly difficult for independent oil companies, because consumers began shopping for the lowest price rather than brand names. Then, when President Eisenhower called for a user tax on shippers and embarked on a study to establish tolls, Blazer feared that Ashland's waterway advantage was at risk. He was in Washington within weeks, testifying before a congressional committee.

Concurrently, though, Blazer took steps to reduce the impact if the waterways user tax legislation were enacted. When Ashland received an invitation to participate in the creation of a pipeline that would originate in Chicago and terminate near its Findlay, Ohio, plant, the company immediately signed on. Ashland would own 20 percent of a 20-inch pipeline — a guarantee of nearly 8,000 barrels of crude oil per day, certain to reduce its dependence on river-borne crude oil.

Wearing New Hats

The relative advantages of entering the petrochemical industry had long been discussed at Ashland, prompted by the young engineers brought aboard during the last decade. "At that point in time, a lot of petroleum companies were looking at acquisitions, and chemicals was the next segment that downstream executives were considering," said Scotty Patrick, Ashland Chemical group vice president of Petrochemicals and Technical in a 1998 interview.[17]

The prospect intrigued Blazer, but he was cautious in the beginning. He listened, he challenged and he probed for flaws. In the end, however, he was convinced.[18] Early in 1956, he approved the installation of a $4.5 million Udex, a Universal Oil Products unit, in Catlettsburg to produce benzene, toluene and xylene.

That same year, the company purchased the R.J. Brown Company of St. Louis for around $2

Everett Wells, who had been with the company since its earliest days, became president of Ashland Oil & Refining in 1957.

That same year, Ashland purchased for $2 million Lynch Oil, a producer with properties in Illinois and Indiana. In October 1956, *Fortune* magazine carried its first directory of the 500 largest industrial corporations in the United States. Based on sales volume, Ashland Oil & Refining was listed at 134. The following year, Paul Blazer, then 67, retired as chairman of the board. Rex became chairman, while Everett Wells was elected president.

Everett Franklin Wells, then 52, had been with Blazer nearly from the beginning. His roots, like Blazer's, were in Aledo, Illinois. Not long after his graduation from the University of Illinois with a major in economics, Wells met Blazer at a social event in their hometown. After some discussion, Wells felt compelled to make the journey to Ashland, as Blazer had suggested. The new recruit began, as nearly all Ashland employees then did, as a trainee in the refinery.

Wells soon moved into sales, quickly moving up the ranks to become Paul Blazer's sales partner. By 1940, at age 35, he became vice president. Over the years he married, had two children and held a variety of positions, including president of Freedom-Valvoline. Tall, quiet and not given to socializing or publicity, he was seen as a solid man who would keep the course steady.

Of course, Paul Blazer's influence and power continued. He remained chairman of the executive and finance committees and was officially in charge of new acquisitions and major transactions. Rex assumed more day-to-day control of the company with a concentration on sales, but Paul remained a significant influence.

The company gradually developed two separate disciplines. One was operational, while the other evaluated opportunities for potential new business.[20]

Meanwhile, the Suez Canal, which provided Western countries a link to oil in the Middle East, became the center of conflict between Britain and Egypt after Gamal Abdel Nasser, president of Egypt, seized the canal from British control in July 1956. These conflicts prompted Ashland to renew its exploration efforts, this time for foreign oil. Ashland joined other oil companies to explore for oil in Venezuela. It was yet another exploration effort that did not live up to expectations, and Ashland lost $220,000 in the venture.

million. R.J. Brown, with sales of around $15 million a year, had plants and offices in Chicago, Cleveland, Detroit, Lansing, Louisville, Memphis, St. Louis and Decatur, Illinois. It sold naphthas, solvents and other specialty products in the eastern United States and Canada. "It was Paul Blazer's theory," said Patrick, "that the company operate in the heartland of the country, and he wanted to have specialty products that could not easily be transported by pipeline or water. He wanted to be able to upgrade and maybe build some sort of economic barrier to competition from the major refining sources on the East and Gulf coasts."[19] Grover Shropshire of Refinery Sales, an Annapolis man and former Naval officer who had been with Ashland's Refinery Sales since 1949, became the Ashland-R.J. Brown liaison.

In 1959, Ashland purchased the Louisville Refining Company and its subsidiary, the Producers Pipeline Company, for nearly $5 million. The firm owned 250 miles of pipeline in western Kentucky and a refinery in Louisville. Furthermore, Ashland's Tom Paulsen in Research and Development disclosed his discovery of a new method to create naphthalene from petroleum and received the patent for a product that would be known as Hydeal.

Tragedy and Growth

In March 1960, Paul Blazer had another close brush with death. While vacationing with his wife in Phoenix, Blazer noticed an odd and ominous noise in his neck. A doctor suspected the worst, and Blazer was flown by the company jet to Houston, where world-renowned surgeon, Dr. Michael De Bakey, confirmed a diagnosis of a blocked carotid artery. The situation was critical, and the surgeon immediately operated to remove the blockage.

The period from 1946 to 1960 had been very profitable. By 1960 there were 5,000 employees, several refineries processing more than 150,000 barrels of crude oil daily, 5,000 miles of pipelines, 26 terminals in 11 states and 3,400 service stations. As author Scott pointed out, "The company had increased by a factor of 15; it had enlarged from sales of $20.4 million to $303 million."[21]

By the beginning of the 1960s, however, profits were flattening, and there seemed little possibility of further operational efficiency. To spur growth, Ashland's pace of acquisition quickened as the company acquired more companies and increased its emphasis on petrochemicals.

The Catlettsburg naphthalene operation, which had gone on line in February, was an example of this new orientation. Contracts for the sale of the product had been signed by a half-dozen chemical companies before the equipment was even installed. By the following year, Hydeal earnings accounted for 20 percent of profits at Catlettsburg.

In the 1960s, the city of Ashland honored Paul Blazer with a school that bore his name. Here Blazer and wife Georgia stand proudly on the school's stairs.

Above: Investigators
examine the site of the
crash that took the lives
of company executives
in September 1962.

Right: Ashland Oil &
Refining Company placed
a granite monument in
Palmyra Cemetery, a few
miles from the crash site.

IN MEMORIAM
JAY PARK ALEXANDER
1911   1962
ARTHUR BLAINE BERKSTRESSER
1913   1962
NEWTON ALBERT BRICKA, JR.
1919   1962
JOSEPH ALOYSIUS COLLINS, SR.
1898   1962
JOHN WILLIAM DRENNEN
1923   1962
JAMES WILEY GOFF
1925   1962
JAMES SLAUGHTER MAHAN, JR.
1925   1962
CLAYTON GEORGE MAXWELL
1902   1962
WILLIAM HENRY PARR
1917   1962
RONALD DALE ROBERTS
1932   1962
JAMES VOLTZ WHITAKER
1910   1962
WAYNE THOMAS WIGGINS
1928   1962
ROBERT FREDERICK WULFF
1925   1962

DEDICATED TO THE MEMORY OF THE THIRTEEN MEN
OF ASHLAND OIL & REFINING COMPANY WHO LOST
THEIR LIVES IN THE CRASH OF A COMPANY AIRPLANE
NEAR LAKE MILTON, OHIO, ON
SEPTEMBER 4, 1962

United Carbon, a significant producer of carbon black, also captured Ashland's attention. Carbon black is primarily used as a reinforcing agent in rubber products, such as tires, and is quite resistant to wear. Blazer and Atkins engaged in intense negotiations to acquire United Carbon. The talks went on for months, from New York to Houston, with Blazer excusing himself periodically to take long draws from the oxygen tank that had accompanied him on trips for more than a decade.

During the United Carbon negotiations, the company suffered a devastating tragedy. On September 4, 1962, one of the company aircraft, carrying executives from Allied Oil in Cleveland and Frontier in Buffalo to a meeting with Rex Blazer in Ashland, crashed in a field near Youngstown, Ohio. All 11 executives, the pilot and the copilot were lost.

It was the worst corporate aircraft accident in the history of U.S. aviation. The exact cause was never established, though investigators concluded it was likely that the Lockheed Lodestar had somehow lost elevator control.

The pilot, A.B. Berkstresser, a former American Airlines pilot, had been with

Ashland since the spring of 1949, when the company had purchased its first aircraft painted with the red and green Ashland Oil & Refining logo. The Frontier and Allied executives had been with the Ashland family for a decade. Their deaths were mourned not only in Cleveland and Buffalo, but also in Ashland, where they had made many friends.

Rex Blazer boarded the company's remaining Lodestar to visit all the widows and families of the deceased. He also attended all their funerals, and the company erected a memorial at a cemetery near the crash site, which listed the names of all the crash victims.

The United Carbon negotiations resumed, complicated and intense. It would be Ashland's largest acquisition thus far — in the neighborhood of $150 million. For Ashland, the acquisition would be a significant diversification, a new venture into the field of rubber, in which it had little expertise.

United Carbon had been the creation of Oscar Nelson, who had assembled in the 1920s a group of small carbon-black manufacturers, building it into one of the world's top three carbon-black producers. When Nelson died in 1953,

Above: This United Carbon tray dryer was the first ever used in the commercial production of carbon black.

Left: United Carbon's official logo, before Ashland acquired the company in 1963.

a few long-time associates managed the company for several years. Then Richard French, a Standard Oil vice president, was recruited as president. He tried a variety of inventive strategies to breathe new life into the company, but by the early 1960s it had slipped to third in the industry.[22]

Finally, in 1963, the deal with United Carbon was finalized, and Ashland was poised to move into the rubber industry. Walker Marx, refinery superintendent at Catlettsburg, was the first Ashland employee transferred to the United Carbon headquarters in Houston. He was quickly followed by young John R. Hall, a Vanderbilt

University grad who had worked for Standard Oil of New Jersey for a year before joining Ashland in 1957. Hall became, at age 31, a chemical engineer for the carbon black company.

Many executives at United Carbon were offered attractive opportunities to depart. After some restructuring, United Carbon soon began reporting a return to positive growth.

John Hall later returned from Houston to become an executive assistant in the Ashland corporate headquarters. Bill Gammon, a graduate of the University of Missouri School of Mine and Metallurgy, who had worked for Sinclair Oil research before joining Ashland in 1956, was made vice president of United Carbon, and soon after, its president.

Acquisitions

Also in 1963, Ashland purchased the central Louisiana pipeline system of Humble Oil & Refining for $5.5 million. The Humble line extended 500 miles in the area and was capable of delivering 50,000 barrels of crude oil a day.

Ashland had done so well in recent years that in 1964, Paul Blazer was placed in *National Petroleum News'* Hall of Fame as a leader in the oil industry.[23] That same year, Ashland Oil was listed as number 153 on the *Fortune* 500 list.[24]

In 1965, there was more movement at the top. Bob Yancey Sr. moved up to senior vice president; John Hall became executive assistant to Paul Blazer; and Bob McCowan moved from refinery sales to become executive assistant. Orin Atkins, at 41, became the company's fourth president, after Everett Wells moved from the presidency to head the executive committee. Bill Seaton had also moved up the ranks in October of the previous year, becoming executive assistant to Rex Blazer.

The new leadership continued Ashland's commitment to further investment in the petrochemical area. The company purchased for $8 million the Catalin Corporation of New Jersey, a manufacturer of antioxidants, phenolic, urea and acrylic resins.

The following year, the company purchased the O.K. Tire and Rubber Company of Littleton, Colorado, for $6.4 million. O.K., with reported sales of $10 million a year, was involved in selling, recapping and repairing tires and had factories in Alabama, Colorado and Washington, as well as franchised dealers across the country. It was considered a logical complement to Ashland's United Carbon business.

Also in 1966, the company acquired Warren Brothers of Cambridge, Massachusetts, among the nation's largest paving contractors, for $37 million. Ashland's own asphalt business had been slowly expanding over the years, and the company had developed substantial expertise in the area.

There were a couple of smaller acquisitions that year as well: the purchase of Chemical Solvents for $1 million and Southern Fiber Glass Products Inc., a pleasure boat builder, for $1 million.

The End of an Era

Paul Blazer was involved in decision-making in all the acquisitions, although he more often left the on-site negotiations to others. Confined most of the time by then to his home, conferring on the telephone with other executives, he returned his attention to the refining end of the company. Upon learning the Catlettsburg Refinery had lost efficiency, he oversaw the development of a new training program for operators. In a short time, throughput had increased significantly. Young John Hall, Blazer's most recent assistant, was promoted to general refinery superintendent and within months was promoted, at age 33, to vice president, the youngest in the company to attain that status. "John Hall was like Mr. Blazer's right arm and his eyes and his ears on a lot of things," said Sam Marrs in a 1998 interview. Marrs, former director of Air Transportation, had the "pleasure of flying on a lot of trips with John Hall."[25]

While Blazer made phone calls day and night, combed the trade publications for plausible acquisitions and was kept informed of company activities, his health continued to fail.

On December 8, 1966, Paul Blazer died at Saint Joseph Hospital in Phoenix, Arizona, at the age of 76. There was no indication, physicians said later, of a heart attack. His body had simply ceased to function. Blazer and his wife had been at their winter home in Scottsdale when he was stricken with profound weakness on December 6. He finished a phone call with his secretary in Ashland, Phyllis Geyer, spoke with Orin Atkins, and then allowed himself to be taken to the hospital. Two days later he died.

The corporate headquarters, its flag at half-staff, remained locked and dark on the Monday Blazer was laid to rest. It was the only non-holiday weekday closing employees could recall in Ashland's history.

The company was flooded with letters of condolence from throughout the state. Lieutenant Governor Harry Lee Waterfield wrote, "He had an unwavering faith in his fellow man, a perceptive mind, compassionate and innovative. All Kentuckians will miss Mr. Paul."[26]

The Ashland Board of City Commissioners rescheduled its regular Monday night meeting to avoid conflict with the funeral services.[27] Two services were held — a memorial service at the high school that bears his name and a private funeral service at Ashland's First Presbyterian Church for close friends, family, business associates and dignitaries. Among those who attended the funeral were the governor of Kentucky Edward T. Breathitt, executives from oil and chemical companies throughout the country, including five top executives of Standard Oil of Ohio and the presidents of several Kentucky colleges.

Newspapers throughout the region paid tribute with adjectives rarely offered the affluent oil industry. "The American success story was never better exemplified than in the career of Paul Blazer," declared Huntington's *Herald-Dispatch*, which termed Blazer an "American industrialist at his best ... compassionate, generous and always approachable."[28]

"Paul Blazer made a deep and lasting imprint on his adopted state. ... Kentucky will mark his death with regret, but with gratitude that he chose to spend his life [in Kentucky]," declared the *Louisville Courier-Journal*.[29]

The tiny and anemic little refining company that in 1924 was valued at just over $200,000 had, by the time of Blazer's death, been nourished by infusions of more than 75 companies and had grown into one of America's 150 largest corporations. In 1966, Ashland Oil & Refining Company was reporting assets of $449 million and net sales of $699 million.

And an era had ended.

Paul Blazer, though always a hard worker, was extremely dedicated to his wife and children. Pictured here from left: Paul Jr., Paul Blazer Sr., Georgia Blazer, Doris and Stuart.

1970 — Now under the leadership of Orin Atkins and Rex Blazer, Ashland Oil & Refining Company changes its name to Ashland Oil, Inc., a reflection of its growing diversification.

1972 — Atkins' zeal for acquisitions leads Ashland to become 70th on the *Fortune* 500 list.

1981 — John Hall (below) becomes chairman of the board and CEO after Orin Atkins is forced to retire.

1985 — *The Gallagher Report* names Hall one of the year's best corporate chief executives for his back-to-the-basics strategy.

THE WINDING ROAD

FROM 1966 UP THROUGH THE LATE 1990s, Ashland Oil went through a series of changes, all of which helped shape the company. Each leader offered unique contributions and steered the company in new directions. Rex Blazer and Orin Atkins landed numerous acquisitions and helped set the foundation for the various divisions of Ashland Inc. John Hall shaped and fine-tuned those acquisitions into profitable segments and set precedents for employee involvement and positive corporate image. The newest chairman and CEO, Paul Chellgren, believed firmly in responsible growth and — unafraid of change — moved Ashland Inc. to new levels of profitability and return on investment. During all of this, Ashland was able to preserve its open, friendly culture and continue its ambitious drive for quality and innovation.

1986 — Ashland Oil successfully thwarts a takeover attempt by the Belzberg brothers, resulting in the establishment of an employee stock ownership plan.

1988 — Hall's excellent handling of an oil spill in Floreffe, Pennsylvania, becomes a model for effective crisis management.

1996 — Paul Chellgren (below) steps up as Ashland Oil's new CEO after Hall retires.

1997 — Ashland embarks in a joint venture with Marathon to form a new subsidiary called Marathon Ashland Petroleum LLC, the nation's sixth largest refiner.

Orin Atkins (left) and Rex Blazer brought different specialties and interests to the company and in tandem propelled huge growth.

CHAPTER SEVEN

NEW FRONTIERS

"We stand today on the edge of a New Frontier — the frontier of unknown opportunities and perils — a frontier of unfulfilled hopes and threats."

— John F. Kennedy, presidential acceptance speech, 1960

PAUL BLAZER'S DEATH HERALDed a transition for Ashland, just as the social disharmony of the 1960s and 1970s marked a significant transition in the history of America. The late 1960s was a period of awakening and turbulence. America was torn by the ongoing conflict in Vietnam, the civil rights debate consumed the country and the domestic balance that had remained in place since the end of World War II was forever upset. Ashland, traditionally a conservative company, tucked among the Appalachian mountains of Kentucky, remained protected from the worst of the strife.

The company, however, did participate in the beginning of one of the 20th century's great awakenings — the environmental movement. By the beginning of the 1970s, all segments of society began paying attention to the land from which they drew nourishment. Citizen groups loudly decried pollutants. The government passed legislation to protect the environment. And Ashland, which as an energy and chemical company operated in the most sensitive of arenas, took proactive steps to join the growing awareness.

The Dynamic Duo

Beginning in 1967, for the first time in the company's history, founder Paul Blazer was no longer involved in the operation. The leadership that would advance the company into the 1970s — gregarious ex-salesman Rexford Blazer, then 59 and chairman of the board; and ex-lawyer Orin Ellsworth Atkins, 42, who had been president for two years and who would become CEO in 1969 — made an unlikely, yet effective, team, as chronicled by newspaper reporter John Ed Pearce in the *Louisville Courier-Journal.*

"The two men had always gotten along well, and the close association — personal and professional — continued [after Paul Blazer's death]. In many ways they complemented each other. ... [Atkins] developed a talent for finance and played a key role in acquisitions. He loved the administrative, legal and financial [aspects of] mergers and purchases. Rex was involved with sales, selecting people for jobs and getting the most out of them. Together they helped build Ashland Oil into a giant."[1]

The separation of powers was, in theory at least, quite clear. "As chairman of the board, Blazer

The Archer-Daniels-Midland (ADM) chemical logo. When Ashland acquired the ADM chemical company in 1967, it also acquired an awakened responsibility to the environment.

had a major role in shaping policy," Pearce noted. "As chief executive officer, Orin Atkins directed most day-to-day operations decisions."[2]

But the exact roles they assumed were ever-changing and highly situational. Moreover, they frequently dipped deep into the organization to find men to handle significant assignments and negotiations. This ever-shifting team approach was one the company had developed in the final years of Paul Blazer's life, and it continued throughout the Atkins-Blazer years.

Otto Scott, who wrote an earlier history of Ashland Oil, was also employed by the company as a writer for several years. His profile of the company illuminated the role each Ashland officer played in these crucial years.

"... when Atkins was still an administrative vice president, Ashland Oil had established — without using the term — what amounted to the 'presidential office.' In practice this meant that the destinies of the firm, long closely held in the hands of Paul Blazer, were being directed by a top-level team who shifted duties, responsibilities

and decisions among one another much as a fast-moving basketball team on the court. Titles were not considered paramount. ... As a result, the elder Blazer was officially retired, but functioned as an advisor. Everett Wells, listed as president with the legal authority of chief executive officer, in reality acted mainly as the chief administrator for the firm's petroleum products activities. Rex Blazer, listed as chairman, was the official presence of the company in public and supervised the sales end of operations. Bob Yancey, an administrative vice president, managed the technical end of the enterprise. That left Orin Atkins and the retired chairman, acting as twins, to plan acquisitions and strategies for the company."[3]

Rampant Acquisitions

Throughout the last half of the 1960s, Ashland went on yet another acquisitions drive, snapping up smaller companies, primarily chemical, and driving sales from $447.7 million in 1965 to $1.4 billion in 1970.

The once obscure overachiever in the hills of Kentucky transmuted into a force that commanded broad national attention. Its activities and developments were recorded in *The Wall Street Journal*, and Ashland and its various officers were frequently featured in *Forbes* magazine and *The New York Times*.

The Northwestern Refining Company in Minnesota added yet another large refinery to Ashland's growing collection.

The acquisition of ADM's Chemical Division placed Ashland among the top chemical companies in the United States.

The rapid-fire acquisitions included New Haven Trap Rock, owner of quarries and concrete plants in Connecticut, which would figure well in Ashland's growing road-building enterprise, and Wanda Petroleum Company of Houston, Texas, the nation's largest independent wholesaler of liquid propane gases. In short order, Wanda's volume increased from 1.8 billion gallons annually to 2.3 billion, due to the added strength of Ashland markets.

In 1969, the company acquired Falley Petroleum, a marketer and transporter of liquefied petroleum gas in the Midwest and upper Midwest. In 1970, Ashland bought the Northwestern Refining Company, based in St. Paul Park, Minnesota. This acquisition brought a 45,000-barrel-per-day refinery with upper-Midwest marketing properties, including the SuperAmerica chain of gasoline/convenience stores and a one-third interest in Minnesota Pipeline Company. Rex Blazer declared that the acquisition would add 15 percent to Ashland's petroleum refining and marketing operations.

At the end of 1971, Ashland purchased for $90 million Union Carbide Corporation's oil and gas holdings, including interests in Louisiana, Gabon, Ghana, Liberia, Sierra Leone, Togo, Spain and Puerto Rico. That same year the company acquired Eastern Seaboard Petroleum Company Inc. in Jacksonville, Florida, a marketer of fuel oil whose customers were primarily industry and public utilities.

The greatest growth spurt during the period came in chemicals. Several small chemical acquisitions included Fisher Chemical Company and Catalin Corporation. The most significant, however, was the 1967 purchase for $65 million of Archer-Daniels-Midland's (ADM) chemical business.

Soon after the ADM purchase, the company's chemical holdings were combined to form the Ashland Chemical group. The $400-million-a-year division — nearly as large as the entire corporation had been five years earlier — was headed by Robert E. Yancey. Then 46, the Ohio-born chemical engineer, a graduate of Marshall University, had joined Ashland in 1943 and had run the refineries and petrochemical units for 11 years.

A New Name

Ashland Oil & Refining had evolved into a multinational enterprise that was experiencing constant change. Long-range planning was instituted for the first time, and the free-flowing ebb of authority among the executive ranks was more rigidly defined. A new campus headquarters building was constructed. And in the first four years of the Rex Blazer-Orin Atkins regime, the enterprise was reorganized into several subsidiaries that included not only Ashland Chemical, but also Ashland Petroleum; Ashland Canada; Ashland Resources, a combination of the company's road-building and coal interests; and London-based Ashland Oil International, to coordinate the company's worldwide petroleum and chemical operations. Later, the coal and asphalt interests would become separate Ashland companies, just as Ashland Chemical did in 1967. (See Section Three.)

Even the company name changed. In 1970 Ashland Oil & Refining Company officially became Ashland Oil, Inc. — a name more representative of the company's expanding diversification.

One thing that did not change was the prodigious work ethic Paul Blazer had instilled in his company. As *Time* magazine pointed out in 1967, Rex Blazer, Atkins and other Ashland executives followed "what is more or less jocularly called 'The Ashland Workweek.'

It begins around 8 a.m., lasts ordinarily until midnight, and runs seven days a week, with only occasional breaks and brief vacations."[4]

As Blazer observed in the article, "I don't think we're any smarter than the competition, but I think we outwork them."[5]

Few in the executive offices had a full day of rest every week, and few at any other level within the corporation enjoyed anything approaching a 40-hour workweek.

By the late 1960s, Rex Blazer was beginning to show signs of heart problems and wore increasingly powerful glasses to counteract a serious vision problem. Nonetheless, he worked constantly, traveled often and entertained business associates at home several nights a month.

A New Leader

Orin Atkins, the tall, prematurely gray Paul Blazer protegé and Ashland wunderkind who had become the company's president by the age of 40, traveled almost non-stop during the week, carrying two large black attaches. One served as his in-basket and one as his out-basket. Because he crisscrossed the country Monday through Friday, the weekends were his

Situated on a lushly wooded hill a couple of miles from the city of Ashland, the new company headquarters was in keeping with the company's culture — sleek and efficient, yet not ostentatious.

designated time to appear in the office. The management team gave reports on Saturdays and conferred in a round of conferences on Sundays.

Described by those who worked with him as a man who preferred action over prolonged conversation, Atkins avoided publicity and personal interviews. During his first few years as president, "Industry watchers barely knew his name," according to a biographical sketch of him prepared by the company.[6]

Atkins had little time for the Bellefonte Country Club, the scene of many of the company's social occasions, and even less to satisfy his great passion for bridge. His wife and two children lived the sort of self-sufficient lives that had been historically required of Ashland families. The rare getaways tended to be brief vacations to Bermuda and the Bahamas, where Atkins developed two new avocations, scuba diving and underwater photography.

Although Atkins would leave the company years later under a cloud, he was, during his first decade in the presidency, widely acclaimed and admired for his vision and creativity, as in testimonials from the Louisville *Courier-Journal*.

"He has led the company from a position as a regional petroleum company into a diversified worldwide business, with important interests in chemical, road building, construction materials and coal mining, as well as petroleum. This diversification was carefully planned, enabling Ashland to overcome difficulties that smaller, undiversified companies may not have been able to handle. Ashland's management, and Atkins in particular, have been honored on numerous occasions ... including by Forbes *magazine, who called it 'one of the best run outfits in the industry.'"[7]*

Still, for all the forward momentum, the company encountered setbacks during this period. Its solid growth was interrupted in fiscal 1967 by a 70-day strike in the rubber industry that cost the company about $3.5 million in pre-tax profits from carbon black. Year-end results showed a decline in profits of more than $500,000, while sales had grown by 15 percent from the previous year. Blazer was unfazed by the reduction in profits, for as *Investor's Reader* indicated in 1967, "The fact that the company was able to achieve the high level of profits being reported reflects the diversity of its sources of income and the high level of operations in the petroleum, petrochemical and chemical areas."[8]

The rebound was quick. In 1968, Rexford Blazer was able to boast at the annual shareholders meeting that the company had a "year of records,"[9] announcing that sales exceeded $1 billion for the first time, while earnings reached $48.3 million. The shareholders at that meeting approved a stock split.

Preventive Measures

This upsurge was not destined to continue. Although 1969 saw an increase in sales and profit, earnings in 1970 plummeted to $38.7 million and in 1971 fell further, to $23.8 million, though sales had increased during both years.

The company took decisive action. In 1970, it reduced top management salaries by 5 to 10 percent and placed a six-month wage freeze on those earning more than $25,000. Further, company cars were eliminated (except for salesmen), Christmas parties were scrapped, trips and meetings were carefully scrutinized, and Ashland downscaled its corporate suite in New York City.[10]

In November 1971, *The Wall Street Journal* proclaimed that "after two years of discontinuing unprofitable or marginally profitable operations, Ashland Oil is confident its earnings for [the coming year] will improve substantially." This was due in large measure to the phasing out or divesting of facilities and operations that produced a pre-tax loss of approximately $8.2 million.[11] Bentonite operations were among those properties Ashland sold.

The strategies had the intended impact. In 1972 Ashland reported net income of $68.3 million — more than twice its 1971 earnings — on sales of $1.78 billion.

Foreign Oil

By the late 1960s, the United States would consume far more oil than it could produce. Domestic oil companies had to look to the Middle East to meet increasing demand.[12] Ashland, of course, was no exception, and in the late 1960s Atkins stepped up his efforts to pursue international oil. It was this overseas exploration, however, that caused difficulty for Ashland's net profit. The company had, in 1967, broken its inland isolation by becoming the largest single owner of Capline, a giant 40-inch pipeline extending from St. James, Louisiana, to Patoka, Illinois. By connecting smaller lines to Capline, Ashland Oil could now obtain foreign crude oil from overseas to feed its refineries, and Atkins was determined to take full advantage of this ability.

He negotiated oil concessions in Libya and later in Brunei and participated in other concessions in Indonesia and offshore California. Ashland's exploration efforts, formerly a small part of the corporate strategy, were expanded and eventually became a separate operating division under Atkins' personal supervision.

The company that had assiduously avoided major crude oil exploration until the late 1950s, and then remained somewhat restrained, was now deeply committed to the effort, an activity Atkins acknowledged to a *Forbes* reporter was always "a real first class crap game."[13]

Forbes further pointed out that as recently as 1966, Atkins had "vehemently and persuasively defended Ashland's practice of buying crude from others" rather than expanding its own exploration, but soon after, he had a change of heart.[14]

"In the past three years, Ashland has poured $43 million into oil exploration in Libya, the north slope of Alaska, Indonesia and North Borneo and off the coast of California. All this is very expensive and does not pay off overnight. Thus, although sales have risen by 24 percent since 1966, earnings per share have decreased from $2.48 to $2.19, while return on stockholders' equity has fallen to 16.5 percent.

"Why did Ashland join the race for crude? Because, says Atkins, Ashland has now become a giant company, and giant companies can't do things the way smaller ones do. ... Ashland can now afford such

fiascoes as occurred when the company drilled for oil in the Santa Barbara channel. It came up with eight dry holes and had to write off $8 million. 'A few years ago,' says Atkins, 'a write-off of $8 million would have been a disaster.' "[15]

By the middle of 1971, the company was so involved in exploration it formed yet another division, Ashland Exploration. The new division would not only oversee oil and gas efforts in Libya, Brunei and Indonesia, but would also manage the firm's extended concessions in Trinidad, Tobago, offshore Puerto Rico, Spain and the African nations of Gabon, Ghana, Liberia, the Spanish Sahara, Sierra Leone and Togo. With headquarters in Houston, Ashland Exploration was headed by George C. Hardin, a geologist who had been executive vice president of the oil and gas division of Ada Oil.

Slow Sinking

Ashland was very busy in Canada during the 1960s and 1970s, eventually consolidating all of its many Canadian properties — including a gas and oil exploration company in Calgary and Columbia Ltd. of Vancouver — with Canadian Gridoil Ltd., an Alberta-based producer.

Atkins wanted even heavier investment in Canada and was prepared to purchase one of Canada's largest oil companies, Home Oil Company. Unfortunately, at that time, Canadians were growing

The United Carbon purchase was one of the first acquisitions to move Ashland beyond its traditional operations in oil.

concerned with the significant level of U.S. investment in their country.

Ashland had already made some aggressive moves into Canadian territory, and Canadian legislators launched a firestorm of sentiment against further Ashland acquisitions. Rhetoric was so animated that an unprecedented all-night session was held to debate the matter in the Canadian parliament. Public uproar ended the negotiations, but Atkins continued to invest heavily in Canadian oil.

In fact, Home was but one of many attempted acquisitions that were unsuccessful. A proposed merger with oil giant Amerada in 1967 fell through due to perceived recoverable reserves, even after headlines in several publications, including the company's own *Ashland Oil Log*, announced the merger, which was billed as "the most significant step yet recorded in a history marked by aggressive growth."[16]

In the spring of 1969, Ashland called off negotiations for the acquisition of the Ayrshire Colleries Corporation of the Ayrshire Assets in New York. Then, in 1970, after months of negotiations, the company terminated discussions with Foster Grant, the plastics concern best known for its trend-setting sunglasses, for a proposed transaction valued at more than $63 million.

Environmental Concerns

As an oil company, Ashland would have fresh challenges to consider, beginning in the 1960s. The industrialized world was beginning to pay closer attention to environmental issues, and Ashland was required to produce more low-lead fuels. In May 1970, Ashland's Bob Yancey stated that while Ashland supported the government's efforts to remove lead from gasoline, the program should be phased in over a long enough time frame to avoid huge costs.

"Many studies have been made indicating that expenditures of billions of dollars would be required to remove all lead from gasoline," Yancey said in a statement to Health, Education and Welfare Secretary Robert Finch. "A program calling for complete removal of lead will certainly be inflationary and should be avoided until more sound information is available, proving beyond question that tetraethyl lead is the culprit."[17]

The debate and additional study continued over the next few years, and in the mid 1970s, the government did mandate the removal of lead from gasoline — phasing out the additive over a number of years, just as Yancey had suggested. Once the mandate became clear, Ashland was among the first to invest in the technology required to produce unleaded gasoline. In the 1980s, Ashland argued strongly in favor of accelerating the phase-out program, largely because of its proven beneficial impact on air quality.

The leaded gasoline issue was, however, merely a tiny corner of the burgeoning environmental movement. Ashland had managed to proceed through the first four decades of its existence with relatively few complaints from neighboring communities. The citizens of Catlettsburg and Ashland occasionally complained of smoke or discharge into the river, but Ashland officials had always been able to offer reassurances.

By the early 1970s, however, growing environmental awareness had triggered a less-patient attitude among the public and government officials. At the same time, Ashland experienced a number of environmental incidents that drew public attention. In 1966, Ashland had acquired a Great Meadows, New Jersey, company that made a variety of synthetic chemical compounds used in products ranging from hair dye to tear gas. Toward the end of the decade, local residents complained of damage from tear-gas dusts that allegedly leaked from the plant on occasion, and state authorities requested that the problems be resolved or the plant shut down.

In 1971, Ashland's carbon black plant near Belpre, Ohio, was criticized for noxious odors.[18] In 1972, the city of Countryside, Illinois, began an inquiry to determine if Ashland Chemical's nearby Willow Springs distribution facility was meeting national, state and county safety requirements. The authorities were reacting to property owner concerns prompted by the explosion a few days earlier of a fireworks plant not affiliated with Ashland in any way.

Not long after, *The Wall Street Journal* took Ashland to task for allegedly discharging a "bluish-black goo" into the Ohio River near Wheeling. An Ashland river barge, docked for cleaning, had indeed spilled 30 gallons — less than one barrel — of oil

Everett Wells (seated), Robert E. Yancey, Rexford Blazer (seated) and Orin Atkins were all leaders in Ashland's diversification into chemicals.

residue into the Ohio, but was not responsible for a continuing problem as the paper had alleged. *The Wall Street Journal* issued a correction.

Taking Responsibility

Ashland acted swiftly to make changes in response to changing public sentiments and from its own concerns for the environment. In 1971, the company announced it would spend more than $4.5 million that year in environmental control efforts. The money was earmarked for new air and water conservation programs — with more than $3 million set aside for Ashland's refineries.

Ashland, like most industries, climbed to higher levels of environmental awareness during this era. Oliver Zandona, head of the company's envi-

ronmental control program, said the company had been environmentally sensitive for decades, but was heightening its efforts. The use of cutting-edge technology would help reduce emissions, and ongoing research and development would render additional improvements. In addition, the company would create extensive training programs for employees.

Over the next several decades, Ashland's environmental efforts were detailed in company publications. *Ashland Oil: An Environmental Overview*, a 1971 production, pointed out that "Solutions will be long-range and costly. We have pledged to devote whatever time, scientific talents, engineering skills and funds necessary to establish and maintain high standards of environmental control in all of our facilities."[19]

Changing of the Guard

Even as environmental issues and the Vietnam War altered the culture of America, the culture of

Ashland was changing as well. Early Ashland employees were fast disappearing from the roster. In 1969, Art Points, an Ashland employee since 1931 and controller since 1945, died. Another, Edward W. (Ned) Seaton, announced his retirement from the board at age 75 after 37 years with the company — 16 years as company treasurer and 33 as a director. He was replaced on the board by son William R. Seaton, an Ashland administrative vice president who had held a variety of positions at Ashland for 20 years.

A day after his 65th birthday, early in 1970, Everett Wells, who was key in the development of the company and company president from 1957 to 1964, announced his retirement. Rex Blazer, too, was rapidly approaching mandatory retirement age and would soon retire as chairman of the board.

A line of succession was forming, with the elevation of Yancey to chief operating officer and the appointments of three new senior vice presidents, all younger men who had joined the company in the 1940s and 1950s: John R. Hall, who had become the company's youngest vice president at age 33; Robert T. McCowan, an expert in marketing who would eventually rise to head Ashland Petroleum and subsequently serve as vice chairman, External Affairs; and William R. Seaton, vice chairman for Law and Administration.

Barely a year after his promotion to senior vice president, Hall, a solidly built Tennessean who had received a chemical engineering degree and acclaim for his football prowess from Vanderbilt University, was named president of Ashland Chemical.

On all levels the company had grown younger, at least in terms of management, and there occurred a subtle shift in expectations for this rising group. Early in 1970, Atkins surveyed the top 200 Ashland executives and observed the average

John Hall, in 1962, was already making a name for himself as an expert in economic analysis. In less than 20 years, he would be chairman of the board of Ashland.

age was middle 40s. "You should begin to groom your successors so you can retire at 60," he said, "and still be able to lead active and purposeful lives thereafter."[20] In other words, Atkins wanted them to give the company their best, but not their whole lives.

The Western Company's drilling vessel, *Pacesetter I,* drilled three wells in the North Sea for Ashland.

CHAPTER EIGHT

ROUGH TERRAIN

"Orin Atkins was really the man who first started getting Ashland away from the refining business. His 17-year tenure included many innovative accomplishments, but we also encountered a lot of problems."

— John Hall, 1998[1]

THE COMPANY SAILED INTO the early 1970s with great confidence and optimism, flush with its recent acquisitions. As it turned out, the decade was destined to be among the most troubled years in the company's history. Ashland Oil, Inc., also known as AOI, was greatly profitable through the 1970s and continued to grow rapidly through acquisition. Orin Atkins, a consummate deal maker, seemingly had an intuitive grasp of the right direction for Ashland.

Nevertheless, at times the bad news seemed to outweigh the good. First in 1973, then again in 1979 and 1980, the world oil market went through fluctuations that hurt Ashland. The environmental movement, which had grown in scope since the late 1960s, found an active voice in national politics. And, in September 1981, Orin Atkins stepped down from his position at the helm of Ashland under a cloud of doubt and recrimination.

To some degree, what happened was an unfortunate twist of circumstance. Not only was Ashland caught in transition, the world itself was changing rapidly as global oil politics assumed center stage. As Paul Chellgren, who eventually became Ashland's chairman of the board and CEO, observed years later, "Someone once said, 'Ashland is a company that can't seem to decide whether it wants to be the world's smallest giant or the world's biggest midget.'"[2] It was an apt characterization.

Giant Steps

In January 1972, the leadership of Ashland was established in the form it would assume for the rest of the decade. In addition to his position as CEO, Orin Atkins was elected chairman of the board in anticipation of Rex Blazer's mandatory retirement later in the year. Robert Yancey was elected president of Ashland Oil, Inc., and Blazer became chairman of the executive committee.

At the board meeting when the management changes transpired, Atkins reiterated that Ashland Petroleum would continue to be "the major source of the company's profit and the single most important area for potential growth."[3]

Acquisitions stand out during those years. The early 1970s were a particularly frenetic time for acquisitions at Ashland Oil, Inc. In fact, the Law Department informally nicknamed this period "The Golden Era of Acquisitions," remembered Thomas L. Feazell, a Washington and Lee Law School graduate who joined AOI in 1965 as a staff attorney and later became general counsel and a senior vice president and secretary. "We sometimes did three a

The Ashland logo. The company would experience difficult times in the 1970s but would bounce back by decade's end.

Orin Atkins (seated right) and J.D. Hughes, vice president of Ashland Oil International (standing right), negotiate with officials from Libya.

month, and the lawyers loved it because it was exciting work."[4]

Atkins, often described as a man of uncommon brilliance, had an insatiable appetite for courting and consummating the deal. Ashland acquired dozens of companies during his reign, including F. H. Ross & Company, a chemical marketing and distributing firm based in Charlotte, North Carolina; Fisher Chemical; and a joint purchase with International Minerals and Chemical Corporation of a methanol plant in Plaquemine, Louisiana.

Atkins' zeal for closing deals and purchasing companies was seemingly boundless, but he at times had no patience for the details that accompany such agreements. Feazell recalled a time not long after he joined the company when Atkins phoned from the West Coast and asked him to fly to Los Angeles to finalize the paperwork on an exploration deal he had worked out with Armand Hammer of Occidental. Feazell jumped the first flight to Los Angeles, checked into the hotel and sought out Bill Gammon, a senior vice president

whom Atkins had said would be with him. He found Gammon, but Atkins had already left L.A., headed for New York, and Gammon had virtually no knowledge of the terms of the agreement. They would have to enter the meeting cold. The next morning, driving to the Occidental offices, Gammon and Feazell worked out the approach they would take. After coffee with Hammer, they lurched ahead.

"We finally said, 'Dr. Hammer, we understand that you and Mr. Atkins have outlined the terms of an exploration project, and we're supposed to reduce it to writing.' He said, 'That's right.' And we said, 'Well, just so there's no misunderstanding, perhaps you could tell us how you envision the transaction.' So he began to outline the transaction, and we madly wrote

it on yellow sheets. So after that, we said, 'Well, maybe we ought to run Mr. Atkins down in New York, and then we'll get together with your staff and try to put words to paper. He said, 'fine.' So we went in the other room, closed the door, got Orin at the hotel in New York, woke him up, and he said, 'Well, what does he say the deal was?' So we told him. And there was a pause and he said, 'Close enough.' And that's the way he operated." [5]

"What he really liked was the transaction, the negotiation. He did not have a great deal of patience with the day-to-day operating problems," remembered Feazell. [6]

Early in 1973, appearing before the New York Society of Security Analysts, Atkins announced fiscal 1972 had been "the best year in our corporate history. On total sales of approximately $1.8 billion, we reported profits of $68 million, equal to $2.65 per share, and cash flow of $156 million. The progress has continued into the current year." [7]

Atkins' pursuit of additional companies sent Ashland on a growth spurt that boosted it to 70th on the *Fortune* 500 list in 1972, with more growth in sight. That year, the company reported $1.78 billion in sales and $68.3 million in income. By the end of the decade, the numbers climbed to $6.74 billion in sales and $526 million in income, including a one-time gain from selling its exploration business. Ashland moved aggressively into chemicals, construction, exploration and coal and embarked on a program of diversification aimed at protecting it from the instability of the worldwide crude oil market.

Financially it was an excellent era, and there were other bright spots early in the decade: AOI was praised for plans to construct a pollution

Ashland entered the chemical business by way of distribution and grew to become the nation's largest distributor of industrial chemical and solvents.

control plant in Catlettsburg three years ahead of federal compliance schedule, and the company announced plans to build a $10 million maleic anhydride plant.

Internal Tragedies

In May 1972, four men were killed and 14 hospitalized in an explosion and fire at an Ashland Chemical plant in Toronto. The plant was completely demolished. The fire consumed 1 million gallons of chemicals, and the intense heat forced the evacuation of 1,000 residents. It was later discovered that the tragedy had probably been caused by an inadequately designed relief valve system. A few months later, in October, an explosion of a gasoline tank truck at an Ashland Petroleum bulk storage plant killed one man and severely injured another.

But perhaps the darkest cloud of publicity to descend over the company was Atkins' confession to the illegal contribution of $100,000 in company funds to President Richard Nixon's re-election campaign.

The story broke in July 1973, when Atkins voluntarily acknowledged he had acquiesced to Nixon re-election officials and made an "extremely regrettable" contribution. He funneled the contribution through an Ashland subsidiary, Ashland Petroleum Gabon Corporation, in the name of Mr. and Mrs. Orin Atkins. Later he told investigators he believed

In the 1960s and 1970s, exploration efforts extended from offshore Louisiana to the shore of Abu Musa, an island off the coast of Sharjah.

he could not reject the request of campaign officials representing the seated president — the man who was likely to win the upcoming election.

Ashland was the second major corporation, but certainly not the last, connected to the illegal contributions. American Airlines had admitted two weeks previously that it had donated $55,000 in company funds to the Nixon campaign. Later, several other companies confessed similar contributions, including Gulf and Goodyear. In all, 21 executives of major corporations admitted making illegal contributions to Nixon's campaign. Two eventually went to jail.

Ashland's contribution had been made without the board's knowledge, and Atkins took full personal responsibility. The money was returned to the company, and in November, Atkins pleaded no contest and was fined $1,000 in federal court, while Ashland Petroleum Gabon pleaded no contest and was fined $5,000.

Although Rex Blazer said he was "not upset" with Atkins, the company was mentioned prominently for months in *The New York Post*, *The Wall Street Journal*, *Time*, *The New York Times*, *The Christian Science Monitor* and other national media publications. In addition to the company's image being tarnished, Atkins himself was subjected to unflattering speculation that his judgment was suspect.

In 1974, the company lost one of its guiding forces. Rex Blazer settled rather happily into retirement. Although suffering from heart problems and extremely bad vision, he remained very active in the company as chairman of the executive committee, working about eight hours a day instead of his usual 16, and enjoying some travel. In an October 1973 interview, he seemed composed and oddly prepared for the inevitable. "Looking back, I have no regrets. It has been a good life, and still is. I hope it can last a while longer, but in any case it has been fine."[8] Less than six months later, he died while being driven to the airport. Later that year, he was selected posthumously to the National Petroleum Council Oil Hall of Fame, the 43rd man so honored.

Oil Crisis

In late 1973, international events once again consumed the company's full attention. Arab nations, angered by U.S. support of Israel in the Yom Kippur War, initiated a complete embargo of oil to the United States. The embargo, the first use of Arab oil as a political weapon, sent the price of crude oil through the roof, prompting allocations and long lines at the gas pumps in much of the nation. Ashland, whose exploratory efforts had not yielded results, depended on foreign crude for roughly 50 percent of its refineries' needs.

Speaking before shareholders in January 1974, Atkins blamed government indecision and its lack of long-range planning for the crisis. Insisting that bad energy management practices had encouraged increased dependence on foreign supplies, he called on Washington to "recognize that the domestic petroleum industry can only be developed in a free economic environment which permits price and profits to reflect the cost of material, capital and a fair return. There is little room in times of stress for the demagoguery that is too often typical of the Washington scene."[9]

The executive operating team in effect in 1974 consisted of Orin Atkins, John Hall, William Seaton and Bob Yancey Sr.

New Developments

Coinciding with an announcement that it would spend $100 million over the next three years on the Catlettsburg refining complex, Ashland instituted a restructuring within the company. In March 1973, the company promoted John R. Hall to executive vice president; he would work directly with Yancey in the Petroleum and Chemical divisions. Hall, formerly president of Ashland Chemical in Columbus, Ohio, was succeeded there by Edward A. Von Doersten, who had been a senior vice president of the division. Robert T. McCowan, well known for his keen sense of the consumer and skilled in public and government relations, was moved up from executive vice president to president of Ashland Petroleum, the largest operating division. A graduate of the University of Kentucky, McCowan was first hired in 1951 as a salesman and was trained

by Palmer Talbutt, one of Paul Blazer's key sales-people. McCowan's early career involved marketing petroleum products, and after 20 years of progressively more responsible positions, he was elected a director in 1971.

Several months later, the company established Ashland Construction Company, an operating division based in Cambridge, Massachusetts, with responsibility for all of Ashland's contract construction and construction materials, including Warren Brothers, as well as New Haven Trap Rock. The new division operated 160 asphalt plants, 35 concrete plants and 30 crushing plants.

Ashland also began delving into the convenience store/gasoline station hybrid. The company had watched with great interest the success of its subsidiary, SuperAmerica, when it began selling gasoline and groceries from the same outlet — something of a rarity at the time. Initiating its own efforts in that direction, AOI called the stores Save Mart and Save More. By the 1980s, the company had 100 such stores in seven states, and the concept was destined to expand even more.

Furthermore, Ashland moved into the coal industry. The company's focus on the increasingly popular fuel source was motivated by the oil embargo and Atkins' desire to move Ashland away from complete dependency on the oil industry while maintaining Ashland Petroleum as its largest operating unit.

Ashland Coal, Inc., a wholly owned subsidiary, was formed in 1975 to produce and sell Appalachian coal. Before the decade was over, the combined annual coal sales of Ashland Coal and Arch Mineral, a 50 percent owned operation that Ashland formed with the Hunt family in 1969, gave AOI a solid foothold in the coal industry.

As Tom Feazell explained, "Mr. Atkins at that time had a theory that energy from oil and hydrocarbons, including coal, was going to be a very important natural resource in the future, because energy was something this country absolutely had to have, and there was nothing on the horizon, nuclear or otherwise, that was going to replace it."[10]

In 1977, Ashland's Catlettsburg refinery looked much different than when the company first started.

Misleading Charges

The cloud of bad publicity that hovered over Atkins and Ashland in 1973 was not to dissipate in 1974. That September, an election year, New York State Attorney General Louis J. Lefkowitz claimed his office had learned the Iranian government, through its National Iranian Oil Company (NIOC), had agreed to acquire a 50 percent interest in Ashland's New York state operations, including the Buffalo refinery.

"Totally inaccurate and misleading," replied Ashland spokesman Harry Wiley, adding that Lefkowitz was making the charge only to get attention during an election year. Wiley acknowledged, however, that Ashland had been studying a proposal by which NIOC would obtain 50 percent interest in refining, marketing and transportation activities in western New York.[11]

Just a few days later, nationally syndicated columnist Jack Anderson wrote a column declaring that Kentucky Senator Marlow Cook, a Republican, was known on Capitol Hill as the "Senator from Ashland Oil." The senator, Anderson said, "champions Ashland's interests on the Senate floor and accepts special favors in return from the oil company."[12]

Finally, in a December hearing before the U.S. District Court, Ashland pleaded guilty and was fined $25,000 for making illegal cash contributions totaling about $170,000 in connection with various election campaigns from 1970 to 1972. Atkins had triggered the contributions and announced he was willing to reimburse the company, as well as pay the legal expenses incurred in connection with the special prosecutor's investigation.

By January, Ashland officers were prepared to take proactive steps to cleanse the company's tarnished image, and on January 11, 1975, senior management decided that outside advice was necessary.

Ashland executives sat for hours with Harold Burson, famed New York public relations impresario, to hash out the most effective way of dealing with current and future difficulties, since the com-

The SuperAmerica chain, an AOI subsidiary, was beginning to prove that the convenience store/gasoline retailer concept could work. Ashland later converted its own branded stations to that concept.

pany "must expect more news stories of a controversial nature in the immediate future," according to a memo from the meeting.[13] The group agreed, among other things, that they would attempt to avoid "no comment" responses.

Advising management that "the heat will dissipate gradually," Burson offered several suggestions. "Stockholders will be unhappy, and the company should take a positive, do-something attitude and consider the prompt restructuring of the board by adding several outside directors whose integrity cannot be doubted."[14] The annual report that came out a few months later listed a new director, Samuel Butler, an attorney with a prestigious New York law firm. The following year another director was added, Dr. Grover Murray, president emeritus of Texas Tech University.

Lost Horizons

Throughout all the controversy, Ashland had continued along a progressive path of increased sales and revenue, but 1978 began with a very poor first six months. The downturn was caused by an industry oversupply of crude oil, a strike by the United Mine Workers and an unusually severe winter that hindered distribution and marketing. While the decline was overcome with an unusually strong second half, company officials took rather dramatic action. As Atkins explained in the 1978 annual report:

"We became concerned earlier this year that Ashland's strengths were not being clearly translated into meaningful values for stockholders. This appeared to result to a considerable degree from today's rapidly changing political and economic environment, and indicated that our previous theory of operations might require modification if we are to be as successful in the future as we have been in the past."[15]

Atkins unveiled a corporate strategy to increase cash flow, reduce debt, expand growth operations, sell assets that were less profitable and buy other, more profitable operations. That year, Ashland sold its 79 percent interest in Ashland Canada for $316 million and embarked on an aggressive reduced capital expenditures program in excess of $300 million.

In his 1978 letter to stockholders, Atkins said the company would also seriously contemplate the future of Ashland Exploration and Ashland-Warren. Both, he said, had been successful, but "it is questionable whether their current modes of operation are compatible with Ashland's plans for the future and if Ashland's stockholders might receive significantly greater benefit from alternative approaches."[16] Moreover, he wrote, negotiations were completed for the sale of part of Ashland Chemical's Resins and Plastics Division soon after the end of the fiscal year in September, "and negotiations are in progress with regard to the possible disposition of the entire Chemical Products Division."[17]

The company withdrew from most of its exploration activities, keeping only its eastern division. "In the late '70s we decided we were too little too late, and we sold almost all those operations," said Senior Vice President, Secretary and General Counsel Thomas Feazell.[18]

A National Oil Crisis

In the early months of 1979, there were growing signals that the country might be on the brink of a second energy crisis. The company newspaper reported in April that "crude oil supply and demand fluctuations are renewing fears of an energy crisis that could approach — or even exceed — the shockwaves created by the 1973–74 oil embargo."[19] The worldwide crude oil supply system simply did not seem capable of meeting expected demand, and pundits were predicting a shortage of oil. To complicate the situation, Iran and Iraq went to war the following year, further disrupting the supply of crude.

After its experience earlier in the decade, Ashland was determined not to be caught short again and took steps to ensure a steady supply. "We were crude poor, so we had to go find deals overseas," Feazell explained.[20]

"This was in the days when you'd get three phone calls a week from somebody that represented a prince, and they claimed to have some oil they were going to sell you at this great price. You had to watch everything you did very carefully. But we got involved, and we obtained a big,

long-term contract with the National Iranian Oil Company. This was that period of time when crude prices went up like a rocket. So we committed to a ten-year contract so as to guarantee a source of supply."[21]

The company also entered a joint venture with the National Iranian Oil Company of Saudi Arabia to build a 5,000-barrel-a-day export lubricating refinery in Rabigh.

The Iranian contract, however, wasn't destined to last long. Once the Shah of Iran was replaced by the Ayatollah Khomeini in January 1979 and the U.S. Embassy in Tehran was seized in November of that same year, the Iranians unilaterally canceled the contract. At that time, Ashland

had three supertankers loaded with crude crossing the seas, and the Iranian government demanded $283 million of payment upon delivery. Ashland refused, on the grounds that Iran had breached the contract and cost Ashland millions of dollars in damages.

Years of litigation followed. There were death threats and negotiations in neutral places like Paris and Vienna, Feazell said. Litigation was filed in New York, London, Bermuda and elsewhere. Ten years later, the company paid the Iranians

The Buffalo, New York, Refinery was one of several the company operated in the 1970s.

just over $300 million, after having had use of the $283 million for a decade.

The three tankers, however, were only a fraction of the 100,000 barrels a day Ashland received from that country, roughly one fourth of the company's total crude oil requirement. Appealing to officials in Washington, Ashland convinced the Department of Energy (DOE) to make an emergency allocation of crude oil to Ashland because of its ability to efficiently supply inland consumers. The DOE then decided which and how many other oil companies would supply Ashland during the crisis.

"We responded very conservatively at first," said then Manager of Media Relations Dan Lacy, "because we were uncertain of what our options were and what was going to happen. But later we were pretty vocal about the need for the country to work together during this time of crisis."[22]

Throughout 1980 the company appeared regularly in Washington on an assortment of issues, but most regularly to ask for an overhaul of the federal crude oil entitlement program. Ashland argued that the Department of Energy had failed in its obligation to maintain the integrity of the program, which was started in 1974 to equalize crude oil prices to refiners, and ultimately gasoline prices to consumers, by offsetting imbalances created by price controls on domestic crude oil. Differences of as much as 18 cents a gallon had appeared between competing marketers, the company complained.

"The customers in the Midwest should not have to bear undue burden or hardship during the winter just because Ashland was a principal supplier for heating oil and fuels in the Midwest," Lacy explained. "If this were a decision of the United States government and a problem for all Americans, then all Americans should bear the burden equally."[23] Ashland's efforts were successful. The Department of Energy ordered some of the other major oil companies to sell their oil to Ashland at market price.

New Frontiers

The turbulence in oil markets in 1979 and 1980 served to convince Atkins that the company needed further diversification. In 1979, Atkins established Ashland Development Inc., a develop-

Bob McCowan was president of Ashland Petroleum Company during the Iranian crisis of 1978–79. In 1980, he was elected vice chairman of the board for external affairs and was an outspoken advocate on behalf of the oil industry, seeking equitable treatment for all fuel users during supply shortages. A member of the board of trustees for the University of Kentucky, McCowan was also a strong supporter of education and instrumental in Ashland's aid to education.

ment company responsible for seeking profit opportunities in new technology in areas outside of Ashland Oil's traditional businesses.

The Development Division was charged with identifying promising new technologies, getting them started, then moving the operation into another division. The first major project was a joint venture with two outside partners to build an ethanol plant in South Point, Ohio.

Above: William R. Seaton proved to be another key leader who spanned the Blazer and modern eras of Ashland history. Seaton joined the company in 1949 during a period of explosive growth. He rose quickly through administrative ranks in personnel and finance and was elected a director in 1969, vice chairman in 1972 and chief financial officer in 1982. Seaton's financial acumen guided Ashland through a number of acquisitions and divestitures and played a key role in the company's drive to regain financial stability in the 1980s.

Below: John Ward served as corporate secretary of Ashland from 1975 until his retirement in 1992. He was also the first secretary and process officer of the core management group created by CEO John Hall in 1982. In a 1998 interview, Hall said: "John's input was always helpful and appreciated. He sincerely made a significant contribution to the direction of the company in his role as counsel to the core group and secretary to the board of directors. He was a person of the highest ethical standards, and his opinion was respected by all." Ward died of a heart attack in December 1995.

Moving Out

By 1979, the company's strategy to manage bad press appeared to be working. Ashland had taken proactive steps to present a positive public face. The image crumbled, however, when that spring Atkins told a local reporter he would seriously consider moving future corporate offices outside the Ashland area, perhaps in Lexington. Rumors of a possible relocation had arisen sporadically through the years, only to dissipate with the passage of time. But this time it was no mere rumor. The chairman had publically disclosed that the possibility was strong, and a tempest was unleashed.

His explanation did nothing to improve the mood of the city fathers, or, indeed, most of the residents of the area. "Frankly," he told a reporter, "over the last several years the perception of Ashland as a community in which to live has gone steadily downhill."[24] Ashland employees working in the field, he said, did not regard a promotion to corporate headquarters as a reward, since it would mean living in the Ashland area. Atkins cited an assortment of deficiencies — poor schools, a floundering library, and insufficient social amenities, hotels and restaurants — which he felt the city did not adequately address.[25]

Fueling his displeasure, according to those close to the situation, was the recent defeat of a measure that would have permitted alcohol to be sold in Ashland. The liquor prohibition, in place for decades, effectively blocked development of major restaurants and hotels, which ultimately created recruiting and retention problems for the company.

Reaction to Atkins' statements was instant and inflammatory. "I think Paul Blazer would turn over in his grave if he knew they were thinking about this," Ashland resident Donna Waggoner told a newspaper reporter.[26]

At that point, Ashland was a huge corporation with 30,000 employees, including 4,500 who lived in Ashland and its environs. It was, by then, the 44th largest industrial concern in the country, and in wages alone, it injected $77 million into the economy every year.

Company officials told *The New York Times* the overall quality of life in Ashland was to blame for at least a half-dozen executives leaving the company each year. As the article pointed out, "the company estimates it loses $112,500 every time an executive voluntarily leaves and a replacement is recruited — a situation that cost Ashland Oil $875,000 in 1977."[27]

Less than a year after Atkins aired his complaints with the city, the company announced it would move 500 employees to a 57-acre plot in Lexington over the next two years. By summer, nearly 200 Valvoline employees had made the move, along with the Real Estate, Insurance, Appraisal and Tax Compliance departments. The other 300 departed two years later. There was discussion in the executive suite for several more weeks about ultimately moving the rest of the corporate operation to the Lexington site. For the time being, at least, the corporate headquarters and about 4,000 employees were to remain in the Ashland area.

Despite the move of some departments to Lexington, the company's office space in Ashland was insufficient to meet the growing company's needs. At the end of 1980, a second sleek brick and glass building, providing 170,000 square feet of space, was built on the hillside site across the Ashland city limits in Russell, Kentucky. The first building, constructed years earlier to serve as the corporate headquarters, would house the petroleum company's administrative offices, as Ashland's 400 corporate employees moved into the new building. A service tunnel linked the buildings.

Reorganization

As the company shifted employees between buildings and cities, another series of significant

Referred to as the Bellefonte office, Ashland's second executive office building was built in 1980.

management shifts took place. Robert T. McCowan was elected vice chairman of Ashland Oil, Inc., with responsibility for external relations, including federal and state government units, public relations and investor relations. McCowan, who had joined the company in 1951, had served in a variety of positions, including six years as president of Ashland Petroleum.

Charles Luellen, who had joined the company in 1952 and served in several sales and marketing positions, became an executive vice president in 1979 and was named to succeed McCowan as president of Ashland Petroleum. He also became senior vice president of Ashland Oil in 1979.

Paul Chellgren joined the company in 1974 as executive assistant to then chairman Orin Atkins. Chellgren became an administrative vice president of Ashland Chemical in 1977 and a group vice president of that division in 1978. He was elected senior vice president and group operating officer of Ashland Oil, Inc. in 1980.

John Hall, who became vice chairman and chief operating officer in 1979, said the company, long known as one of the nation's leading independent oil refiners, would be shifting its emphasis away from gasoline and other traditional petroleum products and toward high technology programs, including synthetic fuels and specialty chemicals. "We cannot rely on the growth of demand for gasoline," he told a reporter for *The New York Times*.[28]

As the article pointed out, in 1978 Ashland Oil, Inc. had initiated a $948 million asset redeployment program to facilitate a change in prod-

A SPARK OF GENIUS

NECESSITY HAS ALWAYS BEEN THE mother of invention. So when the OPEC oil embargo sent world oil prices spiraling upwards in 1974, Ashland Oil took action. Not only was the price of foreign crude oil skyrocketing, but the oil contained more sulfur and heavy metal, making it less valuable for converting into gasoline.

That was when Ashland's George Meyers, vice president of Operational Planning for Refining and an expert in catalytic cracking technology — along with a team of Ashland scientists and engineers — started developing what would later become the company's patented Reduced Crude Conversion (RCC) process. The RCC process would set new standards for refining heavy crude oil into higher-value products, with refineries all over the world using one or more features of the process.[1]

George Meyers was the driving force behind Ashland's RCC process, which produced higher yields of gasoline from lower-quality crude oil.

uct emphasis and make acquisitions more feasible. By 1981, the company had acquired the United States Filter Corporation, a New York-based company known for coal liquefaction technologies and pollution control, as well as the Integon Corporation, an insurance concern headquartered in Winston Salem, North Carolina. Ashland seemed joyous over the two acquisitions.

This continuing strategy of diversification was, in part, motivated by the market for crude oil, which was still tight. At the annual shareholders meeting in 1981, Ashland declared it was bracing itself for the most challenging period in the company's history. "We faced more problems this year than we have ever experienced," Atkins said, including a U.S. economic slump, higher crude oil prices and a petroleum industry caught in transition, all of which led to a decline in profits.[29]

In the meantime, the world oil market was becoming increasingly unstable. Inflation was rampant across the world. The number of oil exporting countries, including Malaysia, China and Angola, increased. The Alaskan pipeline increased its flow from the North Slope. Worse still, the combination of politics, higher prices and environmentalism dampened the demand for oil. At first, analysts predicted a shortage in the world oil supply. But the decrease in demand and the increase in domestic production turned the shortage into a glut. Oil prices slumped, and the market spun into a free-for-all. Instead of prices being determined by American oil companies or OPEC, oil was traded as a commodity, and the

Though Meyers retired in 1978 after 27 years at Ashland, he still worked steadily on the project. That same year, Ashland built a demonstration unit at its Catlettsburg refinery. "What the process does," reported the *Ashland News,* "is to convert residual oil left after conventional processing — the so-called 'bottom of the barrel' — into gasoline and other valuable transportation fuels."[2] The new 20,000 barrel-per-day unit yielded the same amount of gasoline as conventional techniques but used 20 percent less crude — thanks to the RCC process.[3]

On March 31, 1980, Ashland sparked national attention when the RCC process was unveiled to the world, because the process would decrease the United States' dependence on foreign crude. Prior to the RCC method, one barrel of crude oil yielded about 21 gallons of gasoline. The new process increased that yield to 26 gallons. "The significance of RCC ... is not just that it can produce more gasoline," reported the *Ashland News,* "but that it can produce a given amount of gasoline using less crude oil."[4]

Sadly, George Meyers would never see his dream come to fruition. He died on April 10, 1980, just 10 days after the process was announced to the public.[5]

That December, Ashland began construction of a 40,000-barrel-a-day RCC unit in Catlettsburg. By November 1983, the $300 million unit was complete, the first commercial RCC process unit ever built. "This is a great day for Ashland," announced then Chairman and CEO John Hall at the dedication ceremony. "We believe this new unit will play an important part in the future of the company."[6] Hall was right. Not only did the new unit increase Ashland's flexibility, since the company could now produce gasoline from lower-priced, heavier crude, but it also increased the amount of gasoline produced per barrel.[7]

Ashland executives paid tribute to the hard work and dedication of the people who made the unit possible. As Charles Luellen, then senior vice president of Ashland Oil and president of Ashland Petroleum, said, "The RCC project, like all other great and innovative projects, required the imagination, talent and unstinting effort of hundreds of people to bring it to creation. And like other great and innovative projects, there was required a special spark of genius from one individual. That one individual was the late George Meyers."[8]

overall effect of this was quite damaging to companies like Ashland.

A Leader Steps Down

That fall, Atkins, who had served as AOI's leader for 17 years, first as president, then as chairman of the board, was forced to retire while still in his 50s.

"It was the most difficult decision," said William Seaton, who was on the board of directors at the time.[30] John Hall, chief operating officer since 1979, became the new chairman and CEO in October 1981. Seaton later described the transition from Atkins to Hall as the most significant change in the company since he started working there in 1949:

"With Atkins, projects were analyzed and finally, when he made up his mind, he set out to persuade everybody to back his side of whatever it was. John became more of a consensus manager. He wanted to be sure everybody had their say, wanted everybody else to be heard. Orin got something done and then presented it."[31]

An *Ashland News* story stated Atkins had discussed his decision to retire months earlier with the board, "but had postponed the action until the company had solved problems affecting its petroleum refining and marketing operations."[32] The company newspaper praised him for having been instrumental in directing the company's activities for more than 20 years. "If any single person can be credited with giving Ashland its personality and establishing its operating style," the company newspaper stated, "that person would have to be Atkins."[33]

Within days of that story, the company began to change its personality and operating style. Toward the end of his tenure, the board and many Ashland executives had grown increasingly disquieted with Atkins. There was a strong and almost universal feeling that Atkins was leading the company down the wrong road, a feeling that was finally expressed openly during his final months. Corporate headquarters was, during this period, filled with palpable tension.

One problem, many agreed, was that Atkins had grown bored with the company. Years later,

when executives who had been close to the situation struggled to recall memories of Atkins during those final years, that word — "bored" — was used by many. Atkins simply could not muster the interest in the company he once did. He seemed distracted much of the time, according to those once close to him.

Paul Chellgren, who had worked closely with him for two years, noticed a change in Atkins between 1977, when Chellgren began a three-year stint in Columbus as group vice president of the chemical company, and in 1980, when he returned to corporate headquarters. "He was distracted personally," Chellgren said.[34]

In all industries, many talented executives eventually leave, often on less-than-ideal terms, but this does not diminish their contributions. Yet Ashland Oil, Inc. had not experienced an expedited departure at the highest levels since 1951, when J. Howard Marshall left.

Genesis

Years later, many Ashland officials came to regard the Atkins era as a mixed bag of growth and some significant mistakes — many of them the result of an unfortunate confluence of world situations and a peculiar financial environment. But at the time of his departure, there was little interest in context-placement. The focus was on setting new sights and establishing new priorities. Within days of Atkins' retirement announcement, Hall embarked on a series of employee meetings to outline a new corporate resolve. He unveiled a major revision of corporate structure and operating strategies aimed at greater autonomy for the company's operating divisions. The new structure included the formation of Ashland Services Company. He also established a core management group of the most senior people in the corporation and emphasized the need to initiate cost controls throughout all operations.

Pointing out that the company's spectacular growth during the 1970s had stalled, and that the declining return on investment of recent years must be reversed, he declared, "We have gotten too fat, and to preserve our health we are going to have to go on a diet."[35] A task force had recommended ways to slash $10 million, and was aiming to double that, but employees were exhorted to take personal responsibility for ferreting out savings. "Each of us, including top management, will have to sacrifice. … We are going to have to reduce the amount of payments to outside consultants and outside law firms, cut down on travel and entertainment expenses, eliminate unnecessary jobs and do a myriad of other things to get our costs under control," Hall said.[36]

Moreover, he added, AOI had become too large and too diverse for top management to be involved in every detail of the operating divisions. "To effectively make and communicate the decisions needed to direct such a diversified corporation, corporate management must delegate a wide range of decision-making authority to those closest to the situation. Top management itself, in turn, must concentrate more on future strategic needs of the corporation."[37]

The performance of the various divisions, Hall declared, would be monitored by a newly established management group charged with setting strategy jointly with each division. In addition to Hall, the management group consisted of President Robert Yancey Sr. (who retired a few months later); vice chairmen William Seaton and Robert McCowan; along with Secretary of the Corporation John Ward and senior vice presidents Paul Chellgren, Charles Luellen, Richard Spears and William Voss.

"Each division," Hall said, "will be responsible for carrying out its own business strategies, achieving profitability standards and meeting predetermined goals."[38] Under the new system, AOI sought to strengthen existing companies and emphasize efficiency. Operations not providing adequate rates of return would be divested, with the funds used to reduce the company's debt.

Moreover, he expressed hope for new technologies, including Reduced Crude Conversion, coal-oil mixture fuels, carbon fiber technology and new processes from Ashland Chemical's Venture Research group.

Ashland Oil, Inc., he announced, was embarking on a new era.

Robert Yancey Jr. joined Ashland in 1969 as a technical service engineer at the Buffalo, New York, refinery. A graduate of Cornell University, Yancey served as president of Ashland Petroleum Company for 11 years, beginning in 1986.

Unrelenting emphasis on customer service, through people and processes, has made Ashland the supplier of choice in many businesses.

CHAPTER NINE

ASHLAND RISING

"I would like to be remembered as a person who took over a troubled company and solved a lot of problems and left it a much stronger company with a bright future."

— John Hall, 1996[1]

JOHN RICHARD HALL HAD A huge challenge before him. As *Business Week* pointed out in 1983, Hall inherited the company just after Atkins "sold almost all of the company's crude reserves for $1.3 billion and spent the money to maintain dividends and at the same time finance his dream of pushing Ashland beyond its traditional dependence on oil. So, along with an aborted strategy, the new chairman found himself short of cash."[2]

Moreover, Ashland Oil, Inc., in 1982 the nation's largest independent oil refiner, had hundreds of operations employing thousands of people all over the globe. The corporation had become a giant organization, with new business focuses in which no one in the company leadership had any experience.

The Reins of Leadership

It was a disquieting situation for Hall, the solid thinker whose engineer's penchant for details had become well-known throughout the company during his 25-year ascension. "He comes at problem-solving in a very bottoms-up, nuts-and-bolts operations approach," Paul Chellgren observed years later.[3]

Hall's instinct — one supported by the board and executive corps — was to re-evaluate and compress Ashland back into a few key specialties. While focusing on the core refining business, he pushed the company more heavily into growth areas, such as chemicals. He steadied profits and stock prices by divesting incongruent holdings and eventually closing four of the company's seven refineries.

"We had to accept that refining was going to be a slow-growth process, that it was going to go through a long period of rationalization," Hall said in a 1998 interview. "We just had to try to be as efficient as we could be and as quick on our feet as we could be to try to compete."[4]

Problem Solving

It was not easy to solve all the company's problems, however, for the effort was complicated by a steady barrage of unexpected developments. Ashland survived a variety of challenges, ranging from a hostile takeover attempt by a Canadian conglomerate — part of the Wall Street takeover craze of the 1980s — to the largest inland oil spill in U.S. history. All of this was complicated by the

By Ashland's 70th anniversary in 1994, John Hall had helped cultivate the company into a successful worldwide energy and chemical firm.

fact that much of the 1980s was recessionary, and the petroleum business was especially volatile, largely because of the government's decontrol of oil prices.

Crisis management became a Hall specialty. "I think our adrenaline flows a little bit better when the fat's in the fire," Hall told Louisville magazine writer Bruce Allar years later.[5]

Hall had several opportunities to feel that jolt of adrenaline. One occurred when the Securities and Exchange Commission announced in 1983 it would investigate questionable payments related to crude oil purchases from Oman prior to Hall's election as chairman. Ashland's board previously had asked a Pittsburgh law firm to serve as an independent special counsel to investigate the issue. The special counsel presented findings and recommendations to the board in October 1981. The recommendations addressed internal control issues, and every recommendation contained in the report was implemented prior to the SEC inquiry. The special counsel concluded there had been no violation of U.S. laws and that Ashland had no legal obligation to disclose the report.

The SEC concluded its own investigation in July 1986 and sought an injunction against Ashland and Orin Atkins, alleging that one transaction between 1979 and 1981 violated the Foreign Corrupt Practices Act. Ashland and Atkins signed final orders enjoining future violations, without admitting or denying the allegations. No other officer, director or employee was charged in the SEC complaint.

Hall directed Ashland's full cooperation with the SEC inquiry, which attracted considerable media attention. It was during this period, almost immediately after he was elected chairman, that he directed the development of a Code of Business Conduct and a preventive law program that would guard against such problems in the future. The Code states that Ashland and its employees will abide by the letter and spirit of all applicable laws and regulations, adhere to the highest ethical standards in all business activities, and act as responsible citizens in the communities where Ashland does business.

In 1984, two former employees filed wrongful discharge lawsuits against the company, making allegations related to the questionable payments issue. After a lengthy trial in Covington, Kentucky, a jury found in favor of the plaintiffs. Rather than incur the expense of a long appeals process, Ashland subsequently settled the suits. The company emphasized, however, it continued to believe the plaintiffs' allegations were without merit.

Hall's mettle was tested yet again when residents of Kenova, West Virginia, filed suit in 1988, alleging harmful health effects related to emissions from the Catlettsburg Refinery. The plaintiffs originally prevailed in a jury trial in Charleston, West Virginia, in May 1990. However, the West Virginia Supreme Court unanimously reversed the verdict. Ashland later settled the issue out of court.

Through these crises, Hall proved himself to be a skillful crisis manager. But just two years into his administration, long before the worst landmines were encountered, some observers and analysts were questioning whether he was the right man for the job. A 1983 *Business Week* article, while acknowledging that Hall had reduced the company's

Ashland continued its exploration efforts in the 1980s, although the company was never as successful in locating crude as it had hoped.

reliance on foreign oil by almost half, and had "injected new discipline into the company, trimming overhead costs by $50 million and reducing the work force by 16 percent,"[6] pointed out the company was experiencing reduced revenues — $8.1 billion for fiscal 1982, compared with $9.5 billion the preceding year, and earnings were down 43 percent.

Turning that situation around proved difficult. A year later, in 1984, when AOI had fallen from 36 to 45 on the *Fortune* 500 list, the company announced it would undergo a restructuring that would cause a net loss for fiscal 1984 — the first loss for any fiscal year in the company's 60-year history. It was ultimately a successful move, but an emotionally trying one.

While the primary mission of Hall and his team was to shore up the company's performance and return it to profitability, a significant amount of energy was expended on repairing Ashland's diminished public image, something for which Hall was ideally suited. "Absolute integrity" was Hall's defining characteristic, Samuel Butler, a member of the AOI board of directors, said years later.[7]

John Van Meter, an early Hall protegé who went on to become president of Ashland International, described his boss as "extremely fair and honest — a man who will do what he thinks is right" and "sets a wonderful example for employees."[8]

Paul Chellgren was elected senior vice president and chief financial officer in January 1988.

Reshaping

During the 1980s, John Hall and Vice Chairman Bill Seaton, who was well-known for his keen financial insight, worked hard to improve Ashland's financial position. By the time Seaton retired as chief financial officer in 1988, Ashland's finances were in good order.

One of the first priorities when Hall took over in 1981 was to examine Ashland's holdings. The company quickly acquired the Scurlock crude oil gathering company of Houston to ensure a steady supply of domestic crude oil. Over the next decade, Ashland acquired several other properties, including Tresler Oil, a Cincinnati terminal operator and marketer of petroleum products; and scores of chemical operations and highway contractors.

Ashland also put several of its companies on the selling block, including its foreign carbon-black holdings; Globrite specialty chemicals for the automotive and metal-finishing industries; and Ashland Technology Corporation, an architectural and engineering subsidiary.

One of the earliest divestiture decisions was also one of the biggest. It had become obvious that the two giant acquisitions of Atkins' final days — Integon, an insurance company based in Winston-Salem, North Carolina, and U.S. Filter, a conglomerate of several environmental firms based in New York City — had been unwise.

When the acquisitions, which together cost the company nearly $600 million, had been made, they were part of an Atkins "master plan that never made it to fruition," General Counsel and Secretary Thomas Feazell explained years later. "He had at that time a vision of creating a financial services business of which the insurance company was going to be an integral part. He never got it finished. On U.S. Filter, he thought he was going to be able to work out a joint venture with a large European industrial company," which also never happened.[9]

The core management group in the early 1980s included Hall (center), Vice Chairmen of the Board Robert McCowan (left) and William Seaton (right).

"The thinking of the time for buying an insurance company was this," said Vice President of Investor Relations William Hartl in a 1998 interview. "We had a fairly strong leg in other allied industries, which by definition was chemicals, and we were looking then, essentially, for a third leg of a financial aspect. Lots of companies were doing that kind of thing back then."[10] Very shortly, however, the acquisitions would be regarded as perhaps the worst of the company's history.

"Both of these businesses were far outside the mainstream of Ashland's normal activities," said William Sawran, who joined Ashland in 1971 and moved up to vice president of Ashland Inc. and president of Ashland Services Company. "We acquired both of these companies just before there was a serious business downturn in the early 1980s, and it became clear pretty quickly that we had absorbed a great deal of debt."[11]

"We didn't know how to fix the acquisition," Paul Chellgren explained in a 1998 interview, after he had become Ashland's CEO. "We're kind of a hands-on bunch of managers around here, and when something goes wrong, we like to think we know how to fix it. We at least know how to ask the right questions and understand what the problems are, but that one, we just didn't know how to fix."[12]

U.S. Filter was also problematic. It "wasn't a good acquisition," Feazell said. "There were a few parts of it that worked out well, the most noteworthy being the Drew Chemical portion that's still run by Ashland Chemical. But for the overwhelming part, it didn't work out."[13]

A Partial Recovery

When the companies hit the selling block, there was not a long line of would-be purchasers. "We did not recover our investment," Chellgren said. "We lost some hundreds of millions of dollars in the round trip."[14]

"It took us," said Feazell, "a number of years to recover from that. And because of those troubles, we changed our tactics on acquisitions, which continue to this day. We try now to do acquisitions that are related to our core businesses so that we have some expertise in the businesses, and I think that has certainly served us well over the years."[15]

Although Ashland Oil lost vast sums of money on the purchase and quick sale of those two companies, the consequences were not as dire as might have been the case in another place in other times. "Fortunately, it was a very benign economic environment," Chellgren said. "Business was pretty strong. Crude oil was readily available, the economy was good, it was the Reagan era, and the company was doing well."[16]

The Belzberg Incident

Less than five years after Hall took over, he was named one of *The Gallagher Report's* 10 best corporate chief executives for 1985 for his back-

to-basics corporate strategy, which resulted in a $146.7 million net profit.

That year, however, AOI was soon fighting off a hostile takeover attempt by the First City Financial Corporation, which was owned by the wealthy Belzberg brothers of British Columbia.

On March 24, Hall received what the company referred to as a "soft bear hug letter," in which the Belzberg family announced it had accumulated about 8 percent of Ashland's outstanding shares.[17] They wanted to discuss buying AOI for about $1.8 billion, or around $60 a share. Hall and his executives felt $60 a share was too low (and some analysts agreed) and worried that the three Belzberg brothers would simply follow a past script and strip the company of its assets, as they had done with other acquisitions. Immediately upon hearing from First City, which was often referred to as Canada's

Ashland's strategy to invest in energy-related businesses took it into the coal industry. Eventually, Arch Coal, an Ashland affiliate, would become the nation's No. 2 coal producer.

foremost corporate raider, Ashland initiated an action plan. The company worked with investment bankers and inside and outside counsel in New York, revising corporate strategy and enlisting the help of Kentucky lawmakers to enact legislation to help its largest corporation.

"It was Easter weekend in 1986," recalled Vice President of Corporate Communications Dan Lacy years later. "I remember getting a call at home saying 'pack your bags and be ready to go to New York. We've got a hostile takeover attempt.'"[18]

The company put out a press release, beating Belzberg to the punch, and called on the expertise of anti-takeover guru Bruce Wasserstein. It was a difficult meeting of the minds, Hall and his straight-forward, no-frills team, and Wasserstein, a flashy deal-maker. General Counsel Feazell described the intensity and uncertainty of the situation:

"When he came into a room, he came with an aura and entourage of subordinates, all of whom kind of genuflected every time he looked their way, and he liked to just say, 'This is what we're gonna do.' Well, John Hall, being the hands-on CEO he was, had a little trouble with that, and so we had to finally take Mr. Wasserstein and the team in the other room and say, 'Look, Mr. Hall is a quick study, but this situation and even the slang you use is foreign to him. You've got to give him more detail. And he does not take kindly to you telling him what he's going to do. You have to explain why this is the course he ought to follow.' Once we got that straight, things went pretty well."[19]

Ashland also called on the help of state lawmakers, who were happy to take action to help protect what by now had become Kentucky's largest corporation. "As luck would have it, the Kentucky Legislature happened to be in session, though they only meet once every two years," said Feazell, "and we got some legislation passed."[20]

Years after the takeover attempt, Lacy remained amazed at how fast Ashland and the legislature acted. "The Kentucky Legislature passed an anti-takeover law," he said. "It was written, passed almost unanimously, and signed by the governor in about three days."[21]

In the meantime, the situation drove Ashland's stock price to almost $60 a share. After the

Legislature acted, the price plunged. Ashland then negotiated with the Belzbergs to buy their 2.63 million shares for $51 each, bringing the brothers, who bought their shares at an average price of $44.23, a net pretax profit of nearly $16 million. The price Ashland negotiated, however, was less than the closing market price on the day of the transaction.

In little over a week, the company had won the skirmish, and the crisis was averted. To stave off further takeover attempts, Hall spearheaded a restructuring plan to convert about $300 million in excess funding in the pension plan to stock and allocate it to employees over a ten-year period. In return, employees had to accept a lower match on funds they placed in the company savings plan. "This was the beginning of the leveraged employee stock ownership plan that made employees our largest shareholder group," said Lacy.[22]

In addition, the threat seemed to bring the company closer together. "The incident very much reinforced John Hall's leadership," said Administrative Vice President and Treasurer John Dansby. "He was seen as someone who was very capable of handling that threat. It was something that gave the whole company a big boost and a lot of confidence."[23]

Corporate Restructuring

In addition to creating the employee stock ownership plan, the company was going through some restructuring in upper management as well. A core operating group of executives had been established in the fall of 1981, but Hall had been operating solo, without a president, for five years.

In 1986, Charles J. Luellen was elected president and chief operating officer of Ashland Oil, Inc. Luellen, a 1952 graduate of Indiana University, had joined Ashland's Refinery Sales Department right after college and held a variety of positions. He was executive assistant to Rexford Blazer before becoming senior vice president of Ashland Oil and group operating officer and president of Ashland Petroleum in 1980. Married, with two daughters, he was widely regarded as a man with an uncommonly sharp sense for business and a shrewd judge of talent.

Replacing Luellen as senior vice president was Robert Yancey Jr., a 17-year veteran of the company and son of its former president. Yancey Jr. had held positions in refining at Buffalo; St. Paul Park, Minnesota; and Catlettsburg.

Hall announced the company would continue as a modified holding company managed by a core management group. This group consisted of Hall, William Seaton, Robert McCowan, Luellen, William Voss, Paul Chellgren, Richard Spears and Corporate Secretary John Ward. "We will continue to use the same management structure which has worked so well for us in implementing our strategy over the past five years," Hall explained in the company publication. "However, these changes will give still greater coordination among our operating units."[24]

And Hall, echoing the theme espoused by many forward-thinking CEOs of the mid 1980s, said the company would be putting a greater emphasis on grass-roots innovation. Overall, Hall's 1981 to 1985 inventive restructuring program was so successful that, in 1986, he was named one of the 10 most influential individuals in the oil and gas industry.

A Call to Action

Thereafter the company publication was for months filled with articles about innovation and creativity. Letters from the chairman and president appeared regularly. The company blanketed employees with what they called "Real Big Idea" forms, aimed at tapping into the thinking of everyone. Innovators were heralded.

As Luellen said, "We have always enjoyed a reputation for innovation, and it's well deserved." In larger companies, employees sometimes find it more difficult for their good ideas to find a conduit for implementation, and this was an effort to ensure "the maintenance of a small-company attitude."[25]

Throughout Ashland's history, its employees and leaders have described it as a friendly company in which everyone has decision-making power. "Nobody is afraid to suggest something that's not in their field," said William Seaton. "In other words, if someone in the chemical company thought they could do something for somebody in the construction company, it got said. And if it was a good idea, it got done."[26] Retired Vice Chairman Robert McCowan reiterated the company's friendly corporate culture in a 1998 interview: "Everybody gets along well. The people enjoy being part of this corporation."[27]

In another 1998 interview, John Hall commented on the open corporate environment he worked so hard to inspire: "I think some of it came from me," he said, "and I think some of it came from our founder. I just tried to carry on some of his ideas."[28]

By April 1987, a year after the initiative had begun, Hall told the company publication that while the stage had been set, he was still awaiting star performances. "I am satisfied with the progress we have made in introducing the program. But I believe it will be a number of years before we begin to get the response we are looking for, because we want to change the way people think and communicate."[29]

Hall and his team by now had an impact on the company culture. Operations and acquisitions were no longer seen in isolation, but as part of the bigger picture, reflecting a "systems" approach to management that had begun to infiltrate organizations in the 1980s.

From sales trainee to corporation president, Charles Luellen's career with Ashland spanned nearly 40 years. Known for his keen business sense, Luellen retooled SuperAmerica into an industry leader and guided Ashland Petroleum through the turbulent days following oil-industry decontrol.

Changes for the Better

Hall's leadership brought on other changes as well. The company, according to most, became a bit less intense. The hours were still long and the work taken seriously, but the age of routine 70- or 80-hour workweeks was ending for up-and-comers. In times of crisis or times of need, the staff often worked almost around the clock, but in normal times the work pattern was substantially less prolonged than it had been under Blazer and Atkins.

Hall, a golfer and avid Vanderbilt football fan, made a fair effort to maintain something approaching a normal life. He made time for his second wife, Donna, whom he had married not long before becoming CEO of Ashland Oil, and his son, whom he had adopted with his first wife prior to her death from cancer. He told magazine writer Allar shortly before his retirement that he had purposely attempted to set a less hectic pace than his predecessors. "We try to encourage our employees to have a family life," he said.[30]

By the end of 1987, Hall was able to report that AOI had experienced a "reasonably prof-itable year in fiscal 1987, despite near break-even results from refining. This is the first time the company has been able to [report strong profits when refining was down]. It demonstrates that our strategy to increase earnings from non-refining businesses is working. Refining is a good, profitable business over time, but it is subject to volatility. Our growth businesses provide an earnings cushion when the refining industry suffers a downturn."[31]

More structural changes were announced at the end of 1987. In anticipation of the retirement of William Seaton, vice chairman and chief financial officer, 44-year-old Paul Chellgren, senior vice president and group operating officer, was appointed chief financial officer; Fred Brothers, 47, group operating officer for Ashland Chemical, SuperAmerica and Valvoline, became a member of the core operating team; Robert Yancey Jr., 42, became core group member and group operating officer, with responsibility for Ashland Petroleum Company; and David D'Antoni, 42, was appointed executive vice president and chief operating officer of Ashland Chemical. Other members of the core group remained: Robert McCowan, who would retire as vice chairman in 1988,

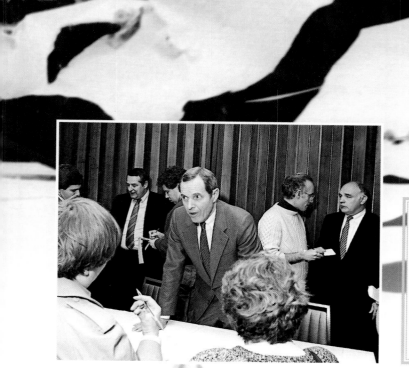

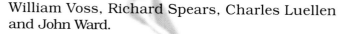

William Voss, Richard Spears, Charles Luellen and John Ward.

The Floreffe, Pennsylvania, oil spill would be a seminal event in how corporate responsibility should be assumed during an environmental crisis. Instead of "the rotten oil company," Ashland would come out of this disaster referred to as the "good guys," and the afterglow would continue, especially when compared with the *Exxon Valdez* disaster in Alaska a year later. Clockwise from the far left, bottom photo: an aerial view of the spill; John Hall surveying the damage; the crumpled 4 million gallon tank; John Hall holding a press conference; Charles Luellen meeting with the press.

The Floreffe Oil Spill

The new team had barely been announced when the company faced what may have been its greatest calamity. On a miserably cold Saturday evening in January 1988, a 4 million gallon storage tank in Floreffe, Pennsylvania, being filled for the first time with diesel fuel, collapsed, unleashing a 3.5 million gallon torrent of oil.

The cascade slammed into the six-foot containment dike and "knocked it all up into the air," said Philip Block, an Ashland vice president and one of the AOI team that dealt with the catastrophe.[32] The flow sluiced into nearby sewer lines, dumping 750,000 gallons of diesel oil into the Monongahela River. The spill quickly spread 100 miles into the Ohio River, fouling drinking water in four states and impacting about 750,000 people. It was, most experts agreed, the largest inland oil spill in the continental United States.

As Ashland officials descended upon the site, the cause of the accident became clear. A 40-year-old tank had been dismantled from Cleveland, removed and shipped to Pittsburgh. "We rebuilt it using 40-year-old steel, welded it and didn't test it properly," said Block,[33] who spent nine months in Floreffe dealing with the situation and its fallout. "Later, the scientists determined that it probably ruptured in less than 10 seconds, basically split from a weak spot."[34]

Ignoring the advice of his lawyers to go slow until all the facts were gleaned, Hall went directly to the spill site, publicly apologized, took full responsibility for the spill and commuted regularly between the corporate offices and Pittsburgh. He made himself and other top executives available around the clock. "It was an all-consuming activity for a number of people," Block recalled.[35]

The company provided drinking water to scores of communities for weeks and also made a grant to the University of Pittsburgh to help finance a study to assess the spill's long-term impact on the river and its aquatic life.

Taking Responsibility

Hall's handling of the situation later won him praise from many, including Carnegie-Mellon University's graduate school of Industrial Administration, which proclaimed him Outstanding Crisis Manager of 1988. And the actions the company took are still being cited — including in a Harvard Business School case study — for proper methods of dealing with corporate calamities.

"One of the things that surprised the press, industry observers and some of our own staff," Hall said, 10 years after the spill, "was when we stood up and said, 'We're responsible. We apologize, and we're going to pay for every consequence of the accident.' It was quite an arresting moment."[36]

Magazine writer Allar, quoting *The New York Times*, observed how Hall took charge of the situation:

"Hall was a little slow out of the blocks, but after a day and a half he began to move heaven and earth. ... He pledged to clean everything up, he visited news bureaus to explain what the company would do, he answered whatever questions were asked. Within 24 hours, he had turned the perception from 'rotten oil company' to 'they are pretty good guys.' "[37]

As expensive as it was — the spill cost at least $40 million ($30 million reimbursed by insurance and $10 million from the company) — the media were impressed, and *The Courier-Journal* of Louisville later pointed out that "the company has come away remarkably unscathed and may well emerge with a better public image than before the disaster."[38]

Hall insisted he and his colleagues simply did the right thing. "Our attitude was, 'Hey guys, we've made a mess here. We've got to clean the thing up, and we've got to try to do anything we can to help all the people who have been inconvenienced, to try to minimize the impact,'" he said in 1990.[39]

That approach did, in fact, have a positive impact on the company's tarnished image, Vice President of Corporate Communications Dan Lacy acknowledged later. The afterglow lasted longer than might have ordinarily been the case, aided by Exxon's somewhat questionable handling of the *Valdez* spill a year later, a study in contrasts to AOI's action. Beyond that, Lacy told a reporter, "the cultural changes we've had within the company" as a result of the spill, including new policies, plans and procedures, "have made us better able to deal with future crises and have spilled over into the industry as a whole."[40]

Another Disaster

As it turned out, Floreffe was the first of two punches. Just two years later, another incident occurred near Bay City, Michigan, when a tanker operated by AOI's subsidiary Cleveland Tankers exploded. On a Sunday morning in September, the *MV Jupiter,* unloading gasoline at a tank farm on the Saginaw River, was torn from its fuel line by a wake. An explosion ripped through the chilly air as nearly 1 million gallons of gasoline on board ignited. One of the 18-man crew was killed, and three were hospitalized. The fire raged for 30 hours. A Texas firm specializing in such disasters assembled a crew and equipment, but a few hours after the blaze was doused with foam, it reignited.

Again, Ashland did not delay. As Luellen explained to *Crisis* magazine in 1991, the Floreffe experience had spurred the company to develop a comprehensive emergency preparedness program to ensure that AOI could "respond to the incident more quickly and with better organization. The perception by the press about how an emergency is handled is very important. We realized quickly that I needed to be in Bay City with the crisis team, participating in handling the accident. My presence showed that Ashland's senior management was committed to all aspects during this crisis."[41]

When it was all over, the Sunday morning episode had caused more than $7 million in damage and cleanup costs, and a stretch of river was blocked for weeks by the sunken wreckage of the *Jupiter.*

A lifelong advocate for education, John Hall attended Vanderbilt University on a football scholarship and was named the college's first Academic All-American.

In fact, environmental issues — emanating from all quarters — required much of the company's focus even into the early 1990s. Ashland faced several lawsuits and paid large fines over illegal emissions during Hall's tenure while also coping with the 1990 federal Clean Air Act Amendments. "We had to double our capital employed in about 36 months between 1990 and 1993 to bring the operations up to new pollution control standards," said Chellgren.[42]

The passage of the Clean Air Act Amendments, directly on the heels of the Iraqi invasion of Kuwait, which forced crude oil prices to $41 a barrel by October 1990, was one of the most profound events of the decade.

It "forced us and the rest of the industry to pump in a huge amount of capital for cleaner fuels," said Fred Brothers, executive vice president.[43]

The practice of expanding refineries to justify expenditures, a pattern that had existed for decades, was once again repeated throughout the industry. "We spent several hundred million dollars," said Brothers, as did other major refiners. "The industry unwittingly brought on so much additional unneeded capacity with those cleaner fuels, and the supply-demand imbalance became so severe, that the industry didn't earn its cost of capital," he added.[44]

Put bluntly, in Chellgren's words, "the business dropped. Profits dropped. So our returns went from very good returns, although admittedly volatile returns, to very poor returns."[45]

Giving Back

Regardless, by the early 1990s, AOI was taking solid steps in the direction of environmental improvement and preservation. Ashland became publicly aligned with several environmental initiatives, including an annual event called River Sweep, in which it teamed up with the Ohio River Valley Water Sanitation Commission as the principal sponsor of the one-day riverbank cleanup project. From 1989 to 1997, the event drew 105,000 volunteers from six states, who cleaned up more than 62,000 tons of trash from the banks of the Ohio and several of its tributaries.

Other environmental initiatives followed, including the Chairman's Challenge Awards, honoring projects and individuals who demonstrate excellence in environmental, health and safety practices. The company also began producing its Environment, Health and Safety annual report, which records and gives updates on company and employee environmental initiatives. Ashland also joined the Wildlife Habitat Council to find ways to preserve and enhance the environment by establishing protected habitats on company properties.

At the same time, the company furthered its push for education, establishing several awards programs for top students and teachers, making large grants to area colleges and universities, and allocating all of its corporate advertising budget to promoting improved education.

Hall himself devoted a great deal of personal time to the cause of education, helping, for example, to form The Partnership for Kentucky Schools, to rally corporate support for changes in primary education. Many argued that this activity generated a lot of public good will and positive public relations in a time when the company was desperate for both. Yet Hall, active on the boards of two universities — Transylvania in Lexington and Vanderbilt,

A Leader in Education

SINCE ITS EARLIEST YEARS UNDER PAUL Blazer, Ashland actively supported education through a variety of means, including hundreds of contributions to educational endeavors. The company pushed lawmakers to improve public education as far back as the 1930s, and a high school in Ashland is even named after Paul Blazer.

Ashland's matching gifts program was among its early, formalized initiatives toward education. Through this program, which was started in 1967, the company matched employees' donations to colleges and universities.

It was in the 1980s, however, that the company championed education as a central corporate cause. Robert D. Bell, administrative vice president, who first suggested that the company spend all of its advertising budget on messages promoting higher education, is widely credited for Ashland's heavy involvement in education during this time. As Bell recalled in a 1998 interview:

"We were having a meeting one day, mainly involving the corporate advertising program, and I said, 'Why don't we spend our entire corporate advertising budget in behalf of messages promoting quality education at all levels?' Well, we couldn't do that without approval of senior management, and as I remember it, Dan Lacy and I went to Bob McCowan, and he immediately approved it. McCowan then took it to John Hall, who also gave the go-ahead. So we got carte blanche to spend all of our budget for corporate advertising in education. And we did just that."[1]

In 1984, Ashland created a package of television commercials aimed at improving the quality of education in Kentucky and West Virginia, and throughout the remainder of the 1980s and the decade of the 1990s, 100 percent of Ashland's corporate advertising budget was devoted to improving education.

Bell was also a founder of the Kentucky Advocates for Higher Education, an advocacy group that played a pivotal role in improved funding for higher education in the 1980s. Before retiring in 1986 as an administrative vice president, he helped install state government relations representatives in key states where Ashland had operations.

John Hall also put a heavy emphasis on education. He served on the boards of two universities, was conferred honorary degrees from several colleges and earned a reputation as a pro-education activist. "John Hall's commitment to move Kentucky education from mediocre to excellent is not mere rhetoric," Carolyn Witt Jones, director of the Partnership for Kentucky Schools, told a writer when Hall retired.[2]

Among Ashland's educational initiatives:

- **Ashland Inc. Teacher Achievement Awards.** Nominations were taken from four states — Kentucky, Ohio, West Virginia and Minnesota — and through a complicated nominating and assessment process, ten teachers were chosen for the award, which included $2,500 in cash.

- **Parent Power.** A thrice yearly publication encouraged parental participation in kids' education, it circulated free to about 70,000 parents nationwide.
- **The Job Center.** A weekly page in the *Lexington Herald-Leader* that offered an in-depth look at a particular field and included the training and steps necessary to follow a particular career path.
- **The Ashland Foundation.** This organization received $60 million in corporate funding from 1967 to 1997 and was a major educational backer. "At least 60 to 65 percent of the Foundation's contributions over the years have gone to education," said Judy Thomas, Foundation president.[3] The remainder was devoted to various cultural, civic, and health and welfare programs.

Among the programs the Foundation financed were "Ashland Scholars," through which children of employees received grants amounting to $1,500 per year for four years; the Governor's Scholars program in Kentucky, a summer enrichment program for top high school juniors; and The Governor's Honors Academy in West Virginia for sophomores and juniors. The Foundation also made substantial grants each year for various public school programs in the two counties closest to Ashland Inc.'s corporate headquarters.

The Foundation was a regular contributor to colleges and universities. It made the first-ever $1 million grant to the University of Kentucky, and was a major sponsor of the Yeager Scholars program at Marshall University, aimed at drawing top scholars from throughout the nation.

Ashland Senior Vice President of Public Affairs Mac Zachem said that among the many benefits of educational contributions numbered "goodwill in the bank. I walk into a congressman or senator's office, … and they say, 'Boy, Ashland is the finest corporate citizen I know, because you support education.' That is part of our culture, and John Hall was a real part of forwarding that. Paul Chellgren is continuing it, and that is very important."[4]

Above: Ashland's Senior Vice President, General Counsel and Secretary Tom Feazell with Judith Langkamer, one of Ashland's West Virginia teachers honored in 1998 as an Ashland Teacher Achievement Award winner.

Left: Bob Bell campaigned tirelessly for education, both inside and outside the company.

his alma mater — as well as in several local and regional initiatives, was credited with being both tireless and genuinely sincere in his efforts.

Telling Figures

The company ended the first year of the 1990s with sales and operating revenues of $9.47 billion, net income of $182 million and operating income of $331 million. The dip was attributed to the summer invasion of Kuwait by Iraq, which precipitated rising crude oil prices. SuperAmerica and Valvoline had added dozens of new outlets that year; equity income from Arch Mineral and Ashland Coal, which had grown massively during the 1980s, increased 31 percent; and APAC, the company's road construction division, was on an upswing after a difficult year. Ashland Chemical had suffered a slump, injured by general economic condi-

Hall, whose roots were in the refinery end of the business, at the Catlettsburg refinery in 1993.

tions that depressed construction and transportation projects.

The following year's results revealed a slight increase in sales and operating revenues, to $9.86 billion, but a decrease to $294 million operating income and a decline in net income to $145 million, as virtually all sectors were impacted by the nation's involvement in Operation Desert Storm to evict Saddam Hussein from Kuwait, and a general downturn in the economy.

In 1992, the company experienced a further decline. Sales and operating revenues had grown to $10.2 billion, but an operating income loss of $63 million was reported, and a net income loss of $68 million, attributable partly to extremely weak petroleum margins and continued recessionary

trends. A major contributor to the loss was the overriding influence of unusual items, including required accounting changes for nonpension retirees' benefits costs, environmental reserves and allocations for a voluntary retirement program.

Company Brat

In 1992, following six years as president and chief operating officer and nearly 40 years with the company, Luellen retired, and Paul Chellgren, who was by then the obvious successor, was elected president and COO.

Paul Wilbur Chellgren, lean and urbane, had made his way into the presidency through a circuitous route that started with a $1.69-per-hour summer job as a company janitor.

Chellgren describes himself as an "Ashland brat."[46] His father, W.E. Chellgren, worked for Ashland for more than 30 years, the last 11 as company controller. Yet Paul Chellgren didn't begin working full time for Ashland until he was in his 30s, with an established track record.

A 1964 graduate of the University of Kentucky, Chellgren went on to Harvard to earn an MBA, and then to London, where he received a degree in developmental economics from Oxford. While there, Chellgren met his British wife, Sheila, with whom he had three children by the time he became Ashland's CEO.

Chellgren had been noticed by the Ashland brass while still in college, during summer and college-break jobs there. Orin Atkins had made frequent entreaties for him to take a position at Ashland. But Chellgren chose a multi-city course away from home for several years. "I wanted to do things on my own," he said later.[47]

In 1974, after holding positions as a management consultant with McKinsey & Company in London and Washington, D.C.; an operations analyst in the office of the Secretary of Defense; a manager with Boise Cascade Corporation in Boise and Los Angeles; and general manager of Universal Capital Company in Kansas City, Chellgren joined Ashland as executive assistant to Atkins. He quickly rose through the ranks, becoming an administrative vice president of Ashland Chemical in 1977, senior vice president of AOI in 1980 and a group operating officer in 1981.

Team Players

Hall and Chellgren were a good match. Hall had an enormous grasp of the operations of the company; Chellgren had an ease with figures and financial statements and a willingness to challenge the company to rethink its goals, approaches and strategies.

During their four years together, the two successfully implemented air-quality improvements that cost hundreds of millions of dollars, oversaw scores of new acquisitions and the launching of an aggressive program to revitalize the Ashland brand of gasoline, and coaxed APAC and Ashland Chemical to record earnings. They also renamed the company Ashland Inc., dropping Oil from the name to better reflect its diverse and less oil-dependent operations. By the end of fiscal 1996, Ashland Inc. would report sales and operating revenues of $13.1 billion, an operating income of $456 million and net income of $211 million.

A Modest Retirement

At the annual meeting in January 1996, Hall announced plans to retire. He would step down as CEO on October 1, 1996, and continue as chairman until February 1, 1997, when he would retire at age 64. Since Ashland had a mandatory retirement age of 65, Hall wanted to retire at an annual meeting and give Chellgren the opportunity to begin the 1997 fiscal year as CEO. Hall's career with Ashland spanned nearly 39 years, the last 15 of which were spent as chairman and CEO.

The Hall years were eventful. It is fair to say that, during his tenure as chairman and CEO, John Hall faced nearly every type of management challenge and that he handled them skillfully. An analysis of the Hall era finds three major accomplishments: First, he successfully altered Ashland's strategic direction to reduce reliance on the volatile refining business and increase earnings from related energy and chemical businesses. In so doing, he unwound the unsuccessful Integon and U.S. Filter acquisitions left over from the Atkins years. Second, he restructured Ashland's board of directors and recruited highly respected leaders

from business and academia. When Hall was elected chairman in 1981, nine of Ashland's 15 directors were officers or retired officers of the corporation. When Hall retired as chairman in January 1997, Ashland's 13-member board included only one company officer, Paul Chellgren, the new chairman and CEO. Third, Hall resolved sensitive corporate governance and litigation issues and renewed the public's confidence in Ashland as a responsible corporate citizen.

Along the way, he successfully managed the Floreffe oil spill crisis, gaining for Ashland a national reputation for effective crisis management. He overcame a hostile takeover attempt by the Belzbergs. He enlarged Ashland's non-refining businesses. The number of SuperAmerica stores nearly quadrupled. Valvoline increased market share, entered the quick-lube businesses and added new product lines. Ashland Chemical's operating income nearly quadrupled, reflecting increased capital employed. Operating profit from APAC nearly tripled. Ashland Coal experienced a fourfold increase in sales tonnage, while Arch Mineral's tonnage more than doubled. In all, during the years between 1981 and 1996, Ashland delivered a total return to shareholders of 10.5 percent.

At the same time, Hall instituted Ashland's Code of Business Conduct and an aggressive preventive law and compliance program to ensure that none of the problems that plagued the company before his tenure would ever be repeated. Finally, he spearheaded Ashland's broad-ranging support for education, creating a lasting difference in the lives of children for generations to come.

Ashland's 1996 annual report paid a fitting tribute to Hall, who had been a leader, not only in the company, but also in the refining industry and the local, regional and national community:

"Known as a consensus builder, and as an admired and respected leader in corporate America, Mr. Hall is personally committed to honesty and human values. He leaves a legacy of dedication to hard work, personal service and a company ready to meet any challenge in the years ahead."[48]

The Ashland
SOURCE

October 1997
Volume III
Number 4

IN THE DRIVER'S SEAT

"Produced for the source of our success," *The Ashland Source* was a key method of communication once the company became so large.

CHAPTER TEN

AN AMBITIOUS COURSE

"Performance ... is more than numbers. It is the will to achieve, to exceed our yesterdays with our tomorrows."

— Paul Chellgren, November 1997[1]

LESS THAN ONE MONTH after Chellgren became chief executive officer in the fall of 1996, Ashland received a formal notice that Providence Capital, a New York investment firm, was nominating a slate of directors to run against Ashland's slate at the upcoming January shareholders' meeting.

Chellgren spent most of November meeting with investors and came away with the certainty, he declared through the company publication *The Ashland Source,* that the company needed to be "less patient, more demanding of performance and drive toward higher return on capital employed."[2]

Moving Fast

In December, Chellgren announced his plans for improving profitability and shareholder return, including the formation of the Petroleum group, which placed Ashland Petroleum, SuperAmerica and Valvoline under the leadership of Ashland Executive Vice President Fred Brothers. The goal was to integrate operations for the best interests of all shareholders, "rather than in the best interests of a narrow profit segment within the petroleum company or SuperAmerica," Chellgren told *The Ashland Source.*[3] The reorganization immediately eliminated 54 positions; 172 more were eliminated in the following months.

In his first 270 days as CEO, Chellgren also sold the domestic assets of Blazer Energy for $566 million, using the proceeds to reduce debt; merged the company's two coal operations, Arch Mineral and Ashland Coal, Inc; and announced the most significant move of recent decades, a proposed joint venture with USX/Marathon, which would merge the companies' refining, marketing and transportation operations.

In explanation, he later told *The Ashland Source* that "one learns over the years to take advantage of opportunities as they arise."[4]

Difficult Decisions

Ashland Inc. was urged to take opportunities by the investment community, which demanded a higher return on its investment. This was something Chellgren understood well. He grew up the son of the company's controller, and "as he says, he learned accounting at the breakfast table," Marvin Quin, senior vice president and chief financial officer, said in a 1998 interview.[5]

The Ashland Source encouraged employees to be "in the driver's seat" by following a road map to their destination of higher performance by the company.

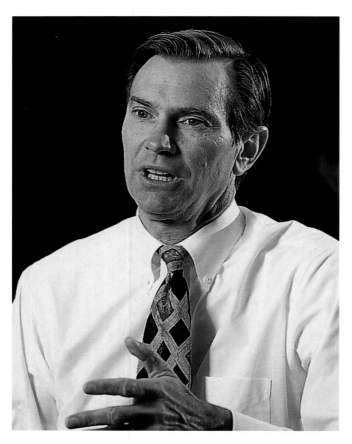

Senior Vice President and Chief Financial Officer Marvin Quin played a major role in the Marathon/Ashland joint-venture discussions.

The reality of the situation was that, like it or not, the company had to change — faster and in more fundamental ways than ever.

"Over the past 40 years we have seen a significant increase in institutional ownership," Quin said early in 1997. "Sixteen years ago institutions owned 5 percent of Ashland's stock. That number was 61 percent at the end of March 1997, and it will continue to grow. Along with the shift in ownership, we have also seen a change in attitude. All shareholders share a common goal of attractive total returns on investment."[6]

Chellgren's plan to accomplish growth and economic certainty within Ashland's petroleum segment struck at the very core of the company's heritage.

"It was a financially easy decision. It was emotionally maybe a little more difficult," said Ashland Executive Vice President Fred Brothers, a 30-year

company veteran.[7] Refining, Brothers pointed out, "was the one business that started the company and sustained the company through so many years," a business that was "very stable, very dependable, very predictable" for decades.[8]

But when the periods of volatility became longer and closer together, Brothers said, "It became increasingly obvious to us and to the industry that business as usual wasn't going to make it. So we, after a lot of tough grappling with strategic options, decided we needed to see if we could become part of a much larger refining-marketing organization, because remaining independent didn't look like a viable financial alternative. It was tough. The board had mixed reactions. … It was a tough time, but we had to come up with a new way of doing business and did so."[9]

"When we started looking for partners," Chellgren recalled, "we began by examining all the refiners in the upper Midwest. We looked at refinery locations, terminals, pipelines, transportation and marketing networks. We had discussions with a number of companies. After extensive analysis, we were convinced Marathon was the best partner for us in terms of compatibility of operations and markets. Plus, we know Marathon. We've been pipeline partners in Capline, in product exchanges and in terminals."[10]

A Partnership of Equals

Both Ashland and Marathon were aiming for 50/50 ownership, and it was with that goal in mind that talks began. But given Marathon's larger size, it eventually became obvious Ashland would have to invest a considerable amount of cash — somewhere in the vicinity of $1 billion — to devise an equal partnership. Three months into the discussions, Ashland concluded it was unwilling to commit that much cash.

Nevertheless, discussions survived that turn of events. "I think if we hadn't been close enough friends with very similar views on a strategic checklist, the negotiations would have ceased at that point," Brothers said.[11]

Two financial teams buried themselves anew in the books, and after weeks of wrangling over percentages of ownership, they settled on a 62/38 split, "which both sides, I believe in retrospect, considered a very fair division," Brothers said.[12] Tom Usher, chairman and CEO of USX, summed up the division nicely when he said, "While we have unequal ownership, we have a partnership of equals."[13]

On December 12, 1997, the agreement was signed to form Marathon Ashland Petroleum LLC. The joint venture would be based in Findlay, Ohio, the home of Marathon before many of its corporate officers moved to Houston in 1990.

With the agreement signed, Ashland Inc. exchanged what had once been the jewel in its corporate crown for a smaller piece of a much larger enterprise. It could then concentrate on what it considered its greater growth markets: Ashland

Chemical, Valvoline and APAC, the highway construction program.

The Pace of Change

The joint venture changed the company landscape forever. Chellgren pointed out that Ashland was not divorcing itself from oil, however, but merely changing its relationship with it.

"Let me emphasize that we have not withdrawn or dis-invested from refining and marketing. We have changed the nature of our investment in response to industry conditions and opportunities, but not the scope of our investment," he declared at the annual shareholders meeting early in 1998.[14]

Still, the cornerstone of the company's heritage had been supplanted. Chellgren, conscious of the identity crisis such wholesale change can precipitate, had been taking pains for months to

Ashland's annual meeting drew hundreds of shareholders to the corporate headquarters in Russell. Paul Chellgren (inset) had much to discuss at the January 1998 meeting, including the recently enacted joint venture with Marathon.

prepare the ranks. Regular updates appeared in *The Ashland Source* where, in a straightforward and unapologetic manner, Chellgren explained the status of the negotiations and why such steps were necessary.

"The pace of change in the refining industry, for example, has been accelerating very rapidly for the past several years," he said. "Industry conditions have become increasingly competitive, much more transparent, and the markets have become much more efficient. To be successful in this environment, a refiner must have low costs, high productivity, economies of scale, higher market shares and additional geographic focus."[15]

A Flair for Leadership

The joint venture created the nation's sixth-largest refiner and the Midwest's largest refiner and marketer of gasoline and petroleum products — a $20 billion company with 5,400 outlets in 20 states. It was a bold, difficult maneuver by the recently seated chairman — and one that sealed his leadership style.

A tenacious problem-solver who met tough decisions without hesitation, Chellgren pulled the company through some difficult straits with relentless determination and optimism. "One of the things that I think has helped him all along the way was he got very much interested in debating in his younger years," his father, W.E. Chellgren, observed. "So he could talk on his feet, and he could think."[16]

Widely regarded as a brilliant strategic thinker with high standards for himself and everyone else, Chellgren quickly made it clear he had no interest in being the source of all power. A fervent delegator, he left the details to his managers, and the compa-

ny moved from a paternalistic bent to a far more self-directed, self-motivated organization.

Chellgren, who throughout his career had always arrived early at the office and stayed late, was devoted, nonetheless, to the concept of balance. He and his wife, avid culture buffs, who also attended cultural events at every opportunity and amassed a substantial and impressive private art collection, did not alter their habits once he assumed the corner office. Further, Chellgren's devotion to physical fitness has become legendary. It was understood throughout the company that his office would be empty at 11:30 every day except in the most extraordinary of circumstances. At that

Top: W.E. Chellgren, father of Paul Chellgren, served as Ashland's controller for many years.

Right: A modern-day Renaissance man, Chellgren is an art connoisseur as well as a financially savvy executive.

hour, he would make his way to the company health club to run and power lift.

On All Fronts

Forward momentum was the message Chellgren sent during his first months as chairman. And while the joint venture took up much of the attention of his top executives during 1997, that process was not the company's entire focus. That year Ashland spent $75 million on 13 acquisitions to strengthen its distribution, specialty chemicals and road construction businesses.

Chellgren also pushed to broaden Ashland's influence in international markets. With trade barriers falling and new markets emerging, he predicted in 1997 that in Europe alone, Ashland was on track to double 1995 revenues by the end of the 1997 fiscal year. While the company had a strong history in Europe — Valvoline had been in Europe since the 1870s, and Ashland Chemical's Foundry Products Division, the world's largest supplier of foundry chemicals, had been there for 30 years — the time was right for even greater penetration into Europe. To ensure more profitability through growth, the company spent the year setting up its European Shared Services Center in Rotterdam to deal with the "back office" functions of dozens of its European entities that had been working independently.

The New Ashland

By the end of fiscal 1997, Chellgren was declaring it "a milestone year."[17] Net income, excluding unusual items, was at an all-time high, the balance sheet was stronger than at any time in the previous decade, and the price of common stock had gone up 37 percent during the year. The company had completed the year, Chellgren declared, "stronger" and "more focused." But, he added, "the journey is not over."[18] The company, he implied, would not be permitted to rest on its laurels.

"Paul has used the term 'responsible growth,'" said CFO Marvin Quin, "and I really like that term. It implies we are going to grow at whatever rates we think we can by making attractive, responsible investments. If there is somewhere we can add value to a particular business and it

APAC, Ashland Inc.'s road construction services company, backed the massive 1996 River Walk project in Augusta, Georgia.

fits something that we're doing very well, we should go after it aggressively. If it's not, we don't want growth for growth's sake."[19]

As if to prove the new Ashland was not just protectively retreating into itself but surging ahead, the company made several announcements early in 1998. It bought Eagle One Industries of Carlsbad, California, to give Valvoline a line of automotive wax, polishes and cleaner products, and would acquire 10 Missouri-based companies for the APAC network. Ashland also announced plans to build a $4.5 million product-development laboratory at Valvoline's Lexington headquarters.

Ashland Inc. in 1998 was quite different from the company that had begun 74 years earlier. Refining was no longer the lifeblood of the compa-

CENTRALIZING EUROPE

THE EUROPEAN SHARED SERVICES Center, the nerve center of the $700-million-a-year business from Ashland's European operations, originated as a vague notion late in 1994, but by early 1998, the office was up and running.

The idea of setting up such an office, providing support services for Ashland's operations in 16 European countries, was conceived in 1994 after Paul Chellgren, then president and COO, encouraged European managers to have a manager's meeting. When that meeting took place in Brussels in November 1994, it was the first time in many years that the European managers had been brought together, and they discussed the potential efficiency in having one support center to deal with accounting and treasury functions, information technology, payroll, human resources, law and environmental health and safety. At that time, Ashland had 39 subsidiaries with 56 different operating sites in Europe, and each was operating as a separate entity.

At the meeting, "it became clear that our European growth objectives couldn't be reached

The June 1998 opening of the European Shared Services Center was an event to be celebrated. From left: Emma Brand, Joe Corry, W.P. Pope, H.J. Simons, Paul Chellgren and Bill Sawran.

without some fundamental change in the administrative cost structure," said company executive William Sawran, who initiated the European Shared Services Center.[1]

But it would not be an easy task to pull off. The countries where the various businesses were operating had different languages, different tax laws, different currencies and different regulations.

A steering committee of European managers was assembled to work with Ernst & Young, commissioned to assist with a thorough review of the structure, and by June 1996, the committee recommended that Ashland Inc. establish not several regional offices but one Pan-European office.

Chellgren instantly approved, with one modification. Chellgren asked that it be put in place within 18 months — in other words, by the end of the first quarter of 1998.

Ashland had to negotiate some obvious hurdles to integrate the functions of so many operations. Every entity had to diminish its own control. Other considerations included the location and staffing of a single office, establishing an accounting infrastructure, selecting computer hardware and training employees.

Rotterdam was selected as the site for the office because it is centrally located in Europe and is a major trade center. Moreover, said Sawran, "The Dutch people have superb language skills, and the transportation facilities are excellent."[2]

The shared services start-up team moved into two floors of a modern high-rise in the center of downtown and set about the daunting task of establishing universal protocols and priorities. Communication was often extremely difficult, as representatives from several different countries, each with different languages and culture, began to work together.

Despite these many challenges, by the middle of 1998 the Rotterdam office could boast 71 full-time employees on site, and many of the business units, which then numbered 62, had been brought into the system.

ny. It was by then in chemicals, automotive products, coal and paving and was a significant part of a refining and marketing empire with more than 5,000 outlets. Ashland Inc. had 2,665 facilities all over the globe and, including Marathon Ashland Petroleum, 39,000 employees. Some of the individual company units were larger than the entire Ashland Oil & Refining operation had been when Paul Blazer died.

The More Things Change ...

But Ashland was, in 1998, a company that had not forgotten its roots or its heritage or its values. Portraits of retired presidents and CEOs and other company builders still lined the walls of the executive offices. Most of the employees who worked there were well aware of the contributions of each, although some of the men in the gallery had died before most employees began working for Ashland.

Ashland continued to be exceedingly respectful of its past leadership. The company maintained a suite of offices and support staff for retired executives in downtown Ashland. "It gives them a place to go and make observations about the current generation of executives, and how they're not doing things the way they should," Chellgren joked. "Some people say, 'Gosh, you're making your own bed of nails.' No, that's part of what we do and who we are."[20]

For retired employees who were not in executive positions, the company sponsored luncheons and dinners and other social events at 17 retiree clubs around the country. The company also published a quarterly newspaper for retirees called *The Next Page*. The editor, a retiree, filled the newspaper

with "those things for which our retirees will have an interest — benefits, public interest stories, messages from our Washington office, issues on health, issues on benefits ... stories on people who have done unique things after they have retired," said Charles Whitehead, director of Selection and Placement for Ashland Inc.[21]

There continued to be in the company a sense of obligation to the children of employees. "We generally maintained summer employment jobs for our children," said Chellgren. "My son has been employed out there. My daughters have been employed by the company. My first exposure to the company was as a summer employee. We have a bit of a tradition of providing summer employment for children of employees."[22]

Of course, Ashland remained deeply committed to its present employees as well. "It was not just a job opportunity," said Michael Toohey, Ashland's director of government relations in Washington, D.C. "It was a commitment to support employees, to provide the best lifestyle they can, to protect them with health care."[23] It was Toohey, after being diagnosed with leukemia and successfully treated through a bone marrow transplant, who encouraged Ashland to team up with Washington, D.C.'s Marrow Foundation.[24] At the time of his 1998 interview, Toohey, on Ashland's behalf, was advocating that Congress change the way health care was delivered in the United States.[25]

As the company moved toward the millennium, Ashland had clearly matured. Much of the company's fabric had changed and would continue to change. But at the same time, much of its essential texture — the texture that Paul Blazer had so devotedly begun molding as far back as 1924 — had endured.

1959 — Valvoline's new growth strategy includes sponsoring the National Hot Rod Association's U.S. National Drag Races, its first association with motorsports.

1967 — Ashland Chemical is formed shortly after Ashland Oil purchases Archer-Daniels-Midland's chemical division.

1969 — Ashland's interest in coal begins when it buys half the stock of Arch Mineral.

1970 — Ashland Oil acquires the Northwestern Refining Company, which includes the SuperAmerica chain of convenience stores.

THE OPERATING UNITS

THE STORY OF ASHLAND INC. WOULD not be complete without chronicling the histories of the company's operating units. As Ashland Oil & Refining Company became more and more diversified — as it evolved into Ashland Inc. — its leaders found it prudent to form additional businesses. Valvoline, Ashland Chemical, SuperAmerica, APAC, Arch Coal, Inc. and Marathon Ashland Petroleum LLC all have unique histories and their own talented leaders. Yet each of these diverse businesses originated from the same parent company, a company that trusted enough in its divisions' leaders to let the businesses flourish, each in its own right.

ARCH COAL, INC.

1974 — Ashland consolidates its construction activities into one company known as Ashland Construction, which will later evolve into APAC.

1986 — Valvoline enters the quick lube business with Valvoline Instant Oil Change.

1997 — Arch Mineral merges with Ashland Coal to become Arch Coal, Inc., a publicly traded company.

1998 — Marathon Ashland Petroleum LLC officially starts operation and begins rolling over Ashland stores to the Marathon name.

MARATHON ASHLAND
Petroleum LLC

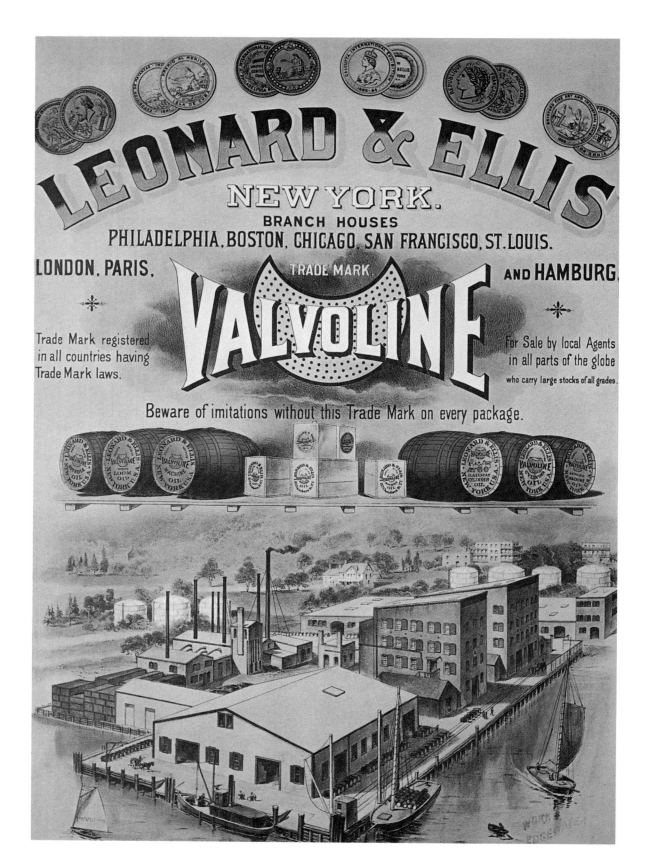

A Valvoline advertisement from the turn of the century pictured the plant in Edgewater, New Jersey, which was destroyed by fire in 1914.

CHAPTER ELEVEN

VALVOLINE

"We want to be viewed as the innovator. That's the type of brand we are, and that's going to be our future."

— James J. O'Brien, president of Valvoline, 1998[1]

O F ASHLAND OIL'S MANY ACQUI-sitions in the late 1940s and early 1950s, Freedom-Valvoline was the one that seemed most likely to lift the company from virtual obscurity to brand-name recognition.

Although Ashland Oil & Refining was well-respected in the oil industry and on Wall Street, few people outside those rarified circles had heard of the company. Valvoline, however, was a company with a 75-year history, recognition and relationships that extended from Pennsylvania to Bombay, and solid brand recognition throughout the industrialized world. Like Ashland, it was a quality-conscious company. Yet until Ashland bought the business, it also seemed more devoted to its reputation than to growth.

Trademarking Lube

Valvoline traces its beginnings to 1865, when Dr. John Ellis, a dynamic Massachusetts-born dentist-turned-physician, turned his attention to pharmacology and became fascinated with various claims relating to the medicinal value of crude oil. At the age of 50, already renowned for pioneering many surgical techniques, he journeyed to the oil-boom area of Pennsylvania. Although he quickly concluded the medicinal claims were unfounded, Ellis became consumed with the notion that it might be possible to create a machinery lubricant from the crude oil oozing from the ground.

There was a great need for lubricants. The machine age was grinding ahead, but the only greasing compounds available were tallow, suet and lard, leavened sometimes with a small dollop of crude. Unfortunately, these poor lubricants tended toward extreme corrosion and gumming.

Ellis was evidently alone in his belief that it might be possible to develop a refining technique to turn crude oil into a denser lubricating substance. At that point, refineries had succeeded only in producing the light oil that was used as an illuminant.

A few months after his arrival in Pennsylvania, Ellis built the world's first mineral lubricating refinery in Binghamton, New York, not far from the oil fields of northwestern Pennsylvania, where the first oil well was drilled, and western New York. Eight years later, in 1873, the product that he called Binghamton Cylinder Oil was given the first mineral lubricating trademark ever registered: Valvoline.

Dr. John Ellis, heralded as a genius by oilmen, created the process that formed the heavy lubricant later named Valvoline.

The product caught on quickly, having received a boost when a young inventor named George Corliss, the nation's top steam engine manufacturer, used it on his steam engine and declared it far superior to all others. On that recommendation, many firms, including three railroads, began using Valvoline.

The original plant quickly proved inadequate to meet growing demand, and in 1869 Ellis opened a new refinery 150 miles away in South Brooklyn, New York. He also established distribution offices in Boston, Chicago, Philadelphia and San Francisco and signed distribution agreements with firms in London, Paris and Hamburg.

Greasing the Competition

The company distinguished itself with laudable and remarkable speed, winning the medal for lubrication excellence at the Centennial Exposition in Philadelphia in 1876, and earning similar recognition at the Exposition Universelle in Paris two years later.

The number of competitors grew as the years passed. Valvoline was rarely the least expensive of the lot, but it was relentlessly consistent. Salesmen emphasized that Valvoline was the highest quality available, and used properly, would be most economical in the long run. Ellis' son, W. Dixon Ellis, who was the company's sales manager from its earliest days, commented about the quality in a letter during the 1870s:

Above: Valvoline products have had a variety of looks over the years, but the name has not changed in more than a century.

Below: Valvoline deliveries were sometimes slow in the early days, but they were always regular.

"A party was in our office a few minutes ago saying that he had used only two gallons of Valvoline per month when he had been using five gallons of someone else's oil."[2]

The elder Ellis was adamant about uniform quality in the products the company sold, and records show him taking his refinery personnel to task for slight deviation from his rigid and exacting standards. The company creed, intact today, was developed in 1868. It says, in part, "Quality is never an accident. It is always the result of high intention, sincere effort, intelligent direction and skillful execution."

Competition became fierce and unscrupulous. And since Valvoline was, in the minds of many — including some of its competitors — the premiere product, Valvoline found it necessary on more than one occasion to take legal steps against companies that were untruthfully attaching the Valvoline name to their own products. Moreover, Valvoline frequently felt compelled to post letters denying the periodically planted rumors that the company had

been taken over by Standard Oil. In one such letter of denial, Valvoline called such statements "slander" and asserted:

"We are today, as we have been for 30 years, absolutely independent, controlled by no trust or company, English or American. We find that the statement mentioned is generally made by some company closely connected with the Standard Oil Company."[3]

The company was exceedingly proud of its quality and archived hundreds of letters sent by pleased customers. In 1909, an official from the Bath Iron Works, renowned shipbuilders in Maine, felt the need to express his enthusiasm for Valvoline, writing: "Your oil gave every satisfaction on the destroyer *Flusser.*"[4]

Testimonials arriving at Valvoline headquarters were tucked away for posterity. In 1946, a letter arrived from the J. Unertl Optical company in Pittsburgh: "Confronted with the ever existing problem of corrosion and rust on steel instrument parts and gauges, we gave your Tectyl #511 an extensive trial," said the letter. "We want to report that Tectyl has really solved our rust problems in every detail and wish to congratulate Freedom-Valvoline Oil Company and its chemists for developing and producing this outstanding product."[5]

20th Century Progression

Although the Valvoline company remained constant for many decades, a significant portion of it

Above: Valvoline products quickly made their way across the seas — to Europe, Asia and points in between. Harry Burk was a distributor in the Hawaiian Islands for many years.

Below: During the war years, Valvoline encouraged careful use of its products.

changed just before the turn of the century. In 1896, the elder Ellis died. His son formed a partnership with T.M. Leonard to expand the company, building a new refinery in Warren, Pennsylvania, and another later in East Butler, Pennsylvania. The company, which had previously made its reputation by serving the railroads, began in the early 1900s to look toward emerging markets of some promise: the automobile and the airplane. Soon after the new century dawned, Valvoline was developing products that would propel it through the 20th century.

The company also made another important strategic move. To ensure its continued independence during an era when Standard Oil seemed intent on encroaching everywhere, Valvoline constructed a pipeline that eventually grew to be 1,200 miles long, the biggest independent refiner pipeline system in the Pennsylvania field.

In 1930, 64 years after the company was founded and 62 years after he started to sell oil for his father, W. Dixon Ellis decided to retire and sold the company to E.W. Edwards, an unusually successful Cincinnati capitalist. Under the new owner-

ship, in 1931, Valvoline purchased the 62-year-old Galena Oil company of Franklin, Pennsylvania. Galena was founded by General Charles Miller to manufacture leaded mineral lubricating oils used by the railroads.

Over the next few years, Valvoline introduced the first-ever all-season, all-purpose gear lubricant; the first lubricating oil for diesel and peak loads in gasoline engines; and its patented Tectyl, a rust-preventive coating developed for the U.S. Army. In 1940, Valvoline became the first company to offer an unconditional money-back guarantee on its motor oil.

Gaining Freedom

In 1944, Valvoline merged with Freedom Oil of Freedom, Pennsylvania, another pioneer in the refining of lubricants.

Founded by Dr. Stephen Craig in 1879, Freedom plied the upper Ohio Valley with distinctive horse-drawn tank wagons that appeared as regularly as the milkman. Housewives would rush from their homes and line up at the spigot on the back of the tank. "I filled the dishpans, buckets and lard cans brought out to the curb by residenters [sic] wishing to replenish their coal oil supplies," Sam Salyers, one of the drivers, recalled decades later.[6]

A Freedom Oil delivery team poses before their vehicle in 1929.

Above: Earle Craig, pictured here with his mother in 1947, was one of two owners of Freedom-Valvoline when it was acquired by Ashland.

Right: Valvoline's packaging sported a new look after Ashland acquired the company.

Freedom covered a radius of more than 150 miles from the refinery in Freedom, Pennsylvania, operating from a series of stations where the oils, greases and other lubricating products were stored for distribution by wagon. Once the automobile became part of American life, the storage stations became service stations, where vehicles could be taken for oil and grease jobs.

The Ashland Campaign

By 1950, William Bechman, one of Freedom-Valvoline's two owners, was aging and worried about inheritance taxes. He saw the merger as a way to alleviate his concerns. Consequently, the company — which employed about 200 people and operated a 1,000-barrel-a-day refinery — became a subsidiary of Ashland Oil & Refining in 1950. The move offered nothing but benefits for the future. In fact, three decades after its affiliation with Ashland, Valvoline would boast a sales increase of more than 900 percent.

The company was slow to start that ascent, however. Until 1959, the Valvoline operation, under former Freedom co-owner Earle Craig, a Yale graduate who had been with Freedom since 1914, maintained its core of loyal customers, but accomplished little in the way of growth. Ashland grew impatient with its great underachiever and in 1959 devised a plan to jumpstart Valvoline. The plan, in essence, required Ashland to recruit a young staff, buy national advertising and make the company grow.

The company built new warehouses and new packaging complexes, adding hundreds of employees. It also spent millions of dollars on national advertising. This advertising push was a foray into new territory for the Ashland board of directors, which until then had never had a product that required more than minimal promotional expenditures.

By 1964, Rex Blazer thought it prudent to justify the expense of a national advertising campaign in writing. In a letter sent to board members that summer, Blazer enclosed a copy of the advertisement that had appeared in the July 10 issue of *Time* magazine and declared, "It is my opinion that extensive national advertising of Valvoline is justified when supported by adequate sales effort."[7]

Racing Toward Success

This image retooling was a calculated part of Valvoline's strategy. To offset its old-line image, Valvoline embarked on a youth-oriented auto racing sponsorship program. The millions of people who watched the Indianapolis 500 or Daytona 500 races from the stands or on television began to see the

Valvoline name everywhere. "We have used racing to prove Valvoline is a quality product," said Marty Kish, vice president of Communications for Valvoline. "The racing platform has given us a unique ability to position the brand."[8]

Of course, the sponsorship between racing and Valvoline has long been a two-way street; Valvoline has come a long way in helping to shape the racing industry, just as racing has helped Valvoline with name recognition. "They've been a world-class sponsor that's been involved with the growth and proliferation of motor sports in many different venues," said Jack Roush, a Valvoline-sponsored NASCAR owner, in a 1997 interview.[9] His driver, Mark Martin, winner of 22 Winston Cup races, described his sponsorship with Valvoline as "symbiotic" in a 1998 interview. "It's a great tie," he said. "Valvoline's been a tremendous supporter when things were good, and they've been

Above: Just another day at the office for Mark Martin, winner of 22 Winston Cup races.

Left: NASCAR owner Jack Roush. *(Photo courtesy of Steven Rose Photography.)*

Inset: Valvoline High Performance Racing Oil was introduced at the 11th annual National Championship Drag Races in Indianapolis.

the first to pat me on the back to say things will get better when they're bad."[10]

Derrick Walker, team owner and president of Walker Racing, who also has had a long-time sponsorship arrangement with Valvoline, agrees. "They're one of the long-lasting sponsors in the history of racing," he said. "They understand the market very well. They're not asleep at the wheel."[11] Racer Gil DeFerran, who drove Walker's Valvoline-sponsored, Indy-style car in the FedEx

Championship series for 1997–98, had nothing but praise for his sponsor. "We want to bring Valvoline yet another success on the track," DeFerran said. "They're very committed to our race program, very responsive. They have obviously contributed to the rise of motor racing as an activity and as a sport."[12]

Valvoline's first venture into motorsports was in 1959, when the company sponsored the National Hot Rod Association's U.S. National Drag Races. Within four years, Valvoline became involved in the Indianapolis 500. Two cars fielded by Andy Granatelli in the 1963 race displayed the Valvoline logo. Although neither car won, they launched the company on a path that would soon make the Valvoline name synonymous with all types of auto racing. By 1969, Valvoline Racing Motor Oil was lubricating most of the starting field at the Indy 500. Valvoline also assumed responsibility for operating the largest service garage at Indy's famed "Gasoline Alley."

Al Unser Sr. gave the company its first Indy 500 win in 1970, setting the pace for the rest of the decade. In 1973, Gordon Johncock won the Indy under the Valvoline banner. In 1974 and 1976 Johnny Rutherford gave Valvoline more Indy wins, and in 1977, A.J. Foyt took Indy for Valvoline. Al

Driver Gil DeFerran and Valvoline create a formidable force on the track.

Unser Sr., had a second Indy win in 1978. Cale Yarborough won three consecutive NASCAR championships with Valvoline in his car's crankcase. In 1978, Valvoline-sponsored Mario Andretti captured the Formula One World Championship.

There were other victories on the racing circuit throughout the 1980s. Gordon Johncock took the Indy again in 1982, and Bobby Rahal in 1986. Shirley Muldowney, using Valvoline, claimed the National Hot Rod Association's top fuel drag racing title in 1980, and Darrell Waltrip claimed a NASCAR crown in 1982.

Roads Less Traveled

For all its nationally televised image-building, Valvoline tried to keep sight of the fact that it should not focus exclusively on its racing activities. Its unofficial motto was "Race on Sunday, sell on Monday." The motorsports activities were intended not to supplant business goals but to enhance them, providing an arena in which to support business relationships, test new products and capture a greater audience.

In 1973, Valvoline bolstered its product line with the purchase of Mac's Super Gloss Inc., a

Above: In his 36-year career, Mario Andretti has won four Indy Car championships and has 52 Indy Car victories.

Left: Jack Boehm , who became Valvoline's president in 1974, was a leader in Valvoline's drive for innovation.

manufacturer of automotive chemicals and appearance products. "We've always been very innovative," said Valvoline's Senior Vice President for North American Products Larry Detjen in 1998.[13] In 1978, for example, Valvoline became the first company to put oil-change instructions on the back of its one-quart cans; and in 1980 it introduced the 12-quart case for do-it-yourselfers. "We had a clear lead on our competitors for at least six months, if not a year," Detjen said.[14] These product breakthroughs transpired under the leadership of Jack Boehm, who was transferred from R.J. Brown to head up Valvoline in 1974. He was assigned to Valvoline jobs in Cincinnati and Ashland before becoming Valvoline president and remained at the helm for nearly two decades.

Late in the 1980s, the company shifted the presentation of its racing image. In 1987,

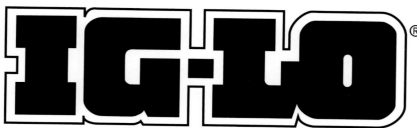

Valvoline brought all its sponsored race car drivers under one umbrella called Team Valvoline and also aligned with the National Federation of Parents for Drug-Free Youth.

Product innovations and additions continued throughout the 1980s. In 1984, Valvoline developed Turbo V motor oil for turbocharged cars; in 1985 it acquired Ig-Lo, the nation's top marketer of automotive refrigerants; in 1986 the company switched from fiber cans to plastic bottles and that same year entered the growing quick-lube business by acquiring the Minneapolis-based Rapid Oil Change chain, renaming the 30 outlets Valvoline Instant Oil Change. "Back in the early 1980s, we started seeing a shift from the do-it-yourselfers, the DIY segment, to the DIFMs, or do-it-for-me segment," said Gerald Wipf, president of Valvoline Instant Oil Change, in a 1998 interview.[15] Valvoline Instant Oil Change became one of America's largest, fastest-growing quick lube chains.

By the end of the 1980s Valvoline had purchased the Pyroil line of automotive chemicals and additives. It also added wholly owned affiliates in Denmark and Sweden to its international distribution network, which included Australia, Canada, the Netherlands and the United Kingdom.

Reaping Rewards

The rejuvenated-image strategy was having success. By the mid-1980s, Valvoline had 950 employees and could claim about 12 percent of the

Above: Valvoline Instant Oil Change is among the leading quick lube chains in the country.

Top and bottom left: Ig-Lo and Pyroil were both acquired by Valvoline in the 1980s.

U.S. market, though it still ranked third, behind Pennzoil and Quaker State. Revenues had skyrocketed to $610 million by 1987, an enormous leap from the $350 million in revenues it reported at the beginning of the 1980s. In fact, the Ashland subsidiary had grown so well and so rapidly that, in the early 1980s, it was moved from corporate headquarters in Ashland into gleaming new division headquarters in Lexington, Kentucky.

In addition, Valvoline was designated a separate profit center in 1986. The profit-center designation was primarily a bookkeeping matter, requiring Valvoline to report expenses and profits on its own, rather than as part of the Ashland Petroleum Division. But the psychological impact was enormous. This was evidence that Ashland felt Valvoline had come far and that the company expected it would go even further.

The Ongoing Glide

The 1990s brought additional growth. The company formed First Recovery in 1990, which

was responsible for the collection and recycling of used motor oil. "We're no longer just an oil company," said Cleve Huston, president of the First Recovery Division for Valvoline, in 1998. "We're focused on our customers' needs. We're providing additional services like used oil collection, and we've been able to figure out ways to recycle products that were historically hazardous."[16]

In 1991 Valvoline introduced synthetic motor oils and greases, and in 1994, the company acquired Zerex, the second most popular brand of antifreeze in the United States. Also in 1994, Valvoline acquired affiliates in Austria, Belgium, France, Germany, Italy and Switzerland and signed joint ventures to build a plant and distribute products in India.

More international progress occurred in 1995: Valvoline signed a joint venture agreement to market, sell and distribute a full line of products in Ecuador and Colombia and also signed an agreement with Cummins Engine Company to promote and market a joint line of heavy-duty lubricants and related products and services.

Valvoline experienced further successes in its racing sponsorships when Al Unser Jr. tallied a victory in 1992. Joe Amato was also a Valvoline-sponsored five-time national champion in the NHRA.

In the early 1980s, Valvoline moved into its own corporate headquarters in Lexington, Kentucky.

Developing a Leader

In 1994 Valvoline had its first billion-dollar year but finished fiscal 1995 with a loss for the first time in its modern history. Escalating raw material and packaging costs were part of the problem. John Barr resigned from the Valvoline presidency in 1995 to take a similar position with Quaker State, and then group operating officer Fred Brothers stepped in to put Valvoline back on track.

Several months later, James O'Brien, a 20-year veteran of Ashland, was named vice president of Ashland and president of The Valvoline company. O'Brien, who was 41 when he took the Valvoline top spot, was recruited from Ohio State during his junior year to be an intern in Ashland Chemical's Accounting Department. The internship was successful, and at the end of his senior year, Ashland offered him a full-time job. As O'Brien tells it, "I graduated from college on Friday, got married on Saturday and started to work full-time a week later in Ashland Chemical."[17]

That was in June 1976, and after a summer of adjusting to full-time employment, he began graduate school funded by Ashland, working at Ashland Chemical's headquarters while attending MBA classes at Ohio State University in Columbus. After receiving his degree, O'Brien held a series of administrative jobs, then was placed in Chemical Sales and Marketing, dealing with specialty chemicals, commodity chemicals and plastics. In 1992, John Hall, then president of Ashland, invited O'Brien to serve as his executive assistant.

It was an invaluable experience, offering quick exposure to the seasoning required to be successful in senior management. It was the kind of position, O'Brien later recalled, that "gets you exposed on how to run a board, what it means to be on a board, how to be an executive versus a manager, how to make decisions, the type of information you need for decisions, for bigger decisions, the timing of decision-making — all those types of things that, unless you can observe it, you learn the hard way."[18]

In 1994, O'Brien was named vice president and general manager of Ashland Petroleum's Branded Marketing Department. He was charged with launching the group's efforts to develop a new jobber/distribution network centered on revitalizing and expanding the company's Ashland-brand gaso-

Valvoline President James O'Brien feels the Valvoline brand has been, and will continue to be, an innovator.

line outlets. Name identification had diminished almost to the point of nonexistence through the 1970s, the result of Ashland having converted all the better Ashland-brand locations to SuperAmerica stores after acquiring the Minnesota-based company.

O'Brien polished up the Ashland-brand image, worked to convince jobbers of the importance of identifying with Ashland and began conversions at dozens of stations. By the end of 18 months, he had opened 110 glittering locations in the Ohio Valley, festooned with the Ashland logo. In the next two years, nearly 400 more locations would become Ashland stations and Ashland image-builders.

A Brand-New Strategy

Pulled out of the gasoline station effort in midstream and named president of Valvoline in

October 1995, O'Brien immediately set about changing the company culture. The organization, while profitable most years, was not sufficiently profitable, he thought, and the Marketing Department was enmeshed in a hodgepodge of various projects that seemed to have no common foundation

or companywide mission. "Valvoline is a branded company," O'Brien said later. "The Valvoline brand is the most valuable asset that we have, and it was always looked at that way but never truly managed that way."[19]

In early 1996, O'Brien launched six cross-functional teams to develop a new vision for Valvoline, establish clear goals and come up with cost-control strategies. "Our planning for Valvoline has become an aspirations-based planning process," said Jim Burkhardt, director of Planning and Analysis, in a 1998 interview. "We'll be more involved in competitive intelligence."[20] In addition, the European structure was reorganized almost immediately to reduce costs and increase effectiveness and efficiency.

The team concept was pressed into the very fabric of the culture, training efforts were acceler-

Eagle One proudly sponsored NASCAR owner Jack Roush and racer Mark Martin (below) at The 1998 Winston Cup. *(Photo courtesy of Steven Rose Photography.)*

ated and "worldwide profitable growth" became the company mantra. The leaders of Ashland, from their headquarters 120 miles away, watched with great interest, but stayed out of the way, no doubt comforted by the positive impact on the bottom line. By the end of fiscal 1996, O'Brien's first year at the helm, Valvoline could claim all-time record profits of more than $82 million.

In 1996, the company signed a five-year contract with ABC-TV to sponsor its halftime scoreboard show, presenting Valvoline in a whole new light to consumers. Valvoline actively positioned itself as a premium brand, while offering new products, like glosses, waxes and wheel cleaners, through the acquisition of Eagle One. This purchase positioned premium Valvoline products both above and below the hood.

Think Globally, Act Locally

By the end of 1997, Valvoline was well-positioned in the world market, but the company's executives wanted the branded motor oil to have even more international reach.

This goal is particularly important, according to Bill Dempsey, vice president and managing director of Valvoline International, in 1998:

"Only 9 percent of the world's population lives in the United States, and only 32 percent of the world's current lubricant demand is in the United States. If you take into consideration that the rest of the world, at some point in time, will have the same standard of living as the United States, 91 percent of the lubricant volume will be outside the States, not within it."[21]

Even as far back as the 1870s, Valvoline had been an international product, but global marketing strategies have come a long way since then. By the end of 1997, Valvoline exported products out of U.S., Canadian, and Australian manufacturing facilities and maintained European packaging facilities in the Netherlands — in addition to overseeing products produced or marketed in foreign countries by licensees and distributors. In 1998, Valvoline also had 13 wholly owned affiliates throughout Europe, Canada, Australia and South Africa.

"The Eagle One acquisition was particularly significant, because it gave us a position in Europe — a position we needed if we were going to be successful internationally," said Valvoline Vice President of Technology Services Fran Lockwood in 1998.[22] That acquisition was just one part of what Dempsey called "acting locally," that is, "employing local managers who understand their countries and markets, and depending on local distributors and licensees who can give us access to emerging markets."[23] Other components of Dempsey's vision for international growth included understanding different cultures and preferences for products and establishing international joint ventures to achieve a more intimate understanding of local marketing practices.

Thinking locally is particularly important because of the differences in how motorists view their car care. For example, "The United States has a more open mind about motor oils," said Jack Gordon, a retiree of Valvoline's International Division. "Americans change the oil themselves or take it to an instant oil change. In Europe, however, people take their cars back to their dealers or to an official garage."[24]

A Bright Future

Throughout its history, Valvoline has succeeded in being at the forefront of new developments, and that spirit of innovation extends into the modern day. "We want to take risks," said Kish in 1998. "Now we're looking for the next big idea, the big new product we're going to introduce."[25]

In February 1998, the company announced plans to build a $4.5 million product-development laboratory in Lexington, to be finished later that year. This research laboratory was just one strategy Valvoline was implementing to stay competitive in the motor-oil industry.[26]

By mid-1998, Valvoline was confident about its future, boasting 500 Valvoline Instant Oil Change outlets and an alliance with Sears Automotive Centers, which will give Valvoline an excellent opportunity for penetrating new markets. "We feel we're well-positioned to meet the needs of the consumer in the automotive market well into the future," Detjen concluded in his 1998 interview. "We have a good strategy with our master branding, and we have the right brands and the right services for our company."[27]

unit in Columbus, Ohio — a conglomeration of 63 manufacturing, research, service and distribution facilities in 22 states and 14 foreign countries. By the time the company began operating in 1967, Ashland Chemical was already a viable contender in the industry. According to an investor publication, "Ten years of growth have placed Ashland in the top six in chemical sales among oil companies."[5]

Despite criticism that the acquisitions seemed random, Yancey defended the growth, saying some of the acquisitions provided opportunities for upgrading other holdings, and others produced materials needed by Ashland divisions.[6]

Right: Bronoco Solvents and Chemicals of St. Louis was one of Ashland's first chemical acquisitions, purchased in 1956.

Below: Robert Yancey Sr. was named the first president of Ashland Chemical when it became a separate operation in 1967.

"One of our strategies was to acquire all these distribution facilities and then produce hydrocarbon solvents and sell them through those distribution facilities," said Patrick. "The other strategy was to see if we could find some downstream chemical or resin plants that we could then upgrade into petrochemicals, which could be used in these downstream manufacturing facilities we'd acquired."[7]

When the chemical company was formed, Yancey told *Chemical Week* that his guiding principals would be two that had worked well for the parent company: "One is no organizational flowchart. The other, 'First, round up the customers.'"[8] It was Yancey, along with Rexford Blazer, Everett Wells and Orin Atkins, who put together a blueprint for the company in 1967 that would divide it into seven operating divisions with a potential of

$300 million in annual sales and a research team of more than 350.[9]

Finding a Niche

Although Yancey was a major player in growing Ashland Chemical, his true love, according to Patrick, was the petroleum company.[10] Yancey remained president of Ashland Chemical until 1970, when Bill Ferguson took over. Ferguson's reign was short-lived. His aggressive management style and forceful pursuit of acquisitions did not blend well with the company culture at that time. He was replaced by John Hall in 1971.

Hall's strategy for Ashland Chemical during his three years at the helm was to fine-tune the company's operations. "During Ferguson's tenure, the bottom fell out of the profits of Ashland Chemical, and we were operating at essentially break-even when I took over," said Hall. "My focus was on returning the company to profitability by cutting costs and focusing the management's efforts on profits from the businesses we had."[11]

As the chemical company grew, it entered new markets for high-performance specialty resins and adhesives such as those used in the manufacture of personal water craft and other pleasure boats.

Above: In 1966, Ashland purchased the Newark, New Jersey, resins plant of Archer-Daniels-Midland.

Left: Edward A. Von Doersten was associated with the chemical industry throughout his career. Named a vice president of Ashland Chemical upon its formation in 1967, he became president in 1974 and presided over much of its early growth.

In 1974, Hall was appointed executive vice president of Ashland Oil, Inc. "I think John was brought back for his refining and crude oil expertise during the OPEC oil crisis of 1973–74," said Fred Brothers, executive vice president of Ashland Inc.[12] Hall was replaced by Edward Von Doersten.

It was during the mid-1970s recession that the specialty chemical business began to really grow while the petrochemical side grew smaller. The advent of the radial tire, with its longer life, precipitated a steep decline in the demand for carbon black, the main component in tires. This forced Ashland Chemical to find new product niches, pushing the company toward the development of specialty chemicals. When Von Doersten became Ashland Chemical's president, the company was producing and distributing hundreds of products, ranging from industrial chemicals and solvents to liquid fertilizers and melamine for the popular dinnerware of the era.

Von Doersten was universally credited with molding a mentoring culture in which professional growth and advancement were paramount. "Ed was absolutely a cheerleader," said Marvin Quin, Ashland's chief financial officer, in 1998. Quin spent most of the 1970s at Ashland Chemical.[13]

"There was a total absence of politics. He created a culture of support for each other, ... and if you ever tried to do something to make a fellow employee look poor, I mean, he would absolutely explode. ... He just created a very positive environment that was a fun place to work, and there was a tremendous amount of growth."[14]

By 1979, chemical company sales exceeded $1 billion, following dozens of acquisitions, a reorganization during Atkins' administration, and somewhat more organizational structure over the years. By 1980, Ashland Chemical had extended its facilities into 28 states and 15 foreign countries. The company was divided into six divisions: carbon black, foundry products, industrial chemicals and solvents, petrochemicals, polyester and chemical systems.

Acquisition Flurry

In 1981, J. A. "Fred" Brothers was appointed chief operating officer of Ashland Chemical, becoming president in 1983. At AOI, meanwhile, Hall designated the chemical business a major driver of Ashland's growth plans. "In the early '80s, there were a few areas of Ashland Oil that were designated as growth companies," recalled Brothers in a 1998 interview. "Chemicals was one, and so when John became chairman and CEO, we were encouraged to grow even faster."[15] Until the end of the decade, in fact, the chemical operation had its most active buying period, acquiring dozens of companies that helped form the nucleus for Ashland Chemical's strong economic engines of the 1990s.

General Polymers, a distributor and compounder of thermoplastic moldings and extrusion materials in Warren, Michigan, was acquired in 1983 and would go on to become one of the fastest

growing segments of Ashland Chemical's thermoplastics distribution business.[16] Other acquisitions that added to the company's thermoplastics distribution included AVI of Deland, Florida; Consource of Spartanburg, South Carolina; and Lambda Plastics of Southern California.[17] "There wasn't much plastics distribution going on in those days," said Brothers. "Our dream was to make Ashland Chemical a national distributor of plastics. And these acquisitions formed the basis for our national thermoplastics distribution business that still goes by the name of General Polymers. ... We became the first national distributor of plastics in North America."[18]

In 1985, the company acquired Lehigh Valley Chemical of Easton, Pennsylvania. "That acquisition laid the foundation for our premier position as the preferred global supplier of electronic chemicals for the micro-electronics industry," said Brothers.[19]

In 1987, the division also took on Berton Plastics, a Teterboro, New Jersey-based distributor of products for fiber-reinforced products;

Fred Brothers helped fine-tune Ashland Chemical by expanding the company's holdings and divesting it of unprofitable businesses.

Above: The company's chemical plant in Neal, West Virginia.

Left: A behind-the-scenes look at Ashland Chemical's electronic chemicals laboratory at Easton, Pennsylvania, reveals a nearly contaminant-free environment where Ashland tests ultra-high-purity chemicals used to make electronic chips and wafers.

and Riberglass, a Dallas-based distributor of resins and other products. Berton and Riberglass would form the basis for the fiber-reinforced plastics (FRP) distribution business, which began in 1988.[20]

Other significant acquisitions during Brothers' tenure included the chemical distribution business of Commonwealth Chemical Company, based near Boston, Massachusetts; Loomis Chemical Company, a distributor of industrial chemicals based in Portland, Oregon; and J.T. Baker Chemical, a worldwide producer of high-purity chemical products based in Phillipsburg, New Jersey.

Ashland Chemical's strategy for growth wasn't just in acquisitions, however. The company also improved its portfolio by divesting itself of unprofitable businesses. "We had to fix what we had," said Brothers. "In the late '70s and early '80s, the economy was not particularly kind to Ashland Chemical."[21] Significant divestitures before Brothers' tenure included the alkyd resins business acquired earlier from Archer-Daniels-Midland, the Chemical Products Division and the carbon black business. The company sold its foreign carbon black business in 1985 and its domestic carbon black business in early 1989.

Hodgepodge Success

In 1988, David D'Antoni, a native of Huntington, West Virginia, and a graduate of Virginia Polytechnic Institute as well as Harvard Business School's Advanced Management Program, became president of Ashland Chemical. First recruited by Brothers, D'Antoni joined Ashland Chemical in 1973 as a project development manager. "David was a student of mine," recalled Brothers. "I was in graduate school working on my doctorate degree in chemical engineering at VPI. ... David was very quick. He had the mind of a chemical engineer but the personality of a salesperson. ... He's a delightful person, not at all like us plodding, introverted engineers."[22] D'Antoni became vice president and general manager of the Polyester Division in 1980 and group vice president in 1982 before becoming president of Ashland Chemical.

The company's flurry of acquisitions did not slow during D'Antoni's reign. As Hall pointed out to shareholders in 1992, between 1988 and 1992, AOI invested more than $400 million in Ashland Chemical for nearly two dozen acquisitions and several plant upgrades.

So diverse were Ashland Chemical's holdings that some in the industry were amazed the company was so successful, according to a 1991 issue of *Chemical Week*: "The company knows manufacturing and knows how to turn a dollar," noted Charles

Schaller, president of consultants for The Southport Group. "It plays in a lot of lucrative markets."[23]

From 1990 to 1995, Ashland Chemical acquired 24 more companies. And in 1996, D'Antoni could make the claim that his division, then 6,000 employees strong, had been the largest contributor of profits to the corporation for four successive years. Ashland Chemical had actually posted record sales every year since 1989, despite some difficult recessionary years during which virtually all sectors experienced depressed performance.

But Ashland Chemical was more than just profitable. It was also voted the top-performing chemical supplier by chemical buyers in April 1996, beating out both Exxon and Eastman Chemical. According to *Purchasing* magazine:

> *"Ashland won or tied more individual performance categories — eight of 14 total — than any other supplier, including all five performance categories under quality and delivery. A very impressive showing, to say the least."*[24]

In 1998, David D'Antoni, president of Ashland Chemical, had ambitious plans to fulfill corporate desires to grow Ashland Chemical.

A Product of Ambition

By 1997, Ashland Chemical had, *Chemical Week* declared, "completed its metamorphosis from a refinery-driven producer and distributor of commodity petrochemicals to a producer and distributor of diverse specialty chemicals."[25]

Ashland Chemical had 48 manufacturing facilities in 11 states and 15 foreign countries and could lay claim to being the leading distributor of industrial chemicals, fiber-reinforced plastic materials and thermoplastics in North America. The Drew Marine Division, a worthy leftover from the infamous U.S. Filter acquisition of Atkins' days, had become the world's largest supplier of shipboard chemical products and services. Furthermore, the Foundry Products Division had become the world's leading manufacturer of foundry chemicals. Ashland Chemical had also succeeded in the international market, serving Asia, Australia, Latin America and New Zealand, with Ashland International President John Van Meter "always looking for more acquisitions for the company."[26] In addition, the company had formed a Fine Ingredients Division and acquired Weinstein Nutritional Products, which markets the rapidly growing nutraceutical products.

Also in 1997, the Petrochemicals Division added an energy services business unit to assist industrial and commercial businesses in the management of their total energy requirements. The company's Petrochemical Division was divided, with Marathon Ashland Petroleum taking over the marketing of cumene, propylene, sulfur, aromatic and aliphatic solvents, leaving Ashland Chemical to focus primarily on the production and marketing of methanol and maleic anhydride.[27]

"We've gone from being a chemical distributor in the Midwest to the largest chemical distributor in North America to a major thermoplastics distributor in North America to a major fiber-reinforced-plastics producer in North America and a major thermoplastics distributor in Europe," D'Antoni told *Chemical Week* late in 1997. "The

RESPONSIBLE CARE CODE IMPLEMENTATION

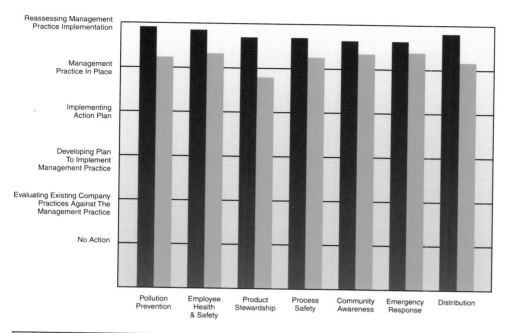

Reassessing Management Practice Implementation

Management Practice In Place

Implementing Action Plan

Developing Plan To Implement Management Practice

Evaluating Existing Company Practices Against The Management Practice

No Action

Pollution Prevention | Employee Health & Safety | Product Stewardship | Process Safety | Community Awareness | Emergency Response | Distribution

Ashland Chemical | Chemical Manufacturers Association

As illustrated in this graph, Ashland Chemical has fully implemented the management systems and programs necessary to achieve Practice in Place (full implementation) for all of the Responsible Care Codes of Management Practice. Ashland Chemical is an industry leader in implementing the Responsible Care initiative. Responsible Care is a registered trademark of the CMA.

list will continue. Our objective is to build leading positions in key markets. We don't want to be all things to all people, just No. 1 or No. 2 to a select group of people."[28]

To bolster that goal, in 1998, Ashland Chemical announced plans to open a $40 million electronic chemicals plant in Pueblo, Colorado, while continuing to make acquisitions and open distribution centers across the globe. The new plant will blend and distribute chemicals for the semiconductor industry. The company's Columbus, Ohio, technical center was also undergoing a $22 million expansion to further research and commercial development.[29]

A Bright Future

By mid-1998, Ashland Chemical was a bright star in the world of chemicals. Not only was the company the leading North American distributor of chemicals and plastics, but its specialty chemicals group was more profitable than it had ever been. It was the No. 1 supplier of foundry chemicals for the metal castings industry and the world's largest supplier of marine chemicals.[30] The company was also showing a deep commitment to Product Stewardship — the safe use and handling of chemicals and plastics — and the Chemical Manufacturers Association's Responsible Care® initiative, which serves to minimize waste and cut emissions. By 1998, Ashland Chemical's pollution-prevention program had reduced toxic chemical emissions by 73 percent since 1987.[31]

When asked what he wanted to see in the future of Ashland Chemical, D'Antoni's answer was threefold: to continue profitability by expanding in current business markets, to expand those markets both product-wise and geographically and to add additional lines of business.[32] "We have the infrastructure and the resources in hand," D'Antoni told *Chemical Week*, "so we're trying to get more new customers for our existing products and more new products for our existing customers."[33]

SuperAmerica stores in the early 1970s began converting to the convenience theme, offering a variety of health and beauty items, quick foods and small appliances.

CHAPTER THIRTEEN

SuperAmerica

"Americans put more value on time and convenience than ever before, and it's our business to provide fuels, rapid services and convenience items at value prices."

— Riad Yammine, executive vice president, Strategic Planning for MAP[1]

WHEN ASHLAND ACQUIRED Northwestern Refining Company in 1970, it got much more than a refinery. The company also acquired a chain of successful gasoline stations with a history of inventive marketing. Northwestern consisted of a refinery founded in 1930 in the Twin Cities of Minneapolis-St. Paul, but it wasn't until 1965 that it began marketing under its own brand name — SuperAmerica. This combination car wash/service station multiplied to 190 stations by the early 1970s, extending from Montana through the Dakotas, Iowa, Minnesota, Wisconsin, Illinois and Ohio, with the bulk of the outlets in Minnesota and Wisconsin.

Something Extra

One distinguishing characteristic of Super-America in the early years was its unusual concept of offering a limited number of relatively high-ticket items, such as clocks, radios and lawnmowers, to its gasoline customers through gift stamps given with every gas purchase. The opportunity to get something for free enticed many customers into brand loyalty. As the number of stations grew, so too did the assortment of items offered, and SuperAmerica came to realize customers were perfectly willing to consider non-automotive items when they filled up at their local gas station. Eventually, the store added merchandise that did not require stamps, and the insides of SuperAmerica stations became floor-to-ceiling assemblages of discount-priced merchandise ranging from soaps and bicycles to garden tools, small appliances and toys.

"We were these small stores selling things you see in Wal-Mart today, and it was obviously very labor-intensive and very hard to control," recalled Bob Hardman, regional vice president of North Central operations, who joined SuperAmerica in 1966. "You can imagine selling bicycles and lawnmowers from small-type convenience stores. We were actually selling radios, televisions, humidifiers. In those days, you didn't have Target or Wal-Mart, but still, that was a hard program to pull off."[2]

Despite this difficulty, SuperAmerica continued to add to its offerings. By the end of the 1960s, a few convenience foods — primarily snack items like boxed cookies, potato chips and peanuts — were added to the mix.

The SuperAmerica logo has long been a symbol of quality and convenience.

A New Convenience

When Ashland Oil, Inc. purchased the Northwestern Refining Company in 1970, it got a little more than it had bargained for. It also got the company's marketing in the form of the SuperAmerica chain. Charles Luellen, who later became chief operating officer of the corporation, was handed the responsibility to either sell it or else improve it. "It was daunting," said Luellen in a 1998 interview. "We had never seen anything like it before, and indeed, there hadn't been anything like it before."[3]

After Luellen persuaded senior managers in Ashland that the chain could be improved, Richard Jensen, who had joined Northwestern Refining in 1965 as a marketing manager and who would later become president of SuperAmerica, led the move to reposition SuperAmerica in the market. As more customers stopped to shop, the tiny stores became cramped, the inventories spotty and the checkout areas congested. SuperAmerica began to offer larger stores with greater emphasis on food, including frozen and refrigerated items, while still stocking its traditional fare of automotive products and accessories, along with such top-selling seasonal products as lawn and garden supplies.

Converting to a convenience store approach was considered a revolutionary move at that time. Hardman had a vivid recollection of the 1971 discussion that propelled the company in that direction. At the end of a regional meeting in Wisconsin Dells, a half-dozen company officials decided the time was ripe to get out of the appliance and sporting goods business and focus on consumer daily necessities. "We were all very excited about getting into a product line that we felt people used every day," Hardman said.

"In our market at that time, I don't recall anyone being in that business. I'm sure there could have been convenience stores in the country that

Left: Charles Luellen is often credited with being the "champion" of SuperAmerica.

Below: The first SuperAmerica store, located in St. Paul, Minnesota, was a combination gasoline station and car wash.

maybe had a gas pump out in front. But this was the first that I know of — a major gasoline retailer with a big gasoline presentation going to a large-scale convenience store."[4]

Save Mart, Ashland's Southern version of SuperAmerica, was eventually converted to the SuperAmerica name.

Conversions

At that meeting in the Dells, company officials decided that the first conversions would take place in a few stores in Milwaukee and one in Beloit, Wisconsin. By 1972, with the conversions well under way, SuperAmerica was operating 109 stores, and the company seemed destined for prosperity. Then in 1973 the oil embargo hit, gasoline prices soared, and consumers did whatever they could to cut gasoline consumption.

It was a crippling time for gas retailers, yet SuperAmerica had an advantage. "What gas stations did was sell their allocation and then close down," said Hardman. "We hooded our pumps when the gas ran out and kept the stores open. That, I think, is what really jump-started the concept of the convenience store and gasoline station going together. It was kind of a wake-up call for everybody."[5]

Competition in the Ranks

Witnessing the success of SuperAmerica's combination gasoline and convenience stores, AOI began converting many of its branded stores in Ohio, Kentucky, West Virginia, Pennsylvania, Michigan and Indiana into Save More or Save Mart gasoline and convenience stores in the mid-1970s. The first one, a Save More, whose name was soon changed to Save Mart, was in Huntington, West Virginia. It was, said Charlie Covey, SuperAmerica vice president in 1998, who had joined Ashland in 1969, "the very first merchandising store in the Southern region that had gasoline, groceries and convenience-store items."[6]

As leading-edge as they may have seemed at the time, Save Mores and Save Marts weren't convenience stores in the 1990s sense, said Phil Collins, director of Design and Construction in 1998, who joined Ashland in 1960. "We were taking the sales rooms in some of the old gasoline stations and selling milk and bread and things like that. It expanded over time until we were remodeling the buildings, making them full-sized stores."[7]

The concept of gasoline/convenience stores was similar in both SuperAmerica and Save Mart, so it seemed wise to rename the Ashland branded stations SuperAmerica, rather than introducing a new name to the public and creating competition in areas where both brands existed. But it was not until 1983 that the 103 Save Mart stores were converted to the SuperAmerica brand (also known as SA), which that year adopted a new logo and capitalized the "A" in America.

Dave Nelson, director of Distribution in 1998, who joined the company in 1968, explained the reason for the two brand names: Two men were in charge of two different operations, one in the North and one in the South, one affiliated with Ashland and one with SuperAmerica. Inter-company competition and "a bit of a power struggle"[8] ensued, so the two were separate and autonomous for several years.

Expanding the Goods

For SuperAmerica, the 1970s ended with a growth spurt. Immediately after the oil embargo, the chain experienced little expansion, but in 1977 the company went on a buying spree, adding 57 stores that year and 40 more the next, for a total of 192.

SuperAmerica was expanding in another realm as well — providing freshly baked goods in many of its northernmost stores. This initiative was an outgrowth of a 1975 experiment in which a Milwaukee SuperAmerica tested an in-store bakery counter program, offering items from local, family-owned Grebe's Bakery. The test was so spectacularly successful that the bakery counter was quickly extended to all SuperAmerica stores in the Milwaukee area. By the late 1970s, SuperAmerica President

This page and next: Bakers at SuperMom's in Minnesota turned out a half-million donuts, cookies, cakes, danishes and breads every week for daily distribution to SA stores within about 100 miles of Minneapolis.

SUPERmom's ®

Richard Jensen was convinced his company could distinguish itself from the growing competition with high-quality bakery goods.

Since the greatest concentration of Super-Americas was in the Minneapolis-St. Paul area, Jensen convinced James Grebe to establish a bakery in the Twin Cities to supply those outlets. Jensen and Grebe agreed on the name SuperMom's for the products that would be created, and over the next two years they worked to set up the bakery, hire the employees and renovate stores to provide bakery counter space. By 1981, the giant bakery was turning out hundreds of items shipped fresh every day to 55 Twin City SuperAmerica stores.

This time, customer response was less than overwhelming, however. For months, sales were sluggish. Customers could not seem to come to terms with going to the gas station for upscale bakery goods. But eventually the concept prevailed, sales escalated, and the bakery also began selling deli-style sandwiches and special-order cakes.

SuperMom's became so regionally appreciated that by 1987 the original bakery, then cramped beyond endurance, was replaced by a new facility and commissary. The new SuperMom's plant, a 24-hour-a-day operation, was, by the mid-1990s, baking 500,000 fresh brownies, cookies, muffins, donuts and breads every week for daily delivery to 180 SuperAmericas within 100 miles of the St. Paul Park bakery. In 1994, SuperAmerica boasted the highest daily average sales of bakery goods of any convenience store in the nation. A scaled-down version of a SuperMom's commissary was constructed in Russell, Kentucky, to serve Southern markets with frozen and fresh sandwiches dropped off for distribution once a week.

The bakery concept was only one of several new initiatives developed for the stores. The first ATM machine was installed in 1981 in the Twin Cities area, and the company launched private label items, including the successful YOURS cigarettes.

Above: John Pettus, who served as SuperAmerica's president until the Marathon/Ashland joint venture, oversaw more than a decade's worth of changes at SuperAmerica.

Below: SuperAmerica stores all over the country evolved to portray the same sleek image.

New Image–New Leader

In 1986, SuperAmerica became a separate division of Ashland Oil, Inc. "We thought the separation would be desirable in terms of focusing attention both outside and inside the company on the size and profitability of SuperAmerica," said Luellen, who by then was president of Ashland Oil.[9] SuperAmerica launched a three-year growth campaign, adding 153 stores between 1985 and 1987. Also in 1986, the chain acquired 100 Rich Oil stations in Kentucky, Ohio and West Virginia. That same year SuperAmerica opened the first in-store dining areas and redefined the company's mission as "compact mass merchandising." At Ashland's year-end presentation in 1986, Jensen explained the position of SuperAmerica's 402 operating stores:

"We are not a convenience store; we are a compact mass merchandiser. We are convenient, yes. But we are not convenience stores in the way the term is usually defined. Our thrust to the customer is a little bit different from the average c-store. We prefer to think of ourselves as niche-power retailers ... a retailer that has found and capitalized upon a market niche that others haven't."[10]

This growth period, however, offered its share of challenges. In 1986, SA was operating 402 stores with an operating income of $37 million. The following year the company was operating 457 stores, but income dropped to $16 million. By the end of 1988, the downward trend had reversed. SA was boasting 500 stores with $50 million in operating income, and one year later, SA had 585 stores and an operating income of $53 million.

In 1988, John Pettus took over as SA president. Widely acknowledged as an unusually accessible president, Pettus quickly established himself as one who lives the "Management by Walking Around" tenant popularized in the 1980s by management expert Tom Peters. In a 1989 story on the company, a newspaper reporter noted with obvious amazement that Pettus often answered his own phone and that he had visited 430 of the company's then 518 stores to rub shoulders with employees.[11]

A natural-born salesman, Pettus grew up in a selling family and learned as a child the importance of constant contact, customer focus and a hands-on approach. He lived in the small rural community of Springfield, Kentucky, and worked summers and after school at his father's lumber company. A week after receiving a degree in management and marketing from Western Kentucky University in 1965, Pettus applied for a job at Ashland and held a variety of positions over the years before becoming vice president of SuperAmerica in 1983, executive vice president in 1987 and president in 1989.

A Downward Slide

The strong performance at the end of the 1980s was not to hold. In 1991, SA had 624 stores, with an operating income of $31 million — 49 more stores than in 1989, and an operating income of $24 million less. Company officials blamed the Gulf War. "The year 1991 was a very challenging time for SuperAmerica," Pettus told newspaper reporters that year. "The war had a significantly negative impact on all retailers; plus crude oil prices were extremely high and gasoline prices were frozen below that crude level."[12]

The situation grew worse in 1992. The company divested itself of 26 stores, and its operating income plummeted to $29 million. The following year, the company sold off 54 more stores. As Pettus explained, "Ashland Oil needed to bring some cash into the corporation. The company decided to close stores in areas generating little return on investment and with no geographical connection to the rest of the company."[13] The strategy worked, and by the end of the fiscal year, SA

In the 1990s, SuperAmerica stores installed machines that allowed gasoline buyers to pay for fuel without ever entering the store.

was operating 588 stores with a record operating income of $65 million.

The Service Edge

With high profitability once again established, stores went through a series of updates. Credit card-activated Express Pumps were installed to allow customers to pay at the pump, and scanners were put in some stores to speed checkout times. "It was this commitment to technology," said Pettus, "that made it possible for us to totally re-engineer our merchandising, marketing and operational functions."[14] Some SA outlets added fast-food franchises or pharmacies, depending on local market needs. There was growing emphasis, too, on seasonal goods, like gardening supplies. All of these services could be included under the general heading of customer service. SA's customer commitment was recognized in a 1989 book, *The Service Edge*, in which author Ron Zemke proclaimed SuperAmerica one of the nation's "101 companies that profit from customer care."[15]

The company's desire to do what it takes to make itself attractive to consumers is clear from the SuperAmerica vision statement: "We pledge to provide our customers with outstanding service. We don't want 'satisfied' customers, we want delighted customers." In this vein, SuperAmerica rewarded employees who provided exceptional customer service. Company newsletters profiled employees who exceeded usual service standards, including a store manager who drove a regular customer home after that

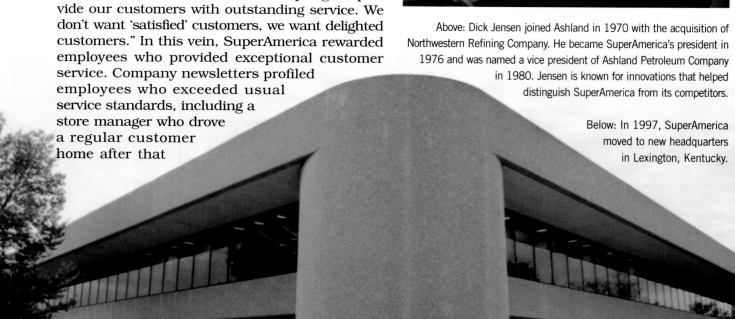

Above: Dick Jensen joined Ashland in 1970 with the acquisition of Northwestern Refining Company. He became SuperAmerica's president in 1976 and was named a vice president of Ashland Petroleum Company in 1980. Jensen is known for innovations that helped distinguish SuperAmerica from its competitors.

Below: In 1997, SuperAmerica moved to new headquarters in Lexington, Kentucky.

person stopped in for a cup of coffee and locked her keys in the car.

Poised for the Future

In 1990, SA's corporate headquarters moved to Lexington, Kentucky, into a newly constructed wing of the Valvoline building. Seven years later it would get its own building, on a plot adjacent to the Valvoline facility.

In 1997, Ashland announced its joint venture with Marathon Oil, which resulted in a merger between SuperAmerica and Marathon's marketing subsidiary to form Speedway SuperAmerica.

When asked about his initial reaction to the joint venture, Pettus, who became executive vice president for Speedway SuperAmerica, said, "I was really pleased. It made a world of sense. Ashland needed to do something downstream, and that something needed to create a lot more critical mass, a lot more leverage, a lot more volume. This meant we had to have some sort of joint venture partnership, and the sooner the better, while there were good players. I'm glad we got involved early so we could be proactive and not reactive."[16]

In July 1998, Marathon Ashland Petroleum announced that SuperAmerica would be moving to Ohio, in a new building planned for the Speedway SuperAmerica headquarters.[17] Also in July, Pettus announced he would retire, after 33 years of service. More structural changes took place that month. Riad Yammine was appointed executive vice president, Strategic Planning and Business Development for the joint venture. Yammine came from the Marathon side of the joint venture and was president of Speedway SuperAmerica LLC for the first half of 1998. John P. Surma was appointed the new president of Speedway SuperAmerica LLC. Surma had been senior vice president of Finance & Administration for Marathon since 1997.

Yammine predicted a bright future for Speedway SuperAmerica, though not without challenges. "We'll be able to carry on our trend of value pricing by continuing to expand our base of services, thus allowing us to absorb the increasing cost of labor," said Yammine in a 1998 interview.[18] "We'll also need to keep pace with technology and use it to better serve our customers. So far, we've put a lot of effort into technology development, because rapid exchange of information is very much a part of Americans' daily lives."[19] In the future, Yammine said, customers can expect to tap into data banks for information on Speedway SuperAmerica's services, which range from ATMs to credit-card-activated pumps, to all the conveniences of one-stop shopping.

APAC completed several projects, including some in Centennial Olympic Park, to help prepare Atlanta for the 1996 Summer Games.

CHAPTER FOURTEEN

APAC

"APAC is built for innovation. The autonomous group of companies quickly adapt to changing markets and the diverse needs of customers. They are the foundation for APAC's substantial bonding capability, financial stability and top performance."

— Charlie Potts, president of APAC, 1998[1]

MUCH OF THE INTERSTATE highway system in the Southeast and Southwest can be traced to Ashland Inc., as can runways at many of the nation's airports. Ashland has also made its mark at many of the country's most compelling tourist destinations, including the 1982 World's Fair in Knoxville, the Charlotte Speedway and 1996 Olympic sites in Atlanta.

The fact that virtually no one outside the business recognizes Ashland as pre-eminent in the paving world is inconsequential to officials at corporate headquarters. Ashland Inc.'s multi-billion-dollar road-building operation, APAC, which consists of dozens of companies in several states, has been a solid, if somewhat anonymous, money-maker for most of the more than three decades since Ashland entered the road-building business. And if few people in South Carolina realize that Ballenger Paving is part of Ashland or few in Texas realize Trotti & Thomson is too, that is, in fact, integral to a philosophy Ashland has abided by over the years.

A Road by Any Other Name ...

Attaching the Ashland name to all its various construction companies was never the corporate strategy. "It's very much a local-service kind of business," Paul Chellgren told reporters early in 1998. "We frequently do business under local names. We keep them because people know them."[2]

Moreover, the high level of autonomy has resulted in various operating units developing some very different and very specific specialties. While this decentralized approach has allowed for a flexibility that has served the various units and the home office well, it is not without challenges. In his presentation to security analysts in Columbus, Ohio, in 1996, APAC President Charlie Potts explained:

"One of the problems we have in describing the company and talking about it is that there is not [another] one that looks exactly like it. We're into a lot of the different facets of the highway construction industry, and we have a very big and significant presence in the many parts of it. Are we a paving contractor? Yes, we are. Are we a hot-mix contractor? Yes, we are. Are we a white-paving or concrete-paving contractor? Yes, we are. Are we a material supplier? We are a big supplier of construction materials in this country."[3]

APAC President Charlie Potts firmly believes that a commitment to employees will lead the company to further success.

Most of the paving and related-materials companies that Ashland acquired over the years had been, prior to their acquisition, local companies run by men with an entrepreneurial bent who understood the local customs, climate and conditions. "That's one of the reasons why we still run the APAC companies, for the most part, under the original names that they had in their local market area," said James Boyd, senior vice president and group operating officer for APAC, Arch Coal and Ashland Services. "People want to work with locals. They trust them."[4]

There is good reason for that trust. Early on, Ashland executives in Kentucky took the position that people from local companies — not chemists or refining experts or oilmen at corporate headquarters — had the knowledge to drive the paving operations to greater success.

This was not modesty on the part of Ashland officials. In fact, they knew very little about the paving business when they first entered it in 1966 with the acquisition of Warren Brothers, a long-established, well-respected and conventional paving firm based in Cambridge, Massachusetts.

Paving the Way

The Warren Brothers acquisition, one of the last orchestrated by Paul Blazer before his death,

was regarded as something of an odd-duck purchase when it was made. The only obvious synergy was that Ashland produced asphalt and Warren Brothers used it.

Warren Brothers, one of the largest paving contractors in the country, was an excellent performer throughout the Northeast, with gross annual sales of $160 million. Ashland Oil & Refining was willing to spend more than $37 million to get it.

It was not, however, regarded as a strong contender within the Ashland ranks for many years. "The list of so-called growth areas has changed somewhat over time," John Dansby, Ashland Inc. administrative vice president and treasurer, observed in 1998. "APAC was an unre-

Above: APAC's broad range of expertise and assets enable it to perform most types of highway construction, from roadway resurfacing to major new interstate exchanges.

Left: An APAC construction team preparing a site for the 1996 summer Olympics in Atlanta.

lated business but, you know, we've been at it now for over 30 years, so there is within the company a high degree of understanding the business and ability to manage it."[5]

Warren Brothers got off to a strong start. By 1972, just six years after becoming part of the Ashland division known as Ashland Resources, headed by Carlton Weaver, Warren Brothers was able to declare itself the largest road-paving business in the world. It operated in 23 states (as well as having an affiliate in Spain) and had begun to broaden its primary emphasis — asphalt paving — to include concrete surfacing, bridges, and sanitary and drainage facilities. By the following year, Warren Brothers boasted 142 asphalt plants, 30 crushing plants, 29 concrete plants and more than 10,000 mobile units.

In 1974, the first of what would be several realignments and restructurings took place. Ashland Construction was formed in October to combine all construction materials and contract construction activities under a central management, based in Cambridge, Massachusetts. The division encompassed 24 semiautonomous units in 23 states and Spain, which performed in both public and private sectors, ranging from surfacing of racetracks and airport runways, to subdivision streets and parking lots.

Over the next few years, Ashland Construction opened a new quarry in Richmond, Virginia, acquired a Jackson, Mississippi, sand-and-gravel operation, purchased a new asphalt paving operation with substantial aggregate reserves and expanded operations in Alabama, Texas and Mississippi.

Twists and Turns

Paving work has always been vulnerable to the weather and the economy. In the early 1970s, as various groups concerned about oil shortages and air pollution searched for solutions, another challenge arose: mass transportation. With 20 percent of business coming from the interstate highway program, and approximately another 30 percent coming from other road projects, road companies were troubled by the notion of a decreasing need for road work. After much study, the construction unit deemed it wise to reassure stockholders in Ashland's 1974 annual report:

APAC's Richmond, Virginia, quarry was a reserve for much of the material needed in Ashland's road-building business.

"The potential impact of mass transit has been given careful consideration. Significant diversion of funds to non-highway use is not anticipated. Mass transit systems will require enormous capital investment and contribute little to enhance common convenience in all but a few locations. Any workable solution to our nation's transit requirements must include the automobile and bus and will involve highway usage."[6]

Still, the mid-1970s witnessed a slight decline in revenues due to a worldwide economic downturn. Although sales in 1975 exceeded a half billion dollars for the first time, operating income decreased, reflecting a lower level of construction in the Northeast and Florida and work stoppages at two major operating entities.

Concerned about the vulnerability to weather, politics and the economy, Ashland embarked on a significant diversification effort in the construction operation, acquiring Levingston Shipbuilding, a Texas manufacturer of marine vessels and equipment, including drilling platforms for the petroleum industry.

By 1976, a recovery was well under way. With sales of $589 million and an operating income of $34.6 million, Ashland Construction generated the highest revenues in its history. Moreover, the diversification efforts allowed Ashland Construction to make the claim that in addition to its capability as a materials supplier and paver, the company also handled site development projects; all

forms of heavy and highway construction; the building of subways, bridges, wharves, docks and mass-transit facilities, sewer drainage and utility installations; erosion control and construction of recreational facilities.

The year 1977 brought another name change. The construction operation officially became Ashland-Warren and made a significant expansion into the Rocky Mountain states by acquiring Nielson's Inc., a heavy construction firm based in Cortez, Colorado. That year it also acquired the MacDougald Construction company of Atlanta.

In 1978 profits were again at a record level — $19.8 million on sales of $748 million. The company had projects through much of the United States, extending from Maine to Colorado.

In 1979 Ashland-Warren's holdings in the region where Ashland's paving operations started, the Northeast, were put on the selling block. The construction season in the Northeast is a short one, crammed into a six- or seven-month window when the weather is warm enough and free enough of snow and ice to permit work.

With its withdrawal from the Northern states, Ashland-Warren, then based in Atlanta, became focused almost exclusively in the rapidly expanding Southeast and Southwest. In these regions, the

APAC's reach extended throughout the country, as indicated by this 1989 project in Arkansas.

growth potential seemed greatest, and the construction season, barring unusually wet years, has traditionally been at least two or three months longer than in the Northeast.

Signs of Trouble

Still, it was a difficult period. In the early 1980s, the country was in the midst of an economic downturn. A shortage in federal and state road funds resulted, which made a tough situation for construction firms that counted on state and federal contracts for up to half of their business. This, coupled with unusually bad weather, created conditions for the most difficult days of what would become APAC.

In 1980, federal authorities, in cooperation with state and local officials, began a sweeping investigation of possible antitrust violations in the highway construction business, and portions of Ashland's operations were called into question. In April of 1982, an agreement was made with the Department of Justice to resolve antitrust matters and close the federal investigation. Ashland subsidiaries in four states were temporarily barred from bidding on highway projects, and the company paid millions of dollars in settlements and fines.

Company officials in Kentucky were caught completely off guard by federal allegations of price fixing. As John Hall, Ashland's CEO at the time, remembered it, "I think the management didn't fully understand what the guys out in the field were doing, and the guys out in the field thought the things they were doing were, on the surface, not too bad. But they were violating the law."[7]

Ashland Oil found itself in the position of having to correct the problem, deal with the employees who were charged and protect the enterprise.

"We decided we were going to protect our people to the extent we could. We'd advance the men their legal fees. If they had to go to jail, we loaned their families money while they were in jail. We tried to be extremely cooperative with the authorities in each area," Hall said. "We told our guys they had to tell the truth, whatever it was, and that we'd work our way out of this. It cost us millions of dollars, but we settled it."[8]

Made aware of risks, the company, Hall said, "put in a compliance system so that this would never ever happen again."[9]

A 1986 paving project in Asheville, N.C., is indicative of APAC's ability to deal with diverse mixes and specifications, from North Carolina to Texas.

Repaving

Another measure taken by Ashland in the midst of the federal investigation was to initiate a 1981 reorganization aimed at providing more oversight. William Voss, who had been an Ashland corporate vice president, became president of the construction group in January 1982. The construction group was divided into 12 operating companies, each held separately by Ashland Oil. The Atlanta-based central administration unit, renamed APAC, provided business and operating support, and each operating company had its own officers and directors.

Although the antitrust investigation had a negative impact at APAC headquarters, the construction groups continued to be successful. They became involved in a string of high-profile projects, including I-45 in Texas, I-75 in Florida, a jetport in the Fort Myers area and site work at the World's Fair in Knoxville. At Knoxville, the Harrison Division of APAC-Tennessee specialized in large earthmoving jobs, transforming 72 acres,

Bridge projects such as this one in Beaumont, Texas, number among APAC specialties.

and the Knoxville Division paved miles of interstate, streets and parking lots.

Such ambitious projects were the mainstay of the APAC group, and soon after becoming its president, Voss narrowed the geographic and strategic focus. Nielson's Inc., located to the extreme west of the general geographic area APAC covered, was sold, as was Levingston Shipbuilding. By 1982, APAC had reduced its focus to 16 states. It had 145 asphaltic concrete plants, 38 aggregate plants, 16 quarries, 20 ready-mix concrete plants and six concrete block plants.

APAC, less than 20 years after Ashland Oil had acquired Warren Brothers, was now a multi-faceted group of subsidiaries that, as the company publication pointed out in 1982, "digs shells in Florida (where they are an approved aggregate for use in asphalt and cement), markets building blocks in Arkansas and drives pilings in Texas."[10]

No Roads Barred

By 1984, APAC was a collection of 26 local independent companies serving an area extending from northern Virginia to Texas. But the markets for APAC's services had changed dramatically. Once again, there was less state money to fund new construction or to finance repairs, the Interstate Highway System was virtually complete, and private business had become increasingly attractive.

By the next year, signs of recovery were apparent. Strong performance by the engineering and construction segment resulted in a 22 percent increase in operating income, equalling $54 million; APAC alone increased its operating income by an astonishing 80 percent. As the 1985 annual report pointed out, declining interest rates had boosted demand in private construction, and in the previous two years, 45 states had passed measures increasing funds available for highway construction.[11]

Bolstered by potential in the days ahead, APAC went on an

expansion binge in 1985, opening new quarries in western Arkansas and eastern Oklahoma and acquiring a quarry in North Carolina. That same year, APAC-Mississippi brought a new asphalt plant on line in Jackson, and APAC-Texas installed a new plant at Fort Worth.

Thanks to increased government funding, favorable weather, lower costs and a healthy private market, APAC President G. William Jones was able to report that 1986 was a record year. Ashland Oil was also viewing APAC as a significant growth segment. The company went through several expansions and acquisitions, including APAC-Alabama's acquisition of Capital City Asphalt of Montgomery and APAC-Arkansas' purchase of a quarry in Harrison.

All road builders were benefiting from the swelling tide of public money, but the APAC companies were determined to compete with the best of them. "Not only do we want to provide the best quality product, we want to work cheaper and smarter than the next guy, and I think we do," declared Ted Mathiesen of the Birmingham Division, explaining an extraordinarily good year in 1986. "We're known for completing projects to specification on schedule, and often ahead of schedule."[12]

The growth continued in 1987 with the acquisition of Tanner Southwest, Inc., a leading Arizona contractor, and of Lehman-Meade of Lexington. Both companies were sold in the early 1990s to raise cash to invest in refining, but at the end of 1987, APAC had operations in 16 states extending from Virginia to Arizona. Holdings included 154 asphalt plants, 48 ready-mix concrete plants, 28 aggregate operations and 39 processing plants.

For the next two years, APAC continued to expand with the acquisitions of Southern Road Builders Inc. of Augusta, Georgia; Ashburn and Gray, a 40-year-old Huntsville, Alabama, contractor; and the addition of plants in Richmond, Virginia, and Memphis.

In 1989, Ashland announced plans to sell Ashland Technology Inc. to its management and employees, and Beaird Industries, another part of the technology segment to a European purchaser. The

This asphalt plant in Columbus, Mississippi, was just one of many plants acquired by APAC in the 1980s.

following year, Ashland took the last step to withdraw from the engineering business, selling Williams Brothers Engineering and Riley Consolidated.

Extending the Infrastructure

Highway projects were poised to get federal attention once again, and in October 1991, as the company had hoped, Congress authorized a significant appropriation — $151 billion — to restore the nation's transportation infrastructure. By the end of that fiscal year, Charlie Potts, who became president of APAC in 1992, announced that as a result of that action, funding in APAC's 14 states jumped by an average of 25 percent. APAC then had 37 operating companies employing 7,200 people.

In the 1980s, APAC built a new asphalt plant in Richmond, Virginia, adding to the company's widespread growth.

The highway appropriation had a long-term impact. By 1996, APAC reported its third consecutive record-breaking year, with operating profits of $83 million. In 1997, APAC "laid more than 20 million tons of asphalt, poured 1 million cubic yards of concrete pavement and produced 17 million tons of crushed aggregate," according to the annual report.[13]

Men at Work

What many don't realize about APAC is the level of hard work and dedication and the attention to detail that goes into each and every operation. "Hard work is the heart of APAC," said Boyd in a 1998 interview. "The sheer number of hours that people at all levels put in is just phenomenal."[14] It's not unusual, in fact, to find APAC's crews putting in 12- to 14-hour days. "Many of the crews are getting mobilized a half an hour before sunrise, and they work hard all day

long in the heat of the summer. They're out there working as long as it's light,"[15] Boyd said.

Of course, it's not just physical labor that makes the work strenuous. Any one project involves myriad decisions at all levels, as Boyd noted.

"You've got to remain on top of all those details. I mean, we're building roads here. ... It's demanding work. You can't just let something slide in this business, because it's our business to not only build these roads, but to make them safe as well. In this business, you can't take that piece of paper and put it on the corner of your desk and say, 'I'll come back to that next week.' You've got to make that decision today because there's machinery going down a highway, and it's not going to stop just because you're sitting there holding a piece of paper.

"... Sometimes, it seems, there's a lack of appreciation for the hard work that APAC does, but Paul Chellgren has been working to try to change that perception."[16]

Road to the Future

By 1998, a change in perception wasn't the only item on Chellgren's agenda. Convinced APAC could be an even greater contributor to Ashland's prosperity, he began eyeing yet more acquisitions. In January, Ashland acquired 10 privately owned Missouri-based road-construction companies, a move that made APAC the largest road contractor in Missouri and positioned it to roll more solidly into the Midwest.

In April 1998, Congress approved another six-year program to update the nation's highway system. "Most of our roads are overtaxed with regards to volumes and loads, and many of the bridges are approaching the need to be rehabilitated," said Potts in a 1998 interview. "A lot of this highway program is aimed at just improving the safety of the system," he continued. "The funding of the program is set up to address each and every one of those levels, and in the APAC organization, we are involved in every aspect of road construction, so we have a vested interest in all aspects of the program itself."[17]

By this time, APAC consisted of 34 divisions organized into seven operating regions covering 13 states: Alabama, Arkansas, Florida, Georgia, Kansas, Mississippi, Missouri, North Carolina, Oklahoma, South Carolina, Tennessee, Texas and Virginia. "We've been ready for the highway bill," said Boyd. "We could see the bill coming. That's one of the reasons why we made all those acquisitions in the last four years."[18]

Being prepared for the future is just one more of APAC's philosophies that keeps the company competitive. "If we're to grow, we've got to grow in several ways," Potts said in 1998. "One is to acquire new companies and to be able to bring them into the organization without having negative impacts on the profit side as we're doing that. We'll also have to grow internally," he continued, "and to do that, to be successful, we're going to have to train and educate and attract high-quality people into this business. Furthermore, we have to look for opportunities that will strengthen our competitive position in the marketplace and to keep a good, steady flow of trained employees who can carry on the rich tradition of this organization."[19]

In 1984, Arch Mineral's Captain Mine in Illinois was the company's largest operation.

CHAPTER FIFTEEN

ARCH COAL, INC.

"We are well-positioned, both strategically and financially, to actively pursue acquisitions and participate in the ongoing consolidation of the coal industry."

— Steven F. Leer, president of Arch Coal, Inc., 1998[1]

IT SEEMED LOGICAL that a fuel-producing company in Appalachia could turn into an abundant local resource for coal. But for decades, Ashland's holdings there did not. While to outsiders, coal and crude oil might seem close cousins, they are actually very different. In fact, geography aside, the two have few similarities.

It wasn't until the mid-1960s that Ashland Oil & Refining eased its way into the coal market by means of a joint venture. Then, in 1975, eager to diversify and become less vulnerable to the volatility of the crude oil market, the company leapt into the coal industry in its own backyard by forming a separate operation named Ashland Coal.

For generations, coal has been a way of life for many of those who live in the Appalachian Mountains. Coal mining had always been a unique enterprise, with a culture all its own. Outsiders were rarely invited within the closely knit industry. While providing income for thousands of mountain families with few resources, the coal industry had long been regarded as an unhealthy industry that decimated both workers and the land. It would clearly be something of a risk for AOI to enter that fray.

Getting Their Feet Black

Ashland first developed an interest in coal in the early 1960s, while Paul Blazer was still alive. Blazer and Orin Atkins met with Merl Kelce of Peabody Coal, a respected St. Louis firm that had merged years earlier with Sinclair Coal. Although the men formed a friendship, no deal was struck, and Kelce eventually sold the family coal enterprise to Kennecott Cooper.

By the end of the 1960s, Kelce, a millionaire many times over through the sale of Peabody, was eager to return to the coal business. Although creating a start-up coal business at that time was considered formidable due to the pre-eminence of a few giant coal operators and the massive expenditures required, Kelce was able to draw in Atkins and Ashland Oil. The joint venture was named Arch Mineral because Kelce's offices overlooked the St. Louis Arch. The company was officially incorporated on June 20, 1969, with Ashland buying half of the Arch stock. Carlton

Ashland's coal operations developed a new logo in 1997, when Ashland Coal merged with Arch Mineral to become Arch Coal, Inc.

"Buck" Weaver, who was president of Ashland Resources, and who was already overseeing the operations of the recently acquired Warren Brothers road building company, was appointed Ashland Oil's representative.

Forging Ahead

Less than ten months after Arch Mineral was founded, in 1970, Merl Kelce died of complications from an operation for colon cancer. He had, prior to being hospitalized, committed to millions of dollars of loans and expenditures. The man with extraordinary expertise in coal was gone, and Ashland was concerned. As Atkins later told Arch biographer Otto Scott, "We

developed a feverish urge to sell Arch Mineral, but there were no takers."[2]

Arch Mineral had no choice but to continue operations. Guy Heckman, a Missourian, Yale graduate and World War II veteran, became CEO. Heckman had joined Peabody in 1958 after stints as an investment broker and in his family's metal manufacturing company.

In the meantime, Ashland Oil was reeling from an unfortunate confluence of events. The company had just lost millions in a vain attempt to find oil in Libya, crude prices were spiking wildly and the economy was enduring a downturn. If those conditions continued, Ashland, already suffering from slumping stock prices, would not likely be able to hang onto a start-up operation with sporadic performance.

Fortunately, the wealthy Hunt family of Texas entered the picture. In 1971, the Hunts made their debut into coal with the unusual step of agreeing to become 50/50 owners in the coal enterprise, rather than insisting on a higher percentage in order to have the power edge. The Hunts' participation, according to author Scott, "saved Arch Mineral from extinction."[3]

Coal on the Fire

Over the next decade, Arch began coal mining operations in Alabama, Illinois and Wyoming and endured a series of financial ups and downs. The company's first-ever profit came three years after start-up, only to be followed immediately with a $3.2-million-loss year. The effort was also disrupted by a variety of environmental concerns, including a ten-month work stoppage in 1976 after a near-extinct black-footed ferret was spotted near Arch's operation in Medicine Bow, Wyoming.

By 1977, however, Arch Mineral's sales had increased from 329,000 tons in 1970 to 13.6 million tons; sales had grown to $156.8 million.

Above: Carlton Weaver, Ashland Oil's representative for Arch Mineral, often encouraged Ashland to persevere when times were tough.

Left: Dragline equipment has long helped increase production and lower costs at Ashland's coal-mining operations.

From its vantage point nearly 400 miles away, Ashland Oil grew increasingly more intrigued with the notion of coal. By the mid-1970s, Ashland executives could no longer ignore the steady cavalcade of heavily loaded coal trucks plying the hills of West Virginia and Kentucky. Fearing a major profit generator was passing them by, AOI formed another coal company — Ashland Coal, Inc.

The new company set up headquarters in Huntington, West Virginia, in 1975 on a hill overlooking the Ohio River. John Kebblish, the son of a coal miner and experienced in coal from years at Pitson Coal, headed the company as president and was determined to put Ashland Coal in a position to take advantage of the growth in coal markets. "I remember saying to myself when I got the job, 'Okay, fellow, we're going to find out how good you are,'" Kebblish recalled in a 1998

Above: Guy Heckman (left), a Missourian, Yale graduate and WW II veteran, became chief executive officer of Arch Mineral just months after its founding in 1970. A graduate of the New Mexico Institute of Mining and Technology, coal industry veteran Gene Samples (right), joined Arch Mineral in 1982 and later became president and chief executive officer.

Right: Ashland Coal reclamation efforts earned the company numerous awards, including the prestigious Director's Award.

interview. "Ashland had a lot of confidence in me, and I had a lot of confidence in it."[4]

A Cleaner Image

Kebblish possessed a vast knowledge of the industry, as well as the locations of quality low-sulfur coal reserves. He reasoned that low-sulfur coal, which was environmentally safer than standard high-sulfur coal, represented the future of the industry. Also, the country was in the midst of an oil shortage, and coal seemed like the most viable alternative fuel source, since it accounted for only about 20 percent of the energy produced in the United States, but 80 percent of the country's energy reserves.

The coal arena, however, had a public image problem akin to that of early oil wildcatters. By the mid-1970s, most coal companies had initiated stronger safety precautions for the miners, and concern about defacing the land resulted in the federal Surface Mining Control and Reclamation Act of 1977, which spelled out minimum mining and reclamation processes.

Turning sentiment around was not an easy task, however. Although government regulations required that the land be returned to reasonably good stead, coal miners were not often welcomed

by mountain residents who lived amid the scarred landscape left by earlier miners.

Even with new methods and new sensitivities that made mining less onerous, the operation still carried with it a certain stigma. The inevitable coal dust turned everything within a several-mile radius a dingy shade of gray, and massive coal trucks were a constant sight hurtling down winding mountain roads. Occasional mining disasters left families fatherless, and not-so-rare sinking houses and pasturelands, the result of subterranean over-mining, contributed to the industry's tainted reputation.

Rough Beginnings

Ashland Oil was entering a new industry fraught with challenge. Yet in 1977, *Business Week* declared coal "Ashland's most promising diversification."[5]

Ashland Coal quickly embraced the coal culture, rapidly bought up huge reserves of low-sulfur coal and found promising markets. It invested in equipment to make coal production more efficient and built a new barge-loading facility called Lockwood Dock, near Catlettsburg in 1979. By 1981, Ashland, through the combined tonnage

The mine in Medicine Bow, Wyoming, was a huge operation for Arch Mineral in the 1970s.

of Ashland Coal and Arch Mineral, was among the top six coal producers in the nation.

But coal was headed for difficult times. After experiencing several boom cycles during the 1970s, the industry began to experience falling earnings as the nation entered a protracted recession.

Environmental regulations were impeding the development of coal markets and increasing the cost of mining. That, coupled with excessive coal supplies and concern over coal's possible role in acid rain, was slowing the forecasted industrial conversions from oil and gas (even though low-sulfur coal, which Ashland Coal mined, did not contribute to acid rain). Thus the significant improvements in profitability projected in the late 1970s did not materialize.

That's when Ashland Coal began looking to the international market. "In 1980 and 1981 there was a worldwide demand for steam coal," Kebblish told the *Ashland News,* the company publication. "Poland couldn't produce, and South Africa was not up to export capacity. As a result, prices in the export market from 1980 to 1982 were better than those within domestic markets. So we made a decision to move into the coal export market."[6]

From 1980 to 1982, Ashland Coal exported nearly 5 million tons of coal, representing about 51 percent of the total tonnage it sold. The company enhanced its hold in Europe through an interesting business approach: Ashland Oil, Inc. sold 25 percent of its coal operation to Saarbergwerke of West Germany in 1981, and in 1982 sold 10 percent to the Spanish firm Sociedad Espanol de Carbon Exterior. That left AOI only 65 percent of Ashland Coal, but the transactions put it in a superior position to market coal in Europe.

Ashland Coal further increased its profitability by entering into a joint venture to construct a vessel-loading terminal at Newport News, Virginia, with a capacity of about 16 million tons per year.

A Burst of Energy

At home, Ashland Coal took steps to position itself at the vanguard of environmental responsibility, winning a variety of awards for its efforts. The company received an excellence in mining and reclamation award from the West Virginia Surface Mining and Reclamation Association for its 1982 activities at its Hobet No. 21 mine. It was the company's fourth such award in its brief existence.

"We are aware of the importance of proper land reclamation in mine operations, and we take our responsibility quite seriously," A.V. Rash, then manager of Government and Public Affairs for Ashland Coal, told a reporter for the *Ashland News.*[7]

In the early 1980s, however, the worldwide market for coal collapsed. That, in conjunction with a depressed domestic market, led to depressed earnings. Even so, the company remained hopeful. The Reagan administration had come into power, and the era was quite favorable to industry.

Much of the coal mined by Ashland Coal was transported on waterways by barges.

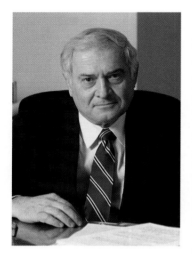

"Decontrol of energy prices is allowing coal to compete on an even footing with other energy sources for the first time in years," Kebblish told a writer for the *Ashland News* in 1982. "President Reagan and Congress are on the verge of bringing a new and proper sense of balance to the regulation of business activities that should benefit both industry and consumers."[8]

A boost came in late 1983 when the company signed a deal with American Electric Power to supply 15 million tons over the following 10 years and 3.5 million tons more over five additional years.

During its first decade, Ashland Coal had concentrated on building asset value by obtaining access to coal reserves, which are the primary growth ingredient for coal companies. From 1988 to 1992 Ashland Coal doubled its revenues, more than tripled its production of low-sulfur coal, and nearly doubled its central Appalachian reserve base — after acquiring three operations at a cost of $427 million and adding state-of-the-art equipment, including a computerized preparation plant. The acquisitions — Coal Mac, The Mingo Logan Coal Company and Dal-Tex — were concentrated in the Appalachian region, where they could maintain competitive mining costs.

Fueling Potential

Such expansion required AOI to change the coal operation's setup. Prior to August 1988, Ashland Oil had a majority interest in Ashland Coal, and as a result, the company was completely consolidated on Ashland Oil's balance sheet and income statements. However, Ashland officials recognized that growing the coal operation would require a huge amount of cash.

"So, to take advantage of Ashland Coal's tremendous potential, we had to find a way to encourage and fuel its growth without compromising Ashland Oil's capital structure," said Paul Chellgren, who was chairman of Ashland Coal in 1992.[9]

The solution came in 1988, when Ashland Coal offered its stock to the public. This resulted in a decrease of Ashland Oil's ownership in the coal company from 65 percent to 46 percent. Ashland Oil made $58 million in pre-tax cash flow. But just as important, the offering separated Ashland Coal debt from Ashland Oil's balance sheet, paving the way for the coal operation to take on its own debt and pursue growth much more aggressively. Not long after the first issuance, Ashland Coal issued more common stock to make an acquisition, reducing AOI's ownership further, to 41 percent.

When Ashland Coal began selling shares, the event was viewed as a novelty, business writer Philip Nussel noted. "Only a few West Virginia-based companies trade on the New York Stock Exchange," he wrote, and "just as unique was the presence of a purely coal-related company on the Big Board."[10] But, as Nussel observed, those who invested got the last laugh. In two years the value of the stock increased by more than 127 percent.

Early in 1991, moreover, *Fortune* magazine declared Ashland Coal one of the 50 best stocks of 1990. The company landed in the magazine's 49th slot, as the local newspaper pointed out, because of its "stock performance, which increased from $17.12 to $23.13 a share ... and the rising demand for low-sulfur coal."[11]

"Going public was a great learning experience," said Steven Leer, who was senior vice president of Marketing for Ashland Coal at the time. "It allowed Ashland Coal to succeed or fail on its own accord. It gave us new opportunities to grow the company and broadened all of the management's horizons."[12]

While AOI reveled in the positive attention Ashland Coal received, just as important was the quiet contribution the coal operation was making to AOI's balance sheet. Equity investments — those companies in which Ashland has an interest of between 20 and 50 percent — had become pivotal to Ashland's financial strategy, providing an

---

John B. Kebblish began his career as a laborer in the mines of Consolidation Coal Co., where he eventually became a vice president. He joined Ashland in 1975, when the company's coal division was formed. He was a vice president of Ashland Oil, Inc. and served as president of Ashland Coal, Inc. in its formative years.

important source of after-tax income, while allowing partially owned operations to finance themselves as needed. By 1992, Ashland Coal, with more than 1,000 employees, was contributing $13 million in equity income to AOI.

A Determined Partner

Arch Mineral, meanwhile, had adjusted to the fluctuations of the 1980s through a variety of measures. In September 1984, Arch Mineral announced the acquisition of three underground mines in Kentucky from USX, formerly U.S. Steel. It was a purchase that surprised many in the industry, partly because it appeared that the company was making a massive change from its traditional surface operations, and partly because Arch was moving into a region and type of coal that put it in direct competition for the first time with Ashland Coal. Arch Mineral, however, felt it was a logical move.

"Arch hasn't been in existence all that many years. ... We are in the business of mining coal, and our purpose is to make money," R. E. Gene Samples, who had been brought in as the company's president in 1982, told the AOI employee publication, the *Ashland News*.[13]

Samples, a graduate of the New Mexico School of Mines, had worked for six different mining companies and became a licensed professional engineer in seven states. He set about to see that his company did, indeed, make money. He insisted upon improved technical expertise in the ranks and a clear line of command. He brought innovative mining techniques to the 39,000-acre reserve area, aggressive marketing and a chance for renewed prosperity for the mining community of Lynch, Kentucky.

Arch posted record earnings in 1984, but an equipment breakdown at the Captain Mine in Illinois, Arch's largest operation, resulted in reduced production, which meant depressed earnings.

The troubles continued. By the mid-1980s, Arch was forced to reduce its highly profitable Western operations. Seminoe No. 1 had been mined of all economically obtainable reserves, and final reclamation was being accomplished prior to closing the mine. Medicine Bow, a joint venture with a subsidiary of Rocky Mountain Energy, would

In 1987, Ashland Coal invested $8 million for a 3.5-mile conveyor belt to improve safety and efficiency at its Hobet No. 21 mine in Boone County, West Virginia.

soon be idle due to market conditions. This left only one active Western mine, Seminoe No. 2, where mining costs were very high because of high severance taxes and royalties imposed by the state.

Still, Arch remained optimistic. As Samples told a reporter for the *Ashland News* in 1985, "If I can see Arch produce in excess of 20 million tons a year profitably by the time I retire — and we have six years to do it — I think I will have adequately discharged my duties to the owners. The goal is achievable. It is stretching, but achievable."[14]

Arch achieved the goal two years earlier than Samples had hoped. In 1989, Arch shipped 20 million tons from its mining operations, and in 1990 the company shipped 24 million tons. Moreover, by 1990 Arch could boast eight years of solid earnings.

Safety and the Environment

For decades, Ashland has been committed to environmental stewardship and employee health and safety in all of its operations, but at the 1996 key managers' meeting, the company articulated its long-time beliefs in an environmental, health and safety (EH&S) vision statement. The doctrine essentially stated that it was the company's goal to earn the trust and confidence of the residents and public officials in the communities where it operates, and of its employees and stockholders.

That year, the company's coal operations (as well as APAC's operations) were making good progress toward meeting that goal. The Huff Creek Mine at Arch Coal's Lone Mountain subsidiary in Pennington Gap, Virginia, won the 1996 Sentinels of Safety award for being the safest mine in the United States. Both Arch Mineral and Ashland Coal, in fact, won numerous safety awards that year, an accomplishment of which the company was very proud.

"We believe safety is good business," said Ashland Senior Vice President James Boyd in a 1998 interview. "We also believe safety is the right thing from a moral standpoint. We've always felt that we have a commitment to our people."[15]

Both coal companies had been acknowledged and awarded for their reclamation efforts as well, receiving dozens of national and state reclamation awards over the years. The Hobet mine in West Virginia won the Director's Award in 1994, the highest national honor given by the Department of the Interior. "We're making the same efforts with environmental initiatives that we have with safety," said Boyd. "We have even over-complied in some cases, just because we believe that preserving the environment is the right thing to do."[16]

The Merging of Great Mines

The first half of the 1990s was a period of sporadic performance, not only for Arch Mineral, but for Ashland Coal as well. In July 1997, the two companies — Arch Mineral Corporation and Ashland Coal, Inc. — merged to form Arch Coal, Inc., with 54 percent owned by Ashland Inc. It was a deal, said Chellgren, that the two companies had been working on for years.

While directors and stockholders of both Arch and Ashland Coal had long felt the two coal operations were often in competition with each other and should be merged, they felt that Ashland Inc. should not participate directly in the negotiations because, being an owner of both, the corporation had conflicting interests. At the same time, each side wanted to make certain it would get the best possible deal.

All things considered, the merger went smoothly, according to Arch Coal President Steven Leer. "Ashland's ownership in both companies did help," he said in 1998, "because we had a lot of contacts in knowing each other in the marketplace. I was at an advantage in that I had worked in both organizations and knew the management talent we had. We were able to form a top team very quickly, actually before the merger was even closed … so that on July 1, 1997 — the day the merger was finalized — we were implementing a plan of action and focusing on value drivers rather than trying to create a plan."[17]

When all was said and done, the merger was one that would lower costs through greater economies

Above: James Boyd, senior vice president and group operating officer for Arch Coal, APAC and Ashland Services, is proud of the company's efforts in safety and environmental awareness.

Left: Steven Leer, president and CEO of Arch Coal, Inc. in 1998, was instrumental in the smooth merging of Arch Mineral and Ashland Coal.

Right: William C. Payne joined Ashland in 1976 as a counsel for Ashland Coal, Inc. He was named vice president of the subsidiary in 1978 and senior vice president in 1981. He became president of Ashland Coal in 1987 and was later named its chief executive officer, a position he held until retiring in 1997.

of scale, Chellgren said. Just as important, there would be no more potential for competition.

Prior to the merger, Arch Mineral and Ashland Coal were the nation's 11th and 14th largest coal producers respectively. The merger created one of the country's largest coal producers — third largest in revenue and sixth largest in tonnage — which company executives projected would produce about 5 percent of the nation's total coal.

The executive headquarters remained in St. Louis, a decision that quickly led to a drop in the number of employees at the Huntington office — from 150 to 60 by year's end.

Future Endeavors

After ending 1997 with such a strong performance, Arch executives announced plans to expand by buying smaller operations. Since most of Arch's existing operations were within a few hours' drive of Huntington, and the new ones were likely to be as well, Huntington was designated as the company's "operating headquarters," which could lead to regrowth in the Huntington region. Furthermore, Chellgren announced that by the middle of 1999, the company would commission a study to establish the most logical and cost-effective location for the combined operating and executive offices.

Just months after the merger, Arch Coal was already growing. The company purchased the western coal holdings of Atlantic Richfield Company (ARCO), closing the purchase on June 1, 1998. The ARCO holdings would make Arch the second-largest coal producer in the United States by tonnage. In addition, the company would supply roughly 10 percent of the U.S. coal supply and could claim bragging rights as the largest low-sulfur compliance coal producer in the Eastern United States.

"The ARCO purchase is a continuation of our low-sulfur strategy," said Leer, just days before the deal was finalized. "All of ARCO's coal is compliance coal, which means it meets Clean Air Act standards for lower sulfur dioxide emissions."[18]

Arch Coal, a publicly owned company, made more than $30 million in 1997, the year of the merger. In January 1998 Leer declared, "We have now substantially completed a seamless integration of the companies merged last year, and we are well positioned, both strategically and financially, to actively pursue acquisitions and participate in the ongoing consolidation of the coal industry."[19]

In pre-joint-venture days, Ashland's gleaming SuperAmerica stores occasionally found themselves competing with Marathon outlets for market share.

CHAPTER SIXTEEN

MARATHON ASHLAND PETROLEUM LLC

"We picked the best people from both companies to be part of this new company. The people are committed, and we're committed as a company, to being a strong competitor, to bringing innovation and the ability to weather whatever future storms might befall the industry."

— J.L. "Corky" Frank, president of
Marathon Ashland Petroleum LLC, 1998[1]

MARATHON IN 1997 WAS a global giant with small-town values, as its executives were fond of pointing out. The company had spent most of its 110 years in Findlay, Ohio, a place where, as one Marathoner observed to management author and Marathon alum Bob Waterman, "It's hard to be a stuffed shirt."[2]

Deep Roots

Marathon began in 1887, when the oil boom had moved out of Pennsylvania into northwest Ohio. Fourteen independent oilmen banded together there, in Lima, Ohio, to form a production company called The Ohio Oil Company. Just two years later, The Ohio, as it was known, was purchased by the Rockefeller oil interests, and in 1905 the headquarters moved to Findlay, farther north, where the oil action seemed to be heading. When The Ohio was separated from Rockefeller's "Standard Trust" as part of Teddy Roosevelt's trust-busting campaign in 1911, and resumed operation as an independent company, it saw no reason to leave the town where, one former executive told Waterman, "There's not much clatter and clang."[3]

For nearly five decades The Ohio operated in the production end of the business, wrestling with the land, the elements and pure chance to find in-ground oil reserves. Operations in western Ohio,

Wyoming and Oklahoma were moderately successful, but nothing in the early days could compare with the day in 1926, when they drilled in Texas on the west side of the Pecos River. Oil gushed forth with stunning force.

Within a year, The Ohio had a small army on site, reaping the benefits of what came to be called the Yates Field. Workers had little water and no privies, and the wind-driven dust pelted them and seeped into their cabins. Despite these hardships, about 400 people earned steady pay from the Yates — the shallowest prolific reservoir in the northwest quadrant of the planet.

By 1929, The Ohio and its partner in the venture, Transcontinental, could boast a solid block of acreage with 70 flowing wells; the following year, Transcontinental's assets were acquired by The Ohio.

Early Preservation

The inclination among all the various companies working the field was to continue pumping until everyone was rich. The operators agreed, however, to be bound by self-imposed rules for

---

Marathon Ashland Petroleum LLC is the nation's sixth largest refiner.

development and production. This ushered in the era of proration and was explained by Rob Wood in a 1987 history of Marathon:

> *"Recognizing that excessive production depleted reservoir energy and shortened the life of the field, the committee voted to limit production and share the results among owners in the field. This practice, called prorationing, was pioneered at Yates and is now standard practice around the world."*[4]

Marathon became principal producer and operator of the field in 1976, and in 1985 the 1 billionth barrel of oil was drawn from the field.

Moving Downstream

If exploration and production were The Ohio's primary mission, they were not, as the years went on, its only venture. By the mid-1920s the company that had been run for nearly 50 years by veteran oil producers

began looking at its surplus crude oil stocks and set a course to move to the downstream portion of the business — refining, marketing and transportation. Henry Ford was turning out motor cars, people were taking to the roadways, and gasoline was suddenly in great demand. O.D. Donnell, managing vice president of The Ohio at the time, and soon to become its president, declared the company must integrate and develop outlets for the company's crude oil.

Having come to that conclusion, Donnell wasted no time formulating an action plan. In 1924, the company purchased the Lincoln Oil Refining company in Robinson, Illinois, and 17 rudimentary service stations in the Robinson and Terre Haute, Indiana, area. Four years later it purchased the Transcontinental Oil Company. This brought not only additional oil in the large Yates Oil Field, but also the Marathon name and the logo —

Marathon adopted its name and the Greek runner logo as far back as 1928, and that logo continued to represent the company in the 1960s.

Ashland brought to the joint venture a strong sense of marketing honed over 75 years in the petroleum refining and marketing business.

the Pheidippides Greek runner and "Best in the long run" slogan.

Eventually the Marathon logo replaced the Lincoln signs, and after World War II, as prosperity returned to the nation, the company experienced enormous growth. By the mid-1950s, the company had 2,700 stations in five states. In 1959 it acquired the Aurora Gasoline company with a refinery in Michigan, and 700 Speedway stations. Three years later it acquired the Plymouth Oil Company, with Texas oil production, a refinery and 18 terminals in 11 states.

In 1962, the company was renamed the Marathon Oil Company to tie it more closely to its brand-name motor fuel and products and to reflect the fact that it had outgrown its provincial beginnings to become a worldwide oil company, active in exploration, production, refining, transportation and marketing.

Like an Old Shoe

In the 1950s, Marathon set off north to Alaska, among the first oil companies to do so, where it accomplished several major oil and gas strikes. As the years passed, it became a presence all over the globe, including such far-flung locales as Canada, Mexico, Guatemala, Egypt and Libya.

In the 1970s, the company purchased Consolidated stations, added Bonded Oil and Gastown to its operations, purchased a new refinery in Garyville, Louisiana, and began moving away from gasoline stations to the gasoline and convenience store concept. By the middle of the 1980s, just 60 years after entering the marketing side of the business, Marathon could lay claim to 1,350 outlets bearing the names of its subsidiaries — Bonded, Gastown, Port, Ecol, Cheker, Speedway, Value and Starvin' Marvin — and 2,350 bearing the Marathon name.

Through all the acquisitions and expansions, the company kept a focus on pipelines, terminals and refineries in the region between Detroit and

Former competitors, Ashland brand, Rich Oil and Speedway outlets become colleagues as part of Marathon Ashland Petroleum.

Florida. It was a deliberate strategy that prevented Marathon from extending its reach into a broader stretch of the United States but also kept distribution costs low.

Another thing that didn't change through all the expansion was the essential texture of the company. "The Ohio never went for the excessive trappings, the bureaucracy, the layers of supervision, the rigid systems, the management fads, the heavy top-down direction that seems to affect so much of corporate America," Waterman observed in 1987. He noted that an "old-shoe, small-town feel" pervades the company.[5] Over the years, Marathon had stubbornly maintained its identity as a company that "sets the standard for integrity and fair dealings," he wrote.[6]

The Drivers

Part of that may be the result of Marathon's consistent quality leadership over the decades. For more than 70 years, the Donnell family piloted the company. First was James C. Donnell, a resourceful wildcatter who took the company to big finds in Wyoming, Oklahoma and Texas. His son, Otto D., took over in 1927. O.D., as he was known, was a strict taskmaster with a warm streak that ran deep. He would chide his employees for missing church or allowing the grass in their yards to get too long, but took pains to keep up with the family members of every employee. And "whenever an employee had a new baby, a pair of booties was forthcoming, presented personally by O.D.," Waterman wrote.[7]

Next came O.D.'s son, also named James C. Donnell, who took charge in 1948 and remained for nearly three decades. Under James C., the company went international and grew its refining and marketing operations.

The last of the Donnells was replaced by Harold Hoopman, a Wyoming wildcatter who moved Marathon even further into the downstream operations and gave employees free rein to innovate and experiment — as long as their activities produced decent returns.

Hoopman's constant refrain, Waterman wrote, was, "you give people a project goal a little out of their reach. That makes them stretch for it, and they grow professionally and individually. The idea is to tell them the ultimate objective and let them figure out how to go about it. It's the only way to cultivate innovation."[8]

Ripe for the Plucking

If one of Hoopman's legacies was an emphasis on innovation, another would be an altered corporate landscape. The era of 1980s takeovers had barely begun when Marathon received word in 1981 that Mobil was making a move on it. This was not regarded as a propitious proposition in the Marathon executive suites, and as top management consulted with anti-takeover experts, the city rallied behind them. Alarmed at the prospect of the equilibrium being upset in a town of only 38,000, 2,100 of them employed at Marathon, townspeople held rallies supporting Marathon's efforts against the takeover. As many journalists covering the episode noted, it may well have been the only time in history that people took to the streets in support of a giant oil company.

Once Mobil's efforts had been thwarted, it was obvious to Hoopman that Marathon was a prime target for further takeover attempts, and he began entertaining discussions with other companies he regarded as more acceptable.

A Lesson in Merging

On March 11, 1982, shareholders approved a merger with U.S. Steel, later to become USX. Although there had been great apprehension in the Marathon ranks during the weeks in which various suitors were making their bids, Marathon "managed to consummate the marriage harmoniously," wrote Boston University professor Dr. Philip H. Mirvis in the company's internally published history.[9]

He credited several things for the smooth merger: regular communication from Hoopman after the merger, which reduced the fear that can be fanned by lack of information and by rumor, and the employees' high degree of trust for Hoopman. Also, he said, U.S. Steel respected Marathon's capital and human assets and lived up to pre-merger promises that Marathon would be permitted to continue to develop its own practices, procedures and policies without interference from the home office. The acid test occurred in the mid-1980s when, during an economic downturn, U.S. Steel initiated layoffs and eliminated vacations. Similar actions were not imposed upon or requested of Marathon.

The actions both parties took, Mirvis wrote, were a "textbook example of how to handle the stress and crisis of a merger."[10] That is not to say there was never disagreement, Mirvis noted, but interference and the clash of company cultures had been kept to a minimum.

Still, there were some difficult times after the merger. As most of corporate America went through downsizing, so, too, did Marathon. In 1986 alone, 1,100 people took early retirement from Marathon, and 300 were terminated.

In 1991 USX issued separate shares of common stock to reflect the performance of its two major businesses — energy and steel — and reinstated Marathon's symbol on the major stock exchanges.

Opportunity Knocks

Six years later, Ashland Inc. proposed a joint venture to allow both Ashland and Marathon to better withstand industry cycles and crude oil price volatility. The letter of intent was signed May 15, 1997, between USX Corporation and Ashland Inc., to pursue a combination of the major elements of USX's Marathon Group and Ashland's refining, marketing and transportation operations. Ashland's exploration, production, chemical and construction businesses were not to be part of the venture, nor was its Valvoline Division, although Ashland's refinery-produced petrochemicals would be included.

Both parties, in announcing their intentions, emphasized the economy of scale that such an enterprise would enjoy.

"The goal of the joint venture is to create a competitive enterprise that capitalizes on the strengths and complementary assets of both companies," said USX Chairman Thomas J. Usher. "Market conditions have dictated that new approaches be explored to improve performance and growth opportunities."[11]

"The petroleum refining and marketing industry in the United States is undergoing a rapid transformation based on the need to improve profitability, create new efficiencies and better serve customers and shareholders," said Ashland Chairman and CEO Paul Chellgren.[12]

Negotiations

The first meeting to discuss the joint venture actually occurred in early November 1996, between Paul Chellgren and Tom Usher of USX. "What sticks in my mind," said Duane Gilliam in 1998, "was how agreeable both parties were. Here we had two companies that had been heads-on competitors for years, and yet they were sitting there saying, 'Look, this makes a lot of sense.'"[13]

Negotiations and due diligence proceeded until both companies reached an agreement. Under the terms, USX-Marathon would have 62 percent ownership and Ashland 38 percent ownership of the joint venture. Determining the ratio of ownership was not an easy task, according to Ken Aulen, administrative vice president and controller for Ashland. "The approach we used was what is called EBITDA," he said. "That's an acronym for 'earnings before interest, taxes, depreciation and amortization.' It's equivalent to a pretax cash flow that the businesses would generate. The 62/38 ratio came from a kind of blending of historical and projected cash flow."[14]

"It was tough on the company to take a minority position in a very large refining company where we had been a very large independent company in our own right," said Fred Brothers, Ashland executive vice president, in a 1998 interview. "But it was a question of stay who we were and play defense all the time because the industry was changing, or we could try to become an

Above: USX Chairman Thomas J. Usher emphasized that, while the ownership percentages were not equal, the joint venture was a partnership of equals.

Right: J.L. "Corky" Frank, a long-time Marathon executive, was named president of Marathon Ashland Petroleum LLC.

offensive player and align ourselves with one or more other players and go on the offense. We chose the latter, and the companies that have not done that are playing defense."[15]

A Done Deal

After months of sorting out the details, the announcement was made at year's end that agreement had been reached and the joint venture, officially called Marathon Ashland Petroleum LLC, or MAP, as it's known to participants, would begin operating January 1, 1998. The headquarters would be in Findlay, Ohio. Both companies would experience workforce reductions and job reassignments, the greater burden borne by Ashland.

"This is a significant departure from Ashland's past," said Gary Peiffer, who came from the Marathon end of the joint venture. Peiffer became senior vice president, Finance and Commercial Services, after the merger was complete. "It took a lot of courage and a lot of thought and consideration by the Ashland management to decide this was the right choice for this business, for this company."[16]

J.L. "Corky" Frank, Marathon's executive vice president for Refining, Marketing and Transportation, was named president of the joint venture; Ashland's Duane Gilliam, then president of Ashland Petroleum and senior vice president for Ashland Inc., was named executive vice president.

Frank, who earned a bachelor's degree at Texas A & M University in petroleum engineering in 1958, began his Marathon career in Hobbs, New Mexico, as a field engineer. In 1973, he became senior production adviser at the headquarters in Findlay and moved up the ranks, eventually becoming president of Marathon Petroleum in 1985 and executive vice president of Refining, Marketing and Transportation in 1991.

Sneak Peek

In a keynote address delivered in May 1998, Frank provided an update of the joint venture's status. "Our sales will be on the order of $20 billion a year," he said. "We will manage more than 10,000 miles of pipeline, one of the industry's largest barge fleets, 85 products terminals and 5,400 gasoline/convenience store stations."[17] Furthermore, Frank continued, "the combination of efficiencies and best practices we have identified should add up to more than $200 million in annual savings, with the first of these savings to be booked this year."[18] In addition, the joint venture was able to buy nearly 1 million barrels of crude a day.

Just months after Marathon Ashland Petroleum began operating, company executives already had plans for ways to cut costs and improve efficiencies, thereby increasing the value of the company for stakeholders.

"We're looking at constructing a pipeline from the Catlettsburg refinery into Ohio," said Kevin Henning, a 28-year veteran of Marathon and senior vice president for supply and transportation of the joint venture. "Marathon has been moving its products from west to east, and Ashland has been moving from east to west. The pipeline will allow us to take product from Catlettsburg

and move it into central Ohio, which for Ashland and Marathon is a major market. And then product from Marathon's Robinson refinery can go to the west."[19]

Company executives were looking at ways to expand as well. "It's ironic that we're sitting here just three months old, but we have a slate of things on our plate that propels us even further," said Randy Lohoff, who became senior vice president of Human Resources, and Health, Environment and Safety for MAP. Lohoff helped ensure that the placement of former Ashland employees within the joint venture was suitable to Ashland's interests. "This venture created many more opportunities, and bringing the two companies together has given us a lot more strategic knowledge."[20]

Marathon Ashland Petroleum's business strategy will continue to evolve as the two companies

Marathon Ashland Petroleum LLC has its headquarters in Findlay, Ohio, in the same building that was Marathon's corporate headquarters until its move to Houston in 1990.

become more synchronized. At the time of the January 1998 announcement, Marathon had four refineries and Ashland three, providing a total capacity of 930,000 barrels of oil per day. Marathon had 51 terminals, and Ashland 34; Marathon had 3,980 outlets in 17 states, and Ashland 1,420 in 11 states. Brand identification for each company was to be maintained, although both companies acknowledged that "future decisions" could be made on brand identification or consolidation. Marathon was marketing under the Marathon brand name, as well as through its Emro marketing company brands: Speedway, Bonded, Starvin' Marvin, United, Gastown, Wake Up and Kwik Sak. Ashland brands included Ashland, SuperAmerica and Rich Oil.

By the middle of 1998, many details still needed to be worked out, particularly as they related to the 5,400 stations, some of which were located literally across the street from each other. "There are different concepts on how the two major operations, SuperAmerica and Speedway, present themselves to the market in terms of facilities and pricing and so forth," said Ashland executive Lamar Chambers, who served as vice president and controller for the joint venture. "Over the course of the next year, a lot of that integration is to be determined, but it was agreed by both parent companies that we wouldn't rush that."[21] Mike Wilder, who was appointed general counsel for the joint venture would help in the decision-making. While at SuperAmerica, Wilder was instrumental in re-engineering SuperAmerica's administrative processes and its overall approach to store operations.

In May 1998, at a meeting of independent gas station owners in Lexington, Kentucky, Marathon Ashland Petroleum "offered to convert Ashland stores to the Marathon label. Those that chose to keep the Ashland name, the company said, would get continued marketing support, but Marathon Ashland would not be adding new Ashland retailers to its brand."[22] The company's other brand names, such as Speedway and SuperAmerica, were not affected by the announcement.[23]

Making Adjustments

The transition into Marathon Ashland Petroleum LLC was not easy for some Ashland employees. Charles Whitehead, director of Selection and Placement for Ashland Inc., admitted that morale suffered somewhat as a result of the layoffs, but stressed that Ashland was doing everything it could to make the transition as painless as possible:

"It's been our role to help all those who didn't go with the joint venture. So far, we are very, very pleased with what we've seen. Our severance package is generous, and our outplacement center provides training on interviewing, use of computers and use of reference materials. We find that people are finding employment elsewhere that's been equal to, or in some cases, better than the positions they were leaving."[24]

Moreover, though both companies previously shared a sense of gritty competitiveness, there was no animosity between former Marathon and former Ashland employees who moved to the joint venture. Rodney Nichols, who worked for Marathon for 20 years and became vice president of Human Resources and Labor Relations for the joint venture, summed it up this way: "Some of the competitiveness just fell away naturally once the joint venture went through. All of a sudden they see the potential — that we're all going to be part of the same company. They start realizing that what they feared the most from their competitors has now turned into an asset for the company."[25]

Fusion

As the adjustments continued, the prevailing feeling among the ranks was similar to that voiced by Richard White, a 42-year Marathon

Left: The Catlettsburg Refinery, Ashland's first asset, joins MAP's highly efficient refining system.

Right: Duane Gilliam, former president of Ashland Petroleum, is executive vice president of Marathon Ashland Petroleum LLC.

veteran. "The sum of the parts is definitely better than the individual companies, without question."[26] The joint venture signified, as White pointed out, "a very dynamic change in the philosophy of both of these companies,"[27] the ramifications of which would unfold for many years to come.

Differences were not seen as a problem, however, but as an asset. "The blend of our two cultures is starting to pay off handsomely," Lohoff said.

"Ashland people, for example, are not reluctant to say what they think to their boss. Marathon people are very much different in that regard, and they've seen that assertiveness in us, and I think some of them like that. On the other hand, we've gotten better because we understand that we've got to have more analy-

sis and data to present something from a management standpoint."[28]

Each company brought with it a different synergy as well — a different way of doing business — and executives knew that both companies would need to make concessions and compromises. "Marathon has been perhaps a little more analytical, a little more reserved than Ashland," said Gilliam. "Ashland has perhaps been a bit more intuitive and aggressive in its business approach."[29]

Despite such differences, many joint venture executives, including Henning, felt the two companies joined with a similar set of values. "In 1996," Henning said, "when both Ashland and Marathon were seeking a joint venture partner, we laid down certain criteria. We said, 'What do we want?' and we were obviously looking for a good physical, financial fit, but we were also looking for a good cultural fit, and when we did our study, we came up with Ashland. And when Ashland did its study, it came up with Marathon."[30]

This illustration of Marathon's and Ashland's marketing regions and refinery locations prior to the joint venture depicts the marketing and distribution synergies gained through Marathon Ashland Petroleum.

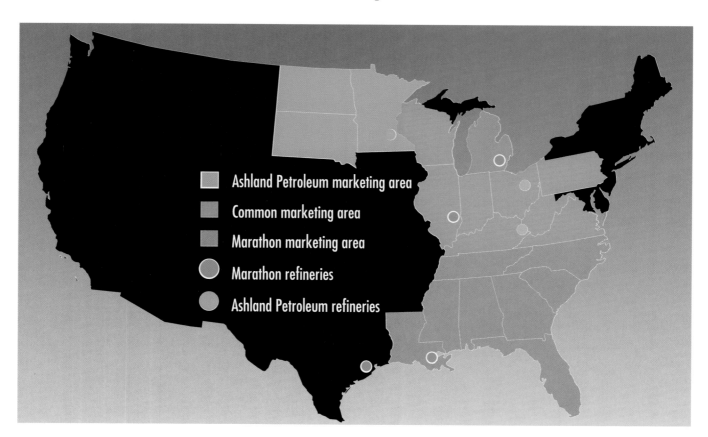

Ashland Petroleum marketing area
Common marketing area
Marathon marketing area
Marathon refineries
Ashland Petroleum refineries

Lohoff agreed. "I think the Marathon people have the same kind of Midwest work ethic that the people in Ashland do. They're loyal to their organization."[31]

Though the merging of two formerly competitive companies was not an easy transition to make, the changes went smoothly — for both personnel and for business. "Everything's new," Lohoff said. "In spite of what the parents' different views are, the people involved in it have an opportunity to create something new, and that's an attitude I want to keep alive for as long as possible."[32]

Moreover, the joint venture placed both companies in a far stronger position than either was in before. "We picked the best people from both companies to be part of this new company," said Frank. "The people are committed, and we're committed as a company to being a strong competitor, to bringing innovation and the ability to weather whatever future storms might befall the industry."[33]

Paul Chellgren, Ashland Inc. CEO, credited the success of the merger to the employees who made it possible and the synergistic opportunities, saying, "Marathon, USX and Ashland employees are to be commended for the hard work, dedication and aggressive pace that they've maintained toward building one of the strongest and most competitive downstream companies in the industry."[34]

Ashland Inc.'s Executive Vice President J.A. Fred Brothers added the operation and functions of MAP to his already long list of responsibilities.

MOVING FORWARD

"There is no Force so powerful as an idea whose time as come."

— Senator Everett Dirksen, 1964

FOR 75 YEARS, ASHLAND INC. HAS BEEN continually evolving. What started as one small refinery back in 1924 has grown into a *Fortune* 500 company with operations in chemicals, motor oil and related automotive products and services, highway construction, petroleum refining and marketing and coal. Much of that evolution has occurred gradually; however, Ashland was founded by an entrepreneur, Paul Blazer, a man known to have a bias for action. Throughout the company's history, its leaders have moved opportunistically to respond to changes in the industrial and economic environment. This entrepreneurial spirit lives on, as evidenced by events in the recent past. In December 1996, Ashland CEO Paul Chellgren announced a profitability improvement plan designed to combat lackluster returns in the refining industry and to focus on growth in the company's chemical, APAC road construction and Valvoline operations.

The plan, implemented over a relatively short 18-month time frame, brought dramatic changes to Ashland. In May 1997, the company announced its intent to form a petroleum and refining joint venture with the USX-Marathon Group. Negotiations continued at a rapid pace throughout the remainder of 1997, and the transaction was completed on January 1, 1998, creating a much more competitive, more profitable entity, Marathon Ashland Petroleum LLC.

Making Hard Choices

Relinquishing its identity as one of the nation's largest independent refiner/marketers was a difficult decision for Ashland. However, as the company entered the second half of the 1990s, management came to the hard realization that it must change course to deliver the type of returns expected by institutional investors. The refining and marketing business, long the lifeblood of the company, was no longer delivering the double-digit returns that many investors sought. Indeed, since the passage of the Clean Air Act Amendments in 1990, the refining industry as a whole had been staggering under the weight of vast sums of capital that had to be invested to produce cleaner-burning fuels and meet the law's other regulatory requirements. As refiners invested to produce the new fuels and further reduce refinery emissions, many also took advantage of the opportunity to "debottleneck" their plants and make other improvements. The end result was often an incremental increase in capacity. Dubbed "capacity creep" by industry observers, the practice led to excess refining capacity. This surplus, coupled with slow demand growth, volatile commodity markets and large capital requirements, resulted in financial returns that for most of the 1990s averaged below the industry's cost of capital.

By May 1997, when Ashland announced its plans to form a joint venture with Marathon, the industry already had begun to consolidate. Between 1995 and mid-1997, fully 31 percent of U.S. refining capacity was involved in some type of merger, strategic alliance or exchange of assets. The transactions involved companies both large and small: Tosco bought Unocal's 76 Products assets; Ultramar merged with Diamond Shamrock and then bought Total, NA; Texaco, Star (itself a joint venture between Texaco and Saudi Aramco) and Shell merged their U.S. downstream operations; and Valero bought Basis.[1] More recently, BP and Amoco announced a worldwide partnership in the largest industrial merger ever. In such an atmosphere, Ashland's decision to combine its refining and marketing operations with Marathon's was clearly a prudent one.

Charting a New Course

Other parts of the profitability improvement plan were driven by Ashland's decision to chart a new course as a multi-industry organization delivering world-class products and services to customers around the globe. As Chairman and CEO Paul Chellgren explained it to key managers at their annual gathering in Cincinnati in 1997, responding to external changes required an internal resolve to improve.

"The need for change is ever constant. Our shareholders demand it in the form of increased value and higher stock prices. Our customers expect it through improved service, quality and price performance. Our communities demand continuous improvement in environmental, health and safety performance. The government mandates it through regulation. Finally, our employees expect it as part of a dynamic workplace. Pressure to perform at increasingly higher levels is relentless, as institutions increase their ownership of corporate America. Institutions currently own 65 percent of Ashland stock, compared to 11 percent 15 years ago. Every investor expects an above-average return, and every institutional portfolio manager seeks to deliver it. Ashland competes against all U.S. stocks for investment dollars, not just other refiners. Our owners are pressuring us for consistent superior returns, and they haven't consistently been there."[2]

In the quest for improved returns, Ashland in the future would focus upon chemicals, which in the 1990s had become the company's fastest-growing business and largest contributor to profits; Valvoline, its best known consumer brand with an opportunity for worldwide growth; and highway construction, its highest return business. The company decided to exit the oil and gas exploration and production business. In the years since 1979, when Ashland had sold most of its oil and gas assets, the company had rebuilt a valuable bank of domestic natural gas reserves. But oil and gas exploration requires significant amounts of "patient money," capital invested in exploration ventures that might take years to earn a return. Ashland decided its shareholders were better served by capturing the Exploration Division's value through selling the assets and using the proceeds to reduce debt.

By July 1 of 1997, Ashland had sold its domestic oil and gas exploration and production (E&P) business. The subsequent debt reduction resulted in a stronger balance sheet that provided the financial might to further expand Ashland Chemical, APAC and Valvoline. (Ashland's relatively small international E&P operations, primarily in Nigeria, were divested in 1998.)

July 1, 1997, also witnessed the merger of Arch Mineral Corporation and Ashland Coal, Inc. Ashland initially owned more than half of this powerhouse coal producer, which after its May 1998 acquisition of Atlantic Richfield's Western coal properties, became the No. 2 coal producer in the nation. A few months later, Ashland decided to deconsolidate Arch from its financial statements, thus giving Arch the ability to grow without affecting Ashland's balance sheet but still providing Ashland with the benefit of equity income.

As a result of these moves, Ashland had streamlined its operating structure. In January 1997, the company had six operating divisions and partial interests in two separate coal companies. By July 1998, Ashland had three wholly owned divisions — Ashland Chemical, APAC and

Valvoline — and interests in Marathon Ashland Petroleum and Arch Coal. Ashland was on its way to achieving some of the key strategic ambitions Chellgren had outlined at the December '97 key managers' meeting: becoming a high-performing competitor delivering world class products and services; occupying the No. 1 or No. 2 spot in the industry categories in which it competes; leading its industries in customer and employee satisfaction; and being perceived as an ethical, responsible corporation by all constituents.

Establishing a New Base

With a new operating structure in place, it was time in the fall of 1998 to fulfill the last goal of the 1996 profitability improvement plan: to evaluate general and administrative expenses and the company's administrative structure. At the same time, the company announced what had been contemplated previously from time to time: Corporate headquarters would move down the Ohio River about 150 miles to Covington, Kentucky, in the Cincinnati metropolitan area, and away from the company's birthplace in Ashland, Kentucky. The move was triggered largely by cost and competitive considerations. "Ashland Inc. isn't the same company it was 18 months ago," said Paul Chellgren. "The adminis-

trative support structure that served us well a year ago from a home office in Ashland is not the support structure that we need or can afford today as a more streamlined organization that is growing on a global basis."[3]

Chellgren explained that, as a public company, Ashland needed to stay competitive. "One way to improve our returns is to become more competitive in our cost structure, including reducing administrative costs."[4]

Ashland chose Covington as its new home for a number of reasons. Importantly, a move to Covington would keep the company in its home state of Kentucky. In addition, Covington is just 10 miles from "America's Most Convenient Gateway," the Cincinnati/Northern Kentucky International Airport. Close proximity to such a major airport would make it more convenient for suppliers, customers and investors to visit the company — a necessity, considering that in 1998, Ashland has sales and operations in all 50 states and more than 140 countries. In addition, the city is centrally located with regard to Ashland's other operations. It is less than 200 miles from the headquarters of all Ashland operating units, except APAC and Arch Coal, both of which are easily accessible via direct flights.

Rumors in Ashland, Kentucky, and surrounding communities circulated at a frenzied pace in the weeks leading up to the decision. Would the company move? If so, would it leave Kentucky? The concerns stemmed from Ashland's contributions over the years to the community and state, as well as its employees' extensive community involvement. "Over the last 15 years, Ashland has set the standard for corporate citizenship in this state," said Bob Sexton, executive director of the Prichard Committee for Academic Excellence.[5] Others agreed. "It is a company that has been involved in nearly every good intention in this state, especially in education," said University of Kentucky President Charles Wethington.[6]

Ashland helped to reduce the impact of the move, both to affected employees and to the community. The company provided generous severance packages and outplacement assistance and offered relocation assistance to those who moved. In addition, Ashland announced it would honor all its existing pledge commitments to the com-

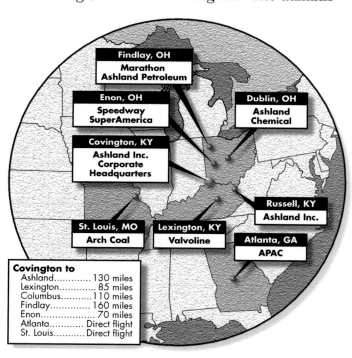

Findlay, OH
Marathon Ashland Petroleum

Enon, OH
Speedway SuperAmerica

Dublin, OH
Ashland Chemical

Covington, KY
Ashland Inc. Corporate Headquarters

Russell, KY
Ashland Inc.

St. Louis, MO
Arch Coal

Lexington, KY
Valvoline

Atlanta, GA
APAC

Covington to
Ashland............130 miles
Lexington............85 miles
Columbus...........110 miles
Findlay..............160 miles
Enon....................70 miles
Atlanta............Direct flight
St. Louis...........Direct flight

Above: Ashland's new headquarters at the RiverCenter complex, located on the Ohio river front in Covington, Kentucky.

Far left: The move to Covington put Ashland's headquarters in the center of its operations.

munity and would phase down its other civic contributions on a gradual basis. To help fill the gap its absence would leave, Ashland donated parts of its 160-acre Russell, Kentucky, office campus to a newly created charitable organization, an arm of the existing Foundation for the Tri-State Community, designed to bring new jobs to the area. The company also provided funds for the

organization to hire nationally recognized community development consultants and pledged to maintain the offices for up to five years.

By the end of 1998, Ashland Inc. will have moved into its new home, three floors of leased space in the 15-story, 240,000-square-foot RiverCenter in Covington. "I think there's a sense of new direction," said Executive Vice President Fred Brothers, when asked about the general atmosphere at the company. "There's a sense of new direction and an opportunity to create a different company, so I think there's a sense of challenge and excitement."[7]

"On a personal level, [the move and restructuring] was an extremely difficult decision," said Chellgren. "This restructuring will pose change for many valuable and dedicated employees. But the reality of doing business today is that we must continue to reduce our costs and continually improve our competitive position."[8]

"At this moment, we stand together at a crossroads in our corporation's history," the CEO advised employees in a message on Ashland's internal electronic news service. "In years to come, this restructuring process will be viewed by future employees as either just another corporate cost-cutting, or as a defining moment when we fundamentally changed the way we do business, particularly the way we do business internally. I want us to use this opportunity to make fundamental changes in the way we do business. To eliminate boundaries between our business units. To provide seamless customer service. To emphasize performance through people working together as partners, all across this corporation."[9]

To continually improve, to find new and better ways of working together, has been Ashland's doctrine since 1924, for without the willingness to change, the company could not have survived a century fraught with economic challenges. Is Ashland's evolution complete? Probably not. But if the first 75 years of its history are any indication, Ashland Inc. has a promising future indeed.

NOTES TO SOURCES

Chapter One

1. Joe Creason, "Blazer and Ashland Oil Have Come a Long Way," *The Courier-Journal,* Louisville, Kentucky, April 22, 1956.
2. Swiss Oil Corporation Annual Report to Stockholders, Feb. 8, 1936.
3. Otto Scott, *The Exception,* McGraw-Hill, Inc., New York, 1968, p. 4.
4. *The Petroleum Engineer,* "Petroleum Profile," September 1956, p. 5.
5. Joe Creason, "Blazer and Ashland Oil Have Come a Long Way," *The Courier-Journal,* Louisville, Kentucky, April 22, 1956.
6. Scott, p. 4.
7. Ibid, p. 6.
8. Ibid, p. 7.
9. Ibid.
10. Ibid, p. 9.
11. Ibid, p. 12.
12. Ibid, p. 13.
13. Ibid, p. 14.
14. Ibid.
15. Ibid, p. 15.
16. Ibid.
17. Ibid, p. 18.
18. Ibid, p. 23.
19. Ibid, p. 24.
20. Ibid, p. 29.
21. Ibid, p. 30.
22. Ibid, p. 34.
23. Ibid, p. 34.
24. Ibid, p. 35.
25. Ibid.
26. Ibid, p. 45.
27. Ibid, p. 39.
28. Ibid, p. 41.
29. Ibid, p. 39.
30. Ibid, p. 41.
31. Ibid, p. 43.
32. Ibid, p. 44.
33. Swiss Oil Corporation Annual Report to Stockholders, Feb. 23, 1925.
34. Ibid.
35. Scott, p. 44.
36. Joseph L. Massie, *Blazer and Ashland Oil.* University of Kentucky Press, Lexington, Kentucky, 1960, p. 32.
37. Scott, p. 50.
38. Ibid, p. 52.
39. Ibid, p. 56.
40. Ibid, p. 57.
41. Ibid, p. 60.
42. Massie, p. 4.
43. Ibid, p. 4.
44. Scott, p. 75.
45. Ibid, p. 79.
46. Swiss Oil Corporation Annual Report to Stockholders, Feb. 20, 1930.
47. Scott, p. 83.
48. Ibid, p. 88.
49. Joe Creason, *The Courier-Journal,* "Blazer and Ashland Oil Have Come a Long Way," Louisville, Kentucky, April 22, 1956.
50. Ibid.
51. Scott, p. 99.
52. Ibid, p. 92.
53. Ibid, p. 103.
54. *The Herald-Dispatch,* "Paul Blazer and the Ashland Oil Co.," Huntington, West Virginia, Dec. 10, 1966.
55. Scott, p. 130.
56. Ashland Oil & Refinery Company Annual Report to Stockholders, March 3, 1937.

Chapter Two

1. Daniel Yergin, *The Prize: The Epic Quest for Oil, Money & Power,* Simon & Schuster, New York, 1991, p. 13.
2. Otto Scott, *The Exception,* McGraw-Hill, Inc., New York, 1968, p. 51.
3. John E. Kleber, Editor, *The Kentucky Encyclopedia,* The University Press of Kentucky, 1992, p. 36.
4. Ibid, p. 170.
5. Carol Crowe-Carraco, *The Big Sandy,* The University Press of Kentucky, 1979, p. 51.
6. Kleber, p. 170.
7. Ibid.
8. *Ashland Oil Log,* Ashland Oil & Refining Co., Dec. 1947, p. 12.
9. Ibid, p. 12.
10. Kleber, p. 692.
11. Yergin, p. 13.
12. Ibid, p. 24.
13. Ibid, p. 29.
14. Ibid, p. 33.
15. George B. Tindall and David E. Shi, *America,* W.W. Norton & Co., New York, 1989, p. 497.
16. Yergin, p. 41.
17. *Encyclopedia Brittanica,* 15th edition, micropedia, Vol. 11, p. 207.
18. Yergin, p. 38.
19. Ibid, p. 53.
20. *Encyclopedia Brittanica,* 15th edition, micromedia vol. 11, p. 207.
21. Ibid, p. 207.
22. Yergin, p. 104.
23. Ibid, p. 110.

Chapter Three

1. Otto Scott, *The Exception,* McGraw-Hill, New York, 1968, p. 160.
2. Ibid, p. 326.
3. Joseph L. Massie, *Blazer and Ashland Oil,* University of Kentucky Press, Lexington, Kentucky, 1960, p. 76.
4. Ibid, p. 51.
5. Paul Blazer, "E Pluribus Unum," speech to the Newcomen Society, April 24, 1956.
6. W.H. Dysard, interviewed by the author, Jan. 22, 1998, transcript p. 2.
7. Veronica Thistle, interviewed by Jon VanZile, April 13, 1998, transcript p. 2.

8. Doris Webb, interviewed by Catherine Lackner, Feb. 11, 1998.
9. James E. Casto, *Towboat on the Ohio*, The University Press of Kentucky, Lexington, Kentucky, 1995, p. 81.
10. Ibid.
11. Massie, p. 125.
12. *Ashland Oil Log*, Ashland Oil & Refining Co., Vol. 1, No. 6, Oct. 1941, p. 2.
13. *The Magazine of Kentucky Affairs*, "Ashland Oil: The Story of Paul Blazer," KEN, July 1955.
14. Otto Scott, *The Exception*, McGraw-Hill, New York, 1968, p. 147.
15. Ibid.
16. Ibid.

Chapter Four

1. Otto Scott, *The Exception*, McGraw-Hill, New York, 1968, p. 172.
2. *Ashland Oil Log*, Ashland Oil & Refining Co., Vol. 2, No. 5, September 1942, p. 4.
3. Ashland Oil & Refining Company 1942 Annual Report, Letter to Stockholders.
4. Scott, p. 172.
5. Ibid, p. 173.
6. *Ashland Oil Log*, Ashland Oil & Refining Co., Vol. 1, No. 10, Feb. 1942, p. 8.
7. Ibid, p. 12.
8. *Ashland Oil Log*, Ashland Oil & Refining Co., Vol. 1, No. 3, July 1941, p. 2.
9. *Ashland Oil Log*, Ashland Oil & Refining Co., Vol. 2, No. 3, July 1942, p. 4.
10. Scott, p. 182.
11. Ashland Oil & Refining Company 1942 Annual Report, Letter to Stockholders.
12. *Ashland Oil Log*, Ashland Oil & Refining Co., Vol. 2, No. 7, Nov. 1942, p. 16.

13. Ashland Oil & Refining Company 1943 Annual Report, Letter to Stockholders.
14. Daniel Yergin, *The Prize: The Epic Quest for Oil, Money & Power*, Simon & Schuster, New York, 1991, p. 409.
15. Ibid, p. 393.
16. Ibid, p. 410.
17. *Ashland Oil Log*, Ashland Oil & Refining Co, Vol. 5, Nos. 3 and 4, July–Aug. 1945, p. 24.
18. Ashland Oil & Refining Company 1943 Annual Report, Letter to Stockholders.
19. *Ashland Oil Log*, Ashland Oil & Refining Co., Vol. 5., Nos. 3 and 4, July–Aug. 1945, p. 24.
20. Ashland Oil & Refining Company 1944 Annual Report, Letter to Stockholders.
21. Ashland Oil & Refining Company 1945 Annual Report, Letter to Stockholders.
22. Ibid.

Chapter Five

1. George B. Tindall and David E. Shi, *America: Brief Second Edition*, New York, W.W. Norton & Company, 1989, p. 815.
2. Otto Scott, *The Exception*, McGraw-Hill, New York, 1968, pp. 231-232.
3. Ibid, p. 237.
4. Ibid, p. 234.
5. Ibid, p. 243.
6. John Ed Pearce, "Ashland Oil's Rex Blazer," *The Louisville Courier-Journal & Times Sunday Magazine*, Louisville, Kentucky, Oct. 14, 1973. p. 12.
7. Scott, p. 246.
8. Ibid, p. 258.

9. W.E. Chellgren, interviewed by the author, March 13, 1998, transcript p. 2.
10. Scott, p. 236.
11. *Ashland Oil Log*, Ashland Oil & Refining Co., Vol. 9, No. 8, Dec. 1949, p. 6.
12. Ibid, p. 9.
13. Statements made at Appreciation Dinner honoring Ashland Oil & Refining Company given by the Ashland Board of Trade, September 9, 1954.
14. Scott, p. 225.
15. Veronica Thistle, interviewed by Jon VanZile, April 13, 1998, transcript, p. 3.
16. Scott, p. 226.
17. Doris Webb, interviewed by Catherine Lackner, Feb. 11, 1998.
18. Ibid.
19. Scott, p. 260.

Chapter Six

1. *The Herald-Dispatch*, Huntington, W. Va., Dec. 10, 1966. p. 4.
2. Paul Blazer, "E Pluribus Unum," speech to the Newcomen Society, April 24, 1956.
3. Ashland file memorandum from Alex Chamberlain, September 12, 1951.
4. John Ed Pearce, "Ashland Oil's Rex Blazer," *The Louisville Courier-Journal & Times Sunday Magazine*, Louisville, Kentucky, Oct. 14, 1973, p. 15.
5. Ibid, p. 12.
6. Johnnie Daniels, interviewed by Catherine Lackner, April 8, 1998, transcript p. 1.
7. James Fout, interviewed by Catherine Lackner, April 7, 1998, transcript p. 6.
8. Doris Webb, interviewed by Catherine Lackner, Feb. 11, 1998.
9. Ibid.

10. Fred Brothers, interviewed by the author, Jan. 22, 1998, transcript p. 2.
11. James Fout, interviewed by Catherine Lackner, April 7, 1998, transcript pp. 1–2.
12. The Ashland Oil & Refining Company 1954 Annual Report, p. 3.
13. The Ashland Oil & Refining Company 1955 Annual Report, p. 2.
14. Otto Scott, *The Exception,* McGraw-Hill, Inc., New York, 1968, p. 307.
15. Ibid, p. 320.
16. Ashland Oil & Refining Company 1955 Annual Report, p. 5.
17. Scott B. Patrick, interviewed by Jon VanZile, April 24, 1998, transcript p. 1.
18. Scott, p. 329.
19. Scott B. Patrick, interviewed by Jon VanZile, April 24, 1998, transcript p. 2.
20. Scott, p. 346.
21. Ibid, p. 377.
22. Ibid, p. 394.
23. Ibid, p. 413.
24. Ibid, p. 414.
25. Sam Marrs, interviewed by Catherine Lackner, April 8, 1998, transcript p. 6.
26. Letter to Rexford Blazer from Harry Lee Waterfield, Dec. 12, 1966.
27. *Ashland Daily Independent,* Dec. 11, 1966.
28. *The Herald-Dispatch,* Huntington, W. Va., Dec. 10, 1966. p. 4.
29. *The Courier-Journal,* Louisville, Kentucky, Dec. 11, 1966.

Chapter Seven

1. John Ed Pearce, *Louisville Courier-Journal & Times Sunday Magazine,* "Ashland Oil's Rex Blazer," Louisville, Kentucky, Oct. 14, 1973, p. 13.
2. Ibid, p. 13.
3. Ashland Oil & Refining Briefing Material, by Otto Scott, Nov. 8, 1972.
4. *Time,* "Outworking the Competition," Nov. 10, 1967, p. 99.
5. Ibid, p. 99.
6. Ashland Oil & Refining Background Briefing Material, by Otto Scott, Nov. 8, 1972.
7. *The Courier-Journal,* "A Company's Progress," Louisville, Kentucky, Nov. 22, 1971.
8. *Investor's Reader,* "Ashland Oil's New Division," Dec. 1, 1967, p. 15.
9. *The Herald-Dispatch,* "Ashland Oil Common Stock Increase Given Shareholders' Approval," Huntington, West Virginia, Jan. 21, 1969.
10. Les Rich, *Houston Chronicle,* "Where Are Big Spenders of Yesteryear," United Feature Syndicate, September 5, 1971.
11. *The Wall Street Journal,* "Ashland Oil Expects Boost," Nov. 30, 1971.
12. Daniel Yergin, *The Prize: The Epic Quest for Oil, Money & Power,* Simon & Schuster, New York, 1991, p. 567.
13. *Forbes,* "A First Class Crap Game," Aug. 1, 1969, p. 41.
14. Ibid.
15. Ibid.
16. *Ashland Oil News,* "Amerada and Ashland Moving into New Era", Vol. VII, No. 3, p. 1.
17. *The Oil Daily,* "Ashland Chief Exec Backs 2 grades of Fuel for Autos," May 11, 1970.
18. *The Sentinel,* "Noxious Odors Come from Plant in Ohio," Parkersburg, West Virginia, April 19, 1971.
19. *Ashland Oil: An Environmental Overview,* Ashland Oil corporate publication, 1971.
20. Ashland Oil & Refining Background Briefing Material, by Otto Scott, Nov. 8, 1972.

Chapter Eight

1. John Hall, interviewed by the author, May 7, 1998, transcript p. 41.
2. Paul Chellgren, interviewed by the author, Jan. 22, 1998, transcript, p. 25.
3. *The Herald-Dispatch,* Huntington, W. Va., "Atkins Takes Top Ashland Oil Seat," Jan. 28, 1972.
4. Thomas Feazell, interviewed by the author, Jan. 21, 1998, transcript p. 4.
5. Ibid, p. 3.
6. Ibid, pp. 3–4.
7. Transcript of presentation by Orin Atkins to the New York Society of Security Analysts, April 10, 1973.
8. John Ed Pearce, *The Louisville Courier-Journal & Times Sunday Magazine,* "Ashland Oil's Rex Blazer," Louisville, Kentucky, Oct. 14, 1973, p. 11.
9. *Ashland Daily Independent,* "Atkins Says Government to Blame for Fuel Crisis," Jan. 31, 1974, p. 1.
10. Thomas Feazell, interviewed by the author, Jan. 21, 1998, transcript p. 12.
11. *Rochester Times-Union* "Call Lefkowitz Statement 'Inaccurate, Misleading,'" by AP, September 27, 1974, p. 1.
12. Jack Anderson, *The Herald Dispatch,* Huntington, W. Va., "The Senator from Ashland Oil," Oct. 1, 1974, p. 4.
13. Ashland internal communication to Clyde Webb from Ed Knight, Jan. 11, 1975, p. 1.

14. Ibid, pp. 1–2.
15. Ashland Oil, Inc. 1978 Annual Report, Letter to Stockholders.
16. Ibid.
17. Ibid.
18. Thomas Feazell, interviewed by the author, Jan. 21, 1998, transcript p. 8.
19. *Ashland News,* "Oil Demand Up, Supply Pinch Growing," April 1979, p. 1.
20. Thomas Feazell, interviewed by the author, Jan. 21, 1998, transcript p. 28.
21. Ibid, p. 29.
22. Dan Lacy, interviewed by the author, April 29, 1998, transcript p. 3.
23. Ibid.
24. Wickliffe R. Powell, *Ashland Daily Independent,* "AOI May Move Operations from City," Aug. 23, 1979, p. 1.
25. Ibid.
26. *Ashland Daily Independent,* "Few Dispassionate About Recent AOI Announcement," Aug. 26, 1979, p. 1.
27. Donna Sammons, *The New York Times,* "Ashland Oil's Dry Kentucky Home," Oct. 21, 1979, p. 15.
28. *The New York Times,* "Ashland's Future May Not Be in Oil," Dec. 1, 1980.
29. *Ashland News,* "Annual Meeting: A Look Back, a Look Ahead," March 1981, p. 1.
30. William Seaton, interviewed by the author, May 7, 1998, transcript p. 12.
31. Ibid, p. 22.
32. *Ashland News,* "Hall Elected Ashland CEO," September 1981, p. 3.
33. *Ashland News,* "Atkins Retirement Ends an Era," September 1981, p. 3.
34. Paul Chellgren, interviewed by the author, Jan. 22, 1998, transcript, p. 31.

35. *Ashland News,* "Hall Outlines New Corporate Structure, Strategies for 1980s," Oct.–Nov., 1981, p. 3.
36. Ibid.
37. Ibid, p. 3.
38. Ibid, p. 3.

Chapter Eight Sidebar

1. *Tri-State Update,* "Ashland's RCC Technology Used Worldwide," Vol. 3, No. 6, Oct. 1990, p. 1.
2. *Ashland News,* "Construction Begins on Catlettsburg RCC Unit," Jan. 1981, Vol. XXI, No. 1, p. 2.
3. Ibid.
4. Ibid.
5. *Ashland News,* "RCC Dedication," Dec. 1983, p. 7.
6. Ibid, p. 6.
7. Ibid.
8. Ibid, p. 7.

Chapter Nine

1. Ameet Sachdev, *Lexington Herald-Leader, Business Sunday,* "He Guided Ashland Inc. Through Trouble to Profits," Lexington, Kentucky, September 29, 1996, p. 15.
2. *Business Week,* "Ashland Oil: Trying to Cope with a Diversification Hangover and a Lingering Scandal," Nov. 7, 1983, p. 17.
3. Paul Chellgren, interviewed by the author, Jan. 22, 1998, transcript p. 29.
4. John Hall, interviewed by the author, May 7, 1998, transcript pp. 12–13.
5. Bruce Allar, *Sky,* "John R. Hall, Chairman and CEO, Ashland Oil, Inc.," July 1990, p. 37.
6. *Business Week,* "Ashland Oil: Trying to Cope With a

Diversification Hangover and a Lingering Scandal," Nov. 7, 1983, p. 19.
7. *The Ashland Source,* "Thanks for the Memories," Jan. 1997. p. 6.
8. Ibid, p. 7.
9. Thomas Feazell, interviewed by the author, Jan. 21, 1998, transcript p. 10.
10. William Hartl, interviewed by the author, Jan. 22, 1998, transcript p. 3.
11. William Sawran, interviewed by Catherine Lackner, April 3, 1998, transcript p. 20.
12. Paul Chellgren, interviewed by the author, Jan. 22, 1998, transcript p. 30.
13. Thomas Feazell, interviewed by the author, Jan. 21, 1998, transcript p. 10.
14. Paul Chellgren, interviewed by the author, Jan. 22, 1998, transcript p. 30.
15. Thomas Feazell, interviewed by the author, Jan. 21, 1998, transcript p. 4.
16. Paul Chellgren, interviewed by the author, Jan. 22, 1998, transcript p. 29.
17. Dan Lacy, interviewed by the author, April 29, 1998, transcript p. 6.
18. Ibid.
19. Thomas Feazell, interviewed by the author, Jan. 21, 1998. Transcript p. 5.
20. Ibid, p. 6.
21. Dan Lacy, interviewed by the author, April 29, 1998, transcript pp. 7–8.
22. Ibid, p. 9.
23. John Dansby, interviewed by the author, Jan. 21, 1998, transcript p. 17.
24. *Ashland News,* "Luellen Elected President of Ashland Oil; Yancey Heads Ashland Petroleum," March 1986, p. 6.
25. *Ashland News,* "Focus on Strategy," May 1986, p. 5.

26. William Seaton, interviewed by the author, May 7, 1998, transcript p. 18.
27. Robert McCowan, interviewed by the author, May 7, 1998, transcript p. 16.
28. John Hall, interviewed by the author, May 7, 1998, transcript p. 29.
29. *Ashland News,* "The Innovative Spirit," April 1987, p. 5.
30. Bruce Allar, *Sky,* "John R. Hall, Chairman & CEO, Ashland Oil, Inc.," July 1990, p. 43.
31. *Ashland News,* "Perspective," Nov. 1987, p. 2.
32. Philip Block, interviewed by the author, Jan. 21, 1998, transcript p. 7.
33. Ibid, p. 9.
34. Ibid, p. 7.
35. Ibid, p. 5.
36. John Hall, interviewed by the author, May 7, 1998, transcript p. 22.
37. Bruce Allar, *Sky,* "John R. Hall, Chairman & CEO, Ashland Oil, Inc.," July 1990, p. 37.
38. *The Courier-Journal,* "Ashland Abounds from Spill," Louisville, Kentucky, April 12, 1988, p. A1.
39. Bruce Allar, *Sky,* "John R. Hall, Chairman & CEO, Ashland Oil, Inc.," July 1990, p. 38.
40. CEO Brief, Supplement to Chief Executive, "Ashland Oil: Go With the Flow."
41. Debbie Phillips, "Crisis, View from the Top: Ashland Oil, Inc." May/June 1991, p. 8.
42. Paul Chellgren, interviewed by the author, Jan. 22, 1998, transcript p. 29.
43. Fred Brothers, interviewed by the author, Jan. 22, 1998, transcript p. 6.
44. Ibid, p. 7.

45. Paul Chellgren, interviewed by the author, Jan. 22, 1998, transcript p. 30.
46. Ibid, p. 7.
47. Ibid, p. 14.
48. Ashland Inc. 1996 Annual Report, p. 67.

Chapter Nine Sidebar

1. Robert D. Bell, interviewed by Jon VanZile, July 31, 1998, transcript p. 12.
2. *The Ashland Source,* "Thanks for the Memories," Jan. 1997, Vol. IV, No. 1, p. 7.
3. Judy Thomas, interviewed by Sharon Peters, May 1, 1998.
4. Mac Zachem, interviewed by the author, Jan. 21, 1998, transcript pp. 21–22.

Chapter Ten

1. Ashland Inc. 1997 Annual Report, "Discussion with the Chairman," Nov. 7, 1997.
2. *The Ashland Source,* "A Familiar Face in a New Place," Jan. 1997, Vol, IV, No. 1, p. 11.
3. Ibid, p. 12.
4. *The Ashland Source,* "Ashland's Changing Complexion," July 1997, p. 4.
5. Marvin Quin, interviewed by the author, Jan. 22, 1998, transcript p. 8.
6. *The Ashland Source,* "Ashland's Changing Complexion," July 1997, Vol. III, No. 3, p. 5.
7. Fred Brothers, interviewed by the author, Jan. 22, 1998, transcript p. 6.
8. Ibid.
9. Ibid, p. 7.
10. *The Ashland Source,* "Ashland's Changing Complexion," July 1997, Vol. III, No. 3, p. 6.

11. Fred Brothers, interviewed by the author, Jan. 22, 1998, transcript p. 9.
12. Ibid, p. 10.
13. Marvin Quin, interviewed by the author, Jan. 22, 1998, transcript p. 11.
14. David Goetz, *The Courier-Journal,* "Proposed Deals Continue Ashland's Shift of Focus," Louisville, Kentucky, Jan. 30, 1998, p. C1.
15. *The Ashland Source,* "Ashland's Changing Complexion," July 1997, Vol. III, No. 3, p. 4.
16. W.E. Chellgren, interviewed by the author, March 13, 1998, transcript p. 6.
17. *The Ashland Source,* "Perspective," Oct. 1997, Vol. III, No. 4, p. 3.
18. Ibid.
19. Marvin Quin, interviewed by the author, Jan. 22, 1998, transcript p. 19.
20. Paul Chellgren, interviewed by the author, Jan. 22, 1998, transcript p. 6.
21. Charles Whitehead, interviewed by Melody Alder, April 28, 1998, transcript p. 2.
22. Paul Chellgren, interviewed by the author, Jan. 22, 1998, transcript p. 6.
23. Michael Toohey, interviewed by Melody Alder, May 5, 1998, transcript p. 5.
24. Ashland Inc. 1997 Annual Report, "Corporate Responsibility," p. 67.
25. Michael Toohey, interviewed by Melody Alder, May 5, 1998, transcript p. 2.

Chapter Ten Sidebar

1. *The Ashland Source,* "Culture Change," July 1997, Vol. III, No. 3, p. 11.
2. *The Ashland Source,* "Postcards from the Road," p. 17.

Chapter Eleven

1. James J. O'Brien, interviewed by the author, Feb. 13, 1998, transcript, p. 23.
2. "85 Years Young: Drama of the Longest Lubricating Oil," a press release from Valvoline Corporate Communications, p. 3.
3. Letter from the Liverpool offices of Valvoline Oil to clients and representatives, 1897.
4. Letter from H.D. Haverfield, Bath Iron Works, September 9, 1909.
5. Letter from John Unertl of J. Unertl Optical Co., May 20, 1946.
6. *Ashland Oil Log*, "Freedom's Great Fleet of Wagons Recalled," Vols. 6–7. Oct.–Nov. 1950, p. 12.
7. Letter from Paul G. Blazer to the Ashland Oil & Refining Company Board of Directors, July 20, 1964.
8. Marty Kish, interviewed by the author, April 29, 1998, transcript, p. 3.
9. Jack Roush, interviewed by Jon VanZile, April 28, 1998, transcript, p. 2.
10. Mark Martin, interviewed by the author, April 6, 1998, transcript p. 4.
11. Derrick Walker, interviewed by Catherine Lackner, April 1, 1998, transcript p. 12.
12. Gil DeFerren, interviewed by Catherine Lackner, March 17, 1998, transcript, p.1.
13. Larry Detjen, interviewed by Jon VanZile, April 29, 1998, transcript, p. 3.
14. Larry Detjen, interviewed by Jon VanZile, April 29, 1998, transcript, p. 3.
15. Jerry Wipf, interviewed by Catherine Lackner, April 8, 1998, transcript p. 1.
16. Cleve Huston, interviewed by Bonnie Bratton, Feb. 12, 1998, transcript p. 3.
17. James O'Brien, interviewed by the author, Feb. 13, 1998, transcript p. 3.
18. Ibid.
19. Ibid, p. 9.
20. Jim Burkhardt, interviewed by Bonnie Bratton, Feb. 12, 1998, transcript p. 4.
21. William Dempsey, interviewed by Jon VanZile, April 22, 1998, transcript pp. 21–22.
22. Fran Lockwood, interviewed by Bonnie Bratton, Feb. 12, 1998, transcript p. 2.
23. William Dempsey, interviewed by Jon VanZile, April 22, 1998, transcript p. 6.
24. Jack Gordon, interviewed by the author, Feb. 13, 1998, transcript p. 6.
25. Marty Kish, interviewed by the author, April 29, 1998, transcript, p. 14.
26. Jamie Butlers, *Lexington Herald-Leader*, "Valvoline to Build Product Laboratory," Lexington, Kentucky, Feb. 27, 1998, p. D1.
27. Larry Detjen, interviewed by Jon VanZile, April 29, 1998, transcript pp. 15–16.

Chapter Twelve

1. *Ashland News*, "Emabond Acquisition Fuels Ashland Chemical Growth," Dec. 1987, p. 10.
2. Carl Pecko, interviewed by Jon VanZile, April 20, 1998, transcript p. 7.
3. *The Ashland Source*, "Thanks for the Memories," Jan. 1997, p. 5.
4. Scott Patrick, interviewed by Jon VanZile, April 24, 1998, transcript p. 24.
5. *Investor's Reader*, "Ashland Oil's New Division," Dec. 1, 1967, p. 15.
6. *Chemical Week*, "A Chemical Company Is Created," Nov. 11, 1967, p. 56.
7. Scott Patrick, interviewed by Jon VanZile, April 24, 1998, transcript p. 6.
8. Ibid.
9. Ibid.
10. Ibid, pp. 7–8.
11. Information provided by John Hall, July 6, 1998.
12. Fred Brothers, interviewed by Melody Alder, July 29, 1998, transcript p. 1.
13. Marvin Quin, interviewed by the author, Jan. 22, 1998, transcript p. 2.
14. Ibid, p. 3.
15. Fred Brothers, interviewed by Melody Alder, July 29, 1998, transcript pp. 6–7.
16. Information provided by Fred Brothers, July 23, 1998.
17. Ibid.
18. Fred Brothers, interviewed by Melody Alder, July 29, 1998, transcript p. 2.
19. Information provided by Fred Brothers, July 23, 1998.
20. Ibid.
21. Fred Brothers, interviewed by Melody Alder, July 29, 1998, transcript p. 7.
22. Ibid, p. 10.
23. Gregory DL Morris, *Chemical Week*, "Ashland Chemical: Culling Success from Diversity," Oct. 9, 1991.
24. Kevin R. Fitzgerald, *Purchasing*, "Chemical Buyers Pick Best-in-Class," April 11, 1996.
25. *Chemical Week*, "Ashland Plan Bears Fruit," Oct. 29, 1997, p. 27.
26. John D. Van Meter, interviewed by the author, June 2, 1998, transcript p. 14.
27. Ashland Inc. 1997 Annual Report, p. 11.
28. *Chemical Week*, "Ashland Plan Bears Fruit," Oct. 29, 1997, p. 29.
29. Ashland Inc. 1997 Annual Report, p. 12.
30. Ibid, pp. 10–11.

31. Ibid, p. 11.
32. David D'Antoni, interviewed by Catherine Lackner, April 7, 1998, transcript p. 8.
33. *Chemical Week*, "Ashland Plan Bears Fruit," Oct. 29, 1997, p. 27.

Chapter Thirteen

1. Riad Yammine, interviewed by Catherine Lackner, April 7, 1998, transcript p. 3.
2. Bob Hardman, interviewed by Matt Hackathorn, Feb. 19, 1998, transcript p. 2.
3. Charles Luellen, interviewed by Melody Alder, Aug. 5, 1998, transcript p. 1.
4. Bob Hardman, interviewed by Matt Hackathorn, Feb. 19, 1998, transcript p. 1.
5. Ibid, p. 2.
6. Charles Covey, interviewed by Matt Hackathorn, March 19, 1998, transcript p. 2 .
7. Phil Collins, interviewed by Matt Hackathorn, Feb. 17, 1998, transcript p. 1.
8. Dave Nelson, interviewed by Matt Hackathorn, March 23, 1998, transcript p. 2.
9. Charles Luellen, interviewed by Melody Alder, Aug. 5, 1998, transcript p. 5.
10. Overview History of SuperAmerica, Corporate Communications, p. 6.
11. Paul Prather, *Lexington Herald-Leader*, "SuperAmerica President Mingles With His People," Lexington, Kentucky, April 17, 1989, p. D3.
12. *Lexington Herald-Leader*, "SuperAmerica Reports Earnings," Lexington, Kentucky, September 5, 1993.
13. Ibid.
14. John Pettus, interviewed by the author, May 7, 1998, transcript p. 9.

15. Zemke, Ron and Schaaf, Dick, *The Service Edge: 101 Companies that Profit from Customer Care*, Penguin, New York, New York, 1989, p. 331.
16. John Pettus, interviewed by the author, May 7, 1998, transcript p. 11.
17. Jim Jordon, *Lexington Herald-Leader*, "Former Ashland Subsidiary Ohio-Bound," July 3, 1998, p. A1.
18. Riad Yammine, interviewed by Catherine Lackner, April 7, 1998, transcript p. 8.
19. Ibid, p. 10.

Chapter Fourteen

1. A Century of Innovation press kit.
2. *The Cincinnati Enquirer*, "Ashland's Future," Cincinnati, Ohio, Feb. 8, 1998, p. E2.
3. Ashland Management Presentations to Security Analysts, Columbus, Ohio, June 25–26, 1996.
4. James Boyd, interviewed by Melody Alder, Aug. 7, 1998, transcript p. 6.
5. John Dansby, interviewed by the author, Jan. 21, 1998, transcript p. 9.
6. Ashland Oil, Inc. 1974 Annual Report, p. 21.
7. John Hall, interviewed by the author, May 7, 1998, transcript p. 26.
8. Ibid, p. 27.
9. Ibid.
10. *Ashland News*, "Innovation, Diversity — the Road to Success," Jan. 1982, p. 3.
11. Ashland Oil, Inc. 1985 Annual Report, p. 28.
12. Ashland News Best in the Business, Nov. 1986, p. 4.
13. *The Ashland Source*, "The Art of APAC," Jan. 1998, Vol. IV, No. 1, p. 15.
14. James Boyd, interviewed by Melody Alder, Aug. 7, 1998, transcript p. 11.

15. Ibid.
16. Ibid, p. 12.
17. Charles Potts, interviewed by Catherine Lackner, April 6, 1998, transcript p. 5.
18. James Boyd, interviewed by Melody Alder, Aug. 7, 1998, transcript p. 5.
19. Charles Potts, interviewed by Catherine Lackner, April 6, 1998, transcript p. 6.

Chapter Fifteen

1. Ken Ward Jr., *The Charleston Gazette*, "Arch Coal Profits Top $30 Million," Jan. 21, 1998, p. 7A.
2. Otto Scott, *Buried Treasure: The Story of Arch Mineral*, Braddock Communications, Inc., Washington, D.C., p. 60.
3. Ibid.
4. John Kebblish, interviewed by Jon VanZile, May 26, 1998, transcript pp. 3–4.
5. *Business Week*, "Crude-Poor Ashland Oil: Prototype of the Future," Jan. 31, 1977, p. 17.
6. *Ashland News*, "Coal," Aug. 1984, p. 3.
7. *Ashland News*, "Reclaiming the Land," July 1983, p. 3.
8. *Ashland News*, "Coal: Ready to Reign Again," Feb. 1982, p. 4.
9. Ashland News, "Steaming Ahead," Nov./Dec., 1992. p. 12.
10. Philip Nussel, *Charleston Daily Mail*, "Investors Hit Jackpot on Ashland Coal," Aug. 21, 1990, p. D1.
11. Jim Ross, *The Herald-Dispatch*, "*Fortune* Magazine Puts Ashland Coal Stocks on Best List," Huntington, W. Va., Jan. 28, 1991, p. B4.
12. Steven Leer, interviewed by Melody Alder, May 27, 1998, transcript p. 3.

13. *Ashland News*, "Arch Mineral," Sept. 1985, p.6.
14. Ibid.
15. James Boyd, interviewed by Melody Alder, Aug. 7, 1998, transcript p. 15.
16. Ibid, p. 16.
17. Steven Leer, interviewed by Melody Alder, May 27, 1998, transcript p. 17.
18. Ibid, p. 13.
19. Ken Ward Jr., *The Charleston Gazette*, "Arch Coal Profits Top $30 Million," Jan. 21, 1998, p. 7A.

Chapter Sixteen

1. J.L. "Corky" Frank, interviewed by the author, April 27, 1998, transcript p. 16.
2. Robert H. Waterman Jr., *One Hundred Years on the Frontier*, "Ourselves As Others See Us," published by Marathon, 1987, p. 8.
3. Ibid.
4. Robert A. Wood, *One Hundred Years on the Frontier*, "West of the Pecos," published by Marathon, 1987, p. 60.
5. Robert H. Waterman Jr., *One Hundred Years on the Frontier*, "Ourselves as Others See Us," published by Marathon, 1987, p. 6.
6. Ibid.
7. Ibid, p. 9.
8. Ibid, p. 12.
9. Dr. Philip H. Mirvis, *One Hundred Years on the Frontier*, "The Future: Change and Renewal," published by Marathon, 1987, p. 132.
10. Ibid.
11. *The Ashland Source*, "USX-Marathon Group and Ashland Inc. Pursue New Venture," May 15, 1997, p. 1.
12. Ibid.
13. Duane Gilliam, interviewed by the author, April 27, 1998, transcript p. 4.

14. Ken Aulen, interviewed by the author, Jan. 22, 1998, transcript p. 4.
15. Fred Brothers, interviewed by Melody Alder, July 29, 1998, transcript p. 12.
16. Gary Peiffer, interviewed by Jon VanZile, April 16, 1998, transcript p. 7.
17. J. Louis Frank, *Hart's Fuel Technology & Management*, "Keynote Address: Downstream Partnerships Can Open New Opportunities and Markets," May 1998, p. 32.
18. Ibid, p. 33.
19. Kevin Henning, interviewed by Catherine Lackner, April 8, 1998, transcript p. 8.
20. Randy Lohoff, interviewed by the author, April 27, 1998, transcript p. 9.
21. Lamar Chambers, interviewed by Melody Alder, April 30, 1998, transcript p. 2.
22. *Lexington Herald-Leader*, "Marathon Ashland to Convert Ashland Stores to Marathon," Lexington, Kentucky, May 15, 1998, p. D1.
23. Ibid, p. D2.
24. Charles Whitehead, interviewed by Melody Alder, April 28, 1998, transcript pp. 8–9.
25. Rodney Nichols, interviewed by Jon VanZile, April 16, 1998, transcript p. 2.
26. Richard White, interviewed by Melody Alder, May 5, 1998, transcript p. 2.
27. Ibid.
28. Randy Lohoff, interviewed by the author, April 27, 1998, transcript p. 5.
29. Duane Gilliam, interviewed by the author, April 27, 1998, transcript p. 8.

30. Kevin Henning, interviewed by Catherine Lackner, April 8, 1998, transcript p. 11.
31. Randy Lohoff, interviewed by the author, April 27, 1998, transcript p. 16.
32. Ibid.
33. J.L. "Corky" Frank, interviewed by the author, April 27, 1998, transcript p. 16.
34. "Definitive Agreement Signed for Marathon, Ashland Joint Venture," Ashland Press Release, Dec. 12, 1997.

Epilogue

1. "International and Domestic Oil," Equity Research, Donaldson, Lufkin & Jenrette, John D. Hervey & Stephanie von Isenburg, June 17, 1997.
2. Paul W. Chellgren, speech to Key Managers' Meeting, Dec. 1997.
3. *The Ashland Source Extra*, "Chellgren Addresses Employees," July 1998, Vol. IV, No. 3.
4. Ibid.
5. Jamie Butlers, *Lexington Herald-Leader*, Ashland Inc.'s Changes May Mean a Move," Lexington, Kentucky, Sunday, June 14, 1998, p. A15.
6. Jack Brammer, *Lexington Herald-Leader*, "Kentuckians Hopeful That Ashland Not Leaving State," Lexington, Kentucky, Sunday, July 19, 1998, p. B3.
7. Fred Brothers, interviewed by Melody Alder, July 29, 1998, transcript p. 14.
8. *The Ashland Source Extra*, "Corporate Headquarters to Move to Covington, Ky.," July 1998, Vol. IV, No. 3.
9. Paul W. Chellgren, *Newslink*, "G&A Restructuring Process Clarified," Aug. 5, 1998.

INDEX